MW01144127

Interactive 3D Graphics
in Windows®

Springer
New York
Berlin
Heidelberg
Barcelona
Budapest
Hong Kong
London
Milan
Paris
Tokyo

Roy Hall
Danielle Forsyth

INTERACTIVE 3D GRAPHICS IN WINDOWS®

Springer

Roy Hall & Danielle Forsyth
Crisis in Perspective, Inc.
1306 NW Hoyt Street, Suite 409
Portland, OR 97209 USA

Microsoft, MS, Windows, Windows 95, Windows NT, MFC, OLE, Visual C++, GDI, AppWizard, ClassWizard, AppStudio and MS Word are registered trademarks of Microsoft Corporation. Pentium is a registered trademark of the Intel Corporation. *JOEY, JOEY* Toolkit, *JOEY* Development Environment, *JOEY* Viewer, and Dr. Zeus are trademarks of Crisis in Perspective, Inc. OpenGL is a registered trademark of Silicon Graphics, Inc. ADI 3D and HEIDI are a registered trademarks of Autodesk, Inc. RenderMan is a registered trademark of Pixar.

Library of Congress cataloging-in-publication data is available from the Library of Congress.

Printed on acid-free paper.

© 1995 Springer-Verlag New York, Inc.
All rights reserved. This work may not be translated or copied in whole or in part without the written permission of the publisher (Springer-Verlag New York, Inc., 175 Fifth Avenue, New York, NY 10010, USA), except for brief excerpts in connection with reviews or scholarly analysis. Use in connection with any form of information storage and retrieval, electronic adaptation, computer software, or by similar or dissimilar methodology now known or hereafter developed is forbidden.
The use of general descriptive names, trade names, trademarks, etc., in this publication, even if the former are not especially identified, is not to be taken as a sign that such names, as understood by the Trade Marks and Merchandise Marks Act, may accordingly be used freely by anyone.

Production managed by Karen Phillips; manufacturing supervised by Rhea Talbert.
Camera-ready copy provided by the authors.
Printed by Hamilton Printing Company, Rensselaer, NY.
Printed in the United States of America.

9 8 7 6 5 4 3 2 1

ISBN 0-387-94573-3 Springer-Verlag New York Berlin Heidelberg

Preface

Today, most graphics books are focused on graphics theory, standards, rendering or specific graphics applications. Windows books address the use and nuances of the Windows environment and programming language books address specific language considerations. There are no books about developing interactive 3D graphic applications in Windows. There are several reasons for this; Windows based tools have not been available to develop 3D interactive applications, Windows historically ran on hardware which could not support interactive 3D graphics applications and very few graphics "experts" used Windows as a development platform. But 3D graphics capability is being added to Windows, Windows now runs on a range of processors which can support interactive graphics applications and "experts" are being forced to work in the environment that users know and use.

For these reasons, we are writing a hands-on book and providing software tools (*JOEY*) which teach application developers how to write good interactive 3D applications in the Windows environment. Originally, it was not our intent to write either *JOEY* or this book. Our goal was to take years of experience in interactive 3D applications, rendering, and architecture and combine them into a next generation architectural modeling system. Unfortunately, there was an almost immediate realisation that the tools to build this type of application didn't exist in Windows. This was followed by an intense effort to build the appropriate tools, and the obvious observation that if we needed these tools, other application developers may need them also.

We worked hard and, generally, had fun writing *JOEY* and this book. There are errors and we need your help to find them. There are also omissions; some are time related, some are related to the scope of the *JOEY* Toolkit and some were not conscious. Your help in identifying both errors and omissions is greatly appreciated. We do not want to drive a user interface standard. We want to use a well thought out, well implemented user interface toolkit in our own applications and we want a wide range of application users to have access to 3D. We hope you enjoy this book and *JOEY*.

Acknowledgments

Lots of application developers gave us great feedback during the development of this book and *JOEY*. We would particularly like to thank Don Brittain from Tsunami Software, Lee Robie and Kevin Linscott from SDRC and Matthew Arrott from Autodesk. Gary Hirsch, the *JOEY* artist, has been a constant delight to work with and has helped us put humour into a topic that is known for its dryness. Wendy Steiner has helped to keep us sane during the long days and nights that led up to the completion of this book. Sam DeSimone has supported our rather unconventional business practices, made them all legal and done it with a great attitude and professional demeanour.

Dr. Zeus has insisted that we retain some reasonable level of balance in our lives and helped immensely by agreeing to handle all customer support.

Our families continue to encourage our efforts with kind words, open minds and lots of love. *JOEY*, well Haydn, has kept us on track. We love him like crazy.

Companion Software: *JOEY*

JOEY is the nickname of a seven year old that we hold dear. *JOEY* is also a set of high level development tools for writing Windows integrated, interactive 3D graphic applications. *JOEY* consists of two major components; a 3D toolkit for application developers and a set of viewers for integration of 3D data into OLE enabled applications. Today, graphic application developers must develop their own graphic support libraries (including the application look & feel). The mechanics of interaction between the user, application and graphic are a challenge. Development of 3D interactive applications is complex, graphics applications have an inconsistent look & feel and 3D data/objects cannot be easily transferred from application to application.

JOEY was developed to solve these problems and will benefit anyone who is writing 3D interactive applications. It will reduce the time that is needed to develop the application, provide the user with new viewing capability within and across OLE applications and minimize the learning time for each application by providing a standard mechanism for interacting with 3D data/objects. *JOEY* provides performance sensitive camera interaction and mechanisms to aid in making application interaction performance sensitive.

Throughout the development of *JOEY*, we were constantly asked where it fits. Is it rendering, a new framework, or a proposed standard? No. It is a thin layer of 3D support classes and services that fit between MFC and the application and provide a component object mapping into the renderer you choose to use.

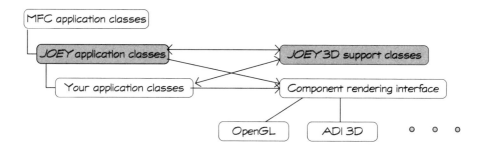

JOEY provides:

♦ 3D graphic windows for SDI and MDI applications
  - *full setup of graphic windows*
  - *interactive camera control*
  - *grids and grid hit testing/locking*
  - *performance sensitive rendering control during interaction*
  - *tools for hit testing*
♦ Camera and grid toolbar and camera feedback for the status bar
♦ OLE linking and embedding for in-place activation of 3D applications
♦ 3D metafiles with OLE server enabled viewers
♦ Clipboard support for 3D metafiles, enhanced metafiles and bitmaps
♦ OLE automation support
♦ Renderer independent access to multiple graphics systems including OpenGL and ADI 3D
♦ Versatile 3D geometric base classes
♦ Context sensitive help templates
♦ Editing dialogues for cameras, grids, materials and lights

JOEY is included with this book in order to explain and allow you to experiment with the functionality described in the book. The version of *JOEY* that you have received is called the *JOEY* Toolkit; it can be copied and shared with other developers. It cannot be distributed as a part of your commercially available application. The *JOEY* Viewer is also included on this disk and can be used, copied and distributed freely.

The *JOEY* Development Environment, a more extensible version of *JOEY* is available for use in commercial applications. Contact Crisis in Perspective, Inc. at 74107.2217@compuserve.com for more details.

Technical support is available to all registered *JOEY* users. Please contact:

Dr. Zeus at 73042.1244@compuserve.com

This is a hands-on book. You need to install the software to use the book. Before installing the software, please read *readme.txt*.

Software Requirements

It is assumed that the *JOEY* user has a working knowledge of Microsoft Windows, C++, Microsoft Foundation Classes (MFC) and OLE and has current releases of all of this software installed on their computer. If this is not the case, you should not attempt to use *JOEY*. It won't work.

JOEY requires a 386, 486 or Pentium class computer. There are no special memory or graphics requirements (other than the requirements of the software above) for *JOEY* but 20 Mb. of available disk space is required.

JOEY will run on Windows NT or Windows 95. The version in this book runs with OpenGL or ADI 3D.

Contents

A detailed section table of contents can be found at the beginning of **Practice**, **Implementation** and **Theory**.

Introduction

There is a belief that interactive 3D graphics applications are hard to write. There are numerous tools available now in Windows, Microsoft Visual C++, and other development environments which help application developers build the repetitive boilerplate required for applications. There are also tools which help to build the custom portions for interacting with data but 3D interactive tools are not yet a standard part of the development environment or user environment. So, application developers spend their time writing both the application and the 3D interaction libraries. This means that 3D application users spend their time learning both the application functionality and the non-standard, non-integrated interaction techniques.

There is nothing inherently difficult about 3D graphics; a developer could spend a lot of time and energy writing vector multiplication routines, worrying about left and right handed coordinates systems, and wondering whether matrices should be pre or post multiplied. Today, these programmatically trivial details consume a huge amount of development time.

Interactive 3D Graphics in Windows provides an easy path to help you build good interactive 3D graphics applications. This book relies heavily on other interactive graphics research and references these writings liberally. *Interactive 3D Graphics in Windows* is not a book to sit down and read without a computer. It assumes that the reader is learning about or actually writing a 3D graphics application and that the goal is to simplify the user interaction with 3D graphical data. This book uses *JOEY* extensively and provides a great deal of sample code and data for use in understanding the principles described. We expect that the reader of this book already believes in the power of visual communication and wants to develop (or extend an existing application to be) a Windows based 3D interactive graphics application.

This book is divided into three major sections: **Practice, Implementation**, and **Theory**. **Practice** is the path to immediate visual gratification (after all, that's what drives people to want and need graphics). **Implementation**, addresses the specific features of the *JOEY* toolkit; what is really behind them and why they work. **Theory**, connects the two previous sections to research that has been done in graphics and explains how it works. This organisation results from the expectation that you will want something to happen immediately. Then, once you start your own application exploration, you will want to explore the full potential of the tools Finally, when things don't seem to work the way you want, you may want to understand how to do something about it.

PRACTICE

Table of Contents: Practice

Figures

1. A Framework for Interactive 3D Applications

It is daunting to be required to absorb 400 pages of material before you can make something useful happen so, instead of dwelling on how or why things work, we jump right in and create a very simple interactive 3D application. This application starts as a 3D object viewer, *viewit3d,* which will resemble the screen snapshot in Figure P-1 after you have completed the exercises in the first section.

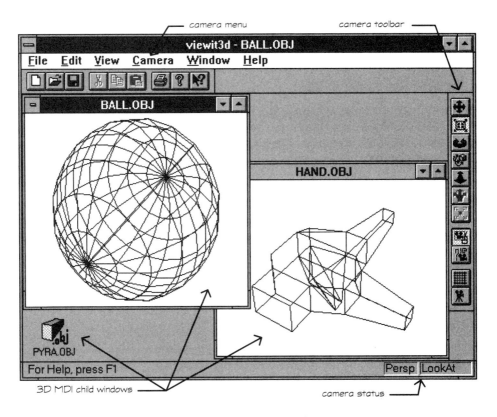

Figure P-1: Screen snapshot of the sample application, *viewit3d.*

Viewit3d is our vehicle for sequentially introducing 3D graphics concepts in the context of a running application. Our progressive development of this application is intended to lead you through features that you may want to use in your own 3D interactive application.

Viewit3d starts as a simple data viewer that reads and displays 3D objects in wireframe. This provides an introduction to the *JOEY* Toolkit and its relationship with MFC.

In the second chapter, *viewit3d* grows to be an OLE server application with support for 3D metafiles and viewers, in addition to standard bitmap and metafile transfer of 2D data to other applications. OLE automation opportunities are also explored.

In the third chapter, *viewit3d* is expanded to have lighting and rendering of solid objects, object and light manipulation and performance sensitivity. In the fourth chapter, opportunities for extending *JOEY* are briefly discussed.

Writing an interactive 3D application that does everything described above would be a monumental task if we worked only with low level tools like Win32 and OpenGL. If we were to use these low level tools, most of our work would focus on structure and framework (which have little relevance specifically to interactive 3D graphics applications).

To minimise the effort spent on underlying structure, we use high level tools to support the building of examples in this text. We use the MFC AppWizard in Visual C++[1] to provide the windows application boilerplate, OLE support and Wizards which minimise programming drudgery. We use *JOEY* to provide similar boilerplate functions for 3D applications. *JOEY* provides 3D window setup, camera control and toolbar, and classes to support 3D graphic elements and manipulations.

We want to make sure that you have created and are running your own interactive graphics application in thirty pages or less, and that each additional exploration can be done in a few pages. As you work through **Practice**, you can build and test your work whenever you see the *JOEY* symbol shown to the right.

---

[1] We are using Microsoft Visual C++ version 2.1 with MFC version 3.1 running under Windows NT version 3.5 for these discussions. If you are using a different version, you may note some differences, but they should not be significant. Note that full OLE support was not provided in Visual C++ before version 2.0 with MFC version 3.0 (32 bit) or version 1.5 with MFC version 2.5 (16 bit).

We use the following application creation process:

♦ Create a project from Visual C++ using the MFC AppWizard, Section 1.1. This provides the basic application framework.

♦ Customise the framework to add *JOEY* interactive 3D capability, Section 1.2. There are application specific instructions which relate to the naming of the project, the data file and extension, the application view class, and the application document class. These application specific instructions are noted so that you can easily make changes specific to any application that you are creating.

♦ Enhance the framework with application specific functionality, Section 1.3.

We assume that you are familiar with Visual C++, MFC, MFC AppWizard, and MFC ClassWizard. If you have not already done so, it is advisable that you go through the "Introducing Visual C++" tutorials for *scribble*, a stand-alone application covering basic MFC concepts and migration to an OLE server and *contain*, a simple OLE container which is used for testing the OLE server version of *viewit3d*.

The framework created in Sections 1.1 and 1.2 is a generic interactive 3D application framework. The steps in these sections are the same for any interactive 3D application using MFC and *JOEY* (except for the application specific class and file names). You are likely to refer to this section frequently as you create other samples from this text or work on your own 3D applications.

Complete application templates for SDI and MDI applications in both OLE-enabled and non OLE-enabled versions are found in the *samples\app_tmpl* directory of the *JOEY* software, included with this text, in the following subdirectories:

Subdirectory:	Contents:
sdi_ole	Single Document Interface application, OLE enabled for embedding, linking, and automation.
mdi_ole	Multiple Document Interface application, OLE enabled for embedding, linking, and automation.
sdi	Single Document Interface Application, no OLE support included.
mdi	Multiple Document Interface Application, no OLE support included.

1.1 Creating a Framework with MFC AppWizard

In this example, we create the application *viewit3d*. This application reads 3D object data files in a *.a3d* ASCII 3D object format (sample objects have been provided on the accompanying disks). We create the view class CObjView in files *objview.h* and *objview.cpp*, the document class CObjDoc in files *objdoc.h* and *objdoc.cpp*, and the OLE server item class CObjSrvrItem in files *objsrvr.h* and *objsrvr.cpp*. If you are creating an application other than the *viewit3d* sample, it is wise to plan this application specific organisation before running MFC AppWizard.[2]

Create a new subdirectory in which you will build the sample application. MS Visual C++ will create subdirectories *hlp*, *res*, *WinDebug*, and *WinRel* by default for help, resources, the debugging version of the build, and the release version of the build respectively. You are now ready to start MS Visual C++ to create an interactive 3D application.

Start MFC AppWizard by selecting menu item File, New.... In the New dialogue box, select Project, then OK. In the New Project dialogue, select the subdirectory you previously created for the sample application and enter the Project Name: *viewit3d*. The Project Type: should be set to MFC AppWizard (.exe) by default. Select Create... to move on to the MFC AppWizard dialogues. Inn our sample application, we are creating a multiple document interface (MDI) application. In this section we also cover creating a single document interface (SDI) application template. Differences in the sequence for creating MDI and SDI applications are noted. Fill in the MFC AppWizard application specific dialogues:

◆ MFC AppWizard - Step 1 dialogue
    Select the appropriate Single Document or Multiple Document application style. The default, Multiple Document is used for the *viewit3d* application. The remaining steps are the same regardless of whether the application is an MDI or SDI application. Then select Next> to move on.

◆ MFC AppWizard - Step 2 of 6 dialogue
    For the examples in this text, we will not be using any database support. Select Next> to continue.

---

[2] This is not a tutorial for using MFC AppWizard. We discuss the MFC AppWizard in the context of creating 3D applications. For specific details of MFC AppWizard, consult the documentation and tutorials supplied with Microsoft Visual C++.

◆ MFC AppWizard - Step 3 of 6 dialogue

To exercise all of the *JOEY* functionality, select Full-Server (for OLE support) and Yes, please (for OLE Automation). The Full-Server selection will result in an application that can be used as a server for OLE linking and embedding of 3D application data.[3] Select Next> to continue.

◆ MFC AppWizard - Step 4 of 6 dialogue

Select Dockable Toolbar, Initial Status Bar, Printing and Print Preview, Context Sensitive Help, and Use 3D Controls. For the sample application, *viewit3d*, *JOEY* will be adding toolbar buttons, reporting feedback on the status bar, and providing context sensitive help.

Select the Advanced... button to bring up the Advanced Options dialogue that allows entry of specific document file information. In the Document Template Strings panel, enter the *viewit3d* specific information as follows:

Doc Type Name: *3D_GEO*

File New Name (OLE Short Name): *3D ASCII*

File Extension: *a3d*

Filter Name: *3D Geometry (*.a3d)*

File Type ID: *ASCII3D.mdi*

File Type Name (OLE Long Name): *ASCII 3D Geometry*

Generally, there is a need to enter only the Doc Type Name and the File Extension and the other fields are generated automatically.

The Main Frame and MDI Child Frame panels provide reasonable defaults for the sample application, *viewit3d*. Select Close to close the Advanced Options dialogue. Select Next> to continue.

◆ MFC AppWizard - Step 5 of 6 dialogue

The default selections are appropriate for the sample application, *viewit3d*. Select Next> to continue.

◆ MFC AppWizard - Step 6 of 6 dialogue

Enter the view and document class names for your application. For the sample application, *viewit3d*, change the MFC AppWizard assigned

---

[3] *JOEY* 3D data can always be linked and embedded for viewing using the *JOEY* data viewer (even if it your application is not an OLE server).

classes `CViewit3dDoc`, `CViewit3dView`, and `CViewit3dSrvrItem` as follows:

◊   `CViewit3dDoc`
    Change Class Name: to *CObjDoc*, Header File: to *objdoc.h*, and Implementation File: to *objdoc.cpp*.

◊   `CViewit3dView`
    Change Class Name: to *CObjView*, Header File: to *objview.h*, and Implementation File: to *objview.cpp*.

◊   `CViewit3DSrvrItem`
    Change Class Name: to *CObjSrvrItem*, Header File: to *objsrvr.h*, and Implementation File: to *objsrvr.cpp*.

Select Finish to complete the selection of options in MFC AppWizard and bring up the New Project Information dialogue. Review this dialogue for accuracy of information. Select OK to accept this information and create the application.

The application frame can now be compiled and run. However, a collection of modifications must be made to give this framework support for interactive 3D graphics.

1.2 Adding the *JOEY* 3D Graphics User Interface to the Framework

The MFC AppWizard framework is now modified to be a framework based on both *JOEY* and MFC. Ideally, using the *JOEY* graphics user interface toolkit would be as easy as selecting the Interactive 3D Graphic box next to the OLE Automation box when you run the MFC AppWizard. However, since there is no 3D Graphic box in the MFC AppWizard, some hand work is required to make the newly created application aware of *JOEY*.

The modifications made in this section are common to any *JOEY* enhanced MFC application that you create. Some of the class names are specific to the *viewit3d* application and will be different for other applications that you write. The complete template files for applications are included in the *samples\app_tmpl* directory of the *JOEY* Toolkit supplied with this book. Within this directory, you will find template subdirectories for OLE enabled MDI applications (*\mdi_ole*), OLE enabled SDI applications (*\sdi_ole*), and MDI and SDI applications that are not OLE enabled (*\mdi* and *\sdi* respectively). The modifications made in this section can be copied from this template directory or the files can simply be replaced by the files in the template directory.

IMPORTANT NOTE: Copying files is fine for all files except the project's *.rc* file and the main project *.cpp* file. Both of these files contain application specific information (including OLE registration information) that is unique to the application you created using AppWizard. For these files it will work better to copy the relevant changes from the template files.

If you have not already done so, install the *JOEY* software supplied with this text as described in the *readme.txt* file on the disk.

Now, you need to decide which graphics subsystem you will use. At this printing, OpenGL and Autodesk's ADI 3D are supported. When a *JOEY* application is run, *JOEY* queries the registration database to determine which graphics subsystem to use. Register OpenGL as the graphics subsystem using $(JOEY_DIR)\reg\joey_gl.reg and ADI 3D by using $(JOEY_DIR)\reg\joey_hdi.reg.[4] Refer to Sections 3.1.2 and 4.2 for information on these graphics subsystems and adding your own graphics subsystem.

1.2.1 Including *JOEY* and Graphics

In the standard application include file *stdafx.h*, add the following:

```
    #include <afxext.h>        // MFC extensions
    #include <afxole.h>        // added by MFC AppWizard for OLE client/server
    #include <afxdisp.h>       // added by MFC AppWizard for OLE automation
➜   #include <joey.h>
➜   __declspec(dllimport) extern CJoeyConfig*    JoeyConfig;
```

This will make the *JOEY* toolkit accessible in all of the project files and it will be built into a pre-compiled header for faster compilation of project files. The class CJoeyConfig contains the configuration and state information for *JOEY*. The application accesses this information through member functions when required.

---

[4] Currently, OpenGL is supplied with Windows NT. ADI 3D is available for Windows NT and Windows 95 and is shipped with this text.

Add the following file to your Project, Files... list: **$(JOEY_DIR)***lib**joey.lib*. In Project, Settings..., add **$(JOEY_DIR)***include* to the list of include directories to search during C++ pre-processing and resource processing.[5] If you compile and run the framework now, the *JOEY* library *joey.dll,*[6] will be loaded and the framework provided by MFC will work. It will not yet have any application or graphics user interface functionality.

1.2.2 Adding the Camera Toolbar

JOEY provides a toolbar to set the camera move mode and access other camera and grid functionality. The application owns the toolbar so that visibility and/or docking can be controlled by the application. *JOEY* is informed by the application of the existence of a camera toolbar by using a `CJoeyConfig` member function. The contents of the camera toolbar are maintained by *JOEY*. Processing of command messages generated by the camera toolbar is performed by *JOEY* and context sensitive help requests for the camera toolbar buttons are mapped into the *JOEY* help templates.

In the main application frame provided by the MFC AppWizard, *mainfrm.h* and *mainfrm.cpp*, the following additions are required:

◆ In *mainfrm.h*, whether it is derived from `CMDIFrameWnd` or from `CFrameWnd`, a declaration for the camera toolbar needs to be added. This should be added after the MFC AppWizard defined application toolbar and status bars:

```
      class CMainFrame : public CMDIFrameWnd
      {
          ◆
      protected:          // control bar embedded members
          CStatusBar      m_wndStatusBar;
          CToolBar        m_wndToolBar;
➔         CToolBar        m_wndCamToolBar;
          ◆
      };
```

---

[5] Instead of changing Project, Settings..., you can simply add **$(JOEY_DIR)***include* to the list of include directories. This can be accessed through the Control Panel (System applet). Alternatively, you can add it to the search path using the Directories panel of the Options dialogue started by Tools, Options.

[6] A number of *.dlls* will actually be loaded. *Joey.dll* will be loaded when the application is started. Other *.dlls* will be loaded as the application begins to use graphic resources. You will not notice the graphics *.dlls* loading at this time, but will notice these being loaded as you make the changes to the view and document described in the next sections.

◆ In *mainfrm.cpp,* the camera toolbar needs to be initialised within the
   OnCreate member function as follows:

```
        int CMainFrame::OnCreate(LPCREATESTRUCT lpCreateStruct)
        {
           ·
           ·
➜          // camera toolbar - create it and let Joey know it's there
➜          if ( !m_wndCamToolBar.Create(this,
➜                WS_CHILD | WS_VISIBLE | CBRS_TOP,
➜                IDM_VIEW_CAMERA_TBAR) ||
➜             !JoeyConfig->CameraToolBar(&m_wndCamToolBar) ) {
➜             TRACE0("Failed to create camera toolbar\n");
➜             return -1;       // fail to create
➜          }
➜          // delete next 2 lines for no toolbar docking
➜          m_wndCamToolBar.EnableDocking(CBRS_ALIGN_ANY);
➜          DockControlBar(&m_wndCamToolBar);
➜          // delete the next line for no tool tips
➜          m_wndCamToolBar.SetBarStyle(m_wndCamToolBar.GetBarStyle() |
➜             CBRS_TOOLTIPS | CBRS_FLYBY);
➜
           return 0;
        }
```

Similar additions need to be made to the in-place frame for OLE server
applications. If you selected **Full** <u>S</u>**erver** while running MFC AppWizard, make
similar changes to the OLE in-place frame. In the OLE in-place server frame
provided by the MFC AppWizard, *ipframe.h* and *ipframe.cpp,* the following
additions are required:

◆ In *ipframe.h,* a declaration for the camera toolbar needs to be added. This
   should be added after the MFC AppWizard defined application toolbar as
   follows:

```
        class CInPlaceFrame : public COleIPFrameWnd
        {
           ·
        protected:
           CToolBar           m_wndToolBar;
           COleResizeBar      m_wndResizeBar;
           COleDropTarget     m_dropTarget;
➜          CToolBar           m_wndCamToolBar;
           ·
        };
```

◆ In *ipframe.cpp,* the camera toolbar needs to be initialised within the
   OnCreateControlBars member function as follows:

```
BOOL CInPlaceFrame::OnCreateControlBars(CFrameWnd* pWndFrame,
     CFrameWnd* pWndDoc)
```

```
         {
            .
            .
→           // camera toolbar - create it and let Joey know it's there
→           if ( !m_wndCamToolBar.Create(pWndFrame) ||
→              !JoeyConfig->CameraToolBar(&m_wndCamToolBar) ) {
→              TRACE0("Failed to create camera toolbar\n");
→              return -1;     // fail to create
→           }
→           // so messages go to the right app
→           m_wndCamToolBar.SetOwner(this);
→           // delete next 2 lines for no toolbar docking
→           m_wndCamToolBar.EnableDocking(CBRS_ALIGN_ANY);
→           pWndFrame->DockControlBar(&m_wndCamToolBar);
→           // delete the next line for no tool tips
→           m_wndCamToolBar.SetBarStyle(m_wndCamToolBar.GetBarStyle() |
→              CBRS_TOOLTIPS | CBRS_FLYBY);
            return TRUE;
         }
```

We now begin to use *JOEY* resources to control menu items in the application.
You add menu items for *JOEY* to handle message handling, interface updating,
and menu/tool tips. The first step is to include *JOEY* resources in the project
resource file.

♦   Include the *JOEY* resources in your project resource file. From within MS
    Visual C++, open the project resource file, *viewit3d.rc*, for editing. From the
    menu, select Resource, Set Includes... to bring up the Set Includes
    dialogue. Within the Read-Only Symbol Directives, add the line #*include*
    <*joey\joey_res.h*> as the first directive. Within the Compile-Time Directives,
    add the line #*include* <*joey\joey_res.rc*> as the first directive. Close the
    project resource file (saving the changes) and re-open it for editing so that
    the *JOEY* resources can be read in and available for use, Figure P-2.

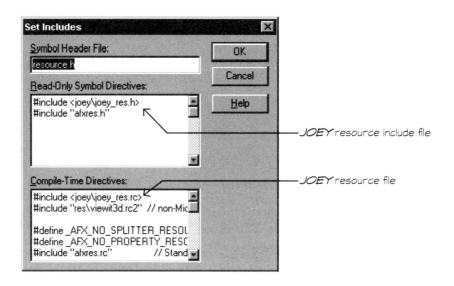

Figure P-2: Including *JOEY* resources in project resources.

In order to control the visibility of the camera toolbar, use AppStudio to add a menu item to the <u>V</u>iew pulldown menu for the SDI main menu (IDR_MAINFRAME in an SDI application), or the document object menu (IDR_3D_GEOTYPE in an MDI application). In OLE server applications, add the same item to the item server menus (IDR_3D_GEOTYPE_SRVR_EMB and IDR_3D_GEOTYPE_SRVR_IP in an MDI OLE server enabled application, and IDR_SRVR_EMBEDDED and IDR_SRVR_INPLACE in an SDI OLE server enabled application). Also, add the message handling for these in the appropriate frame windows.

◆   Add a selection with the ID: IDM_VIEW_CAMERA_TBAR (selected from the pre-defined IDs), and the Caption *&Camera Toolbar*, to the affected <u>V</u>iew pulldown menus. With the MFC ClassWizard, add processing for this message to both the application main frame, CMainFrame, and the OLE in-place editing frame, CInPlaceFrame (if the application is OLE server enabled). In both cases, add functions to process the command and to update the command user interface.

Start MFC ClassWizard and use the **Message Maps** panel to add these message handling functions. Select **Class <u>N</u>ame:** CMainFrame and in the **Object <u>I</u>Ds:** listbox select IDM_VIEW_CAMERA_TBAR. In the **Messages:** listbox, double-click on COMMAND and UPDATE_COMMAND_UI to create the message handler templates. Accept the names suggested by MFC ClassWizard for these message handlers. Repeat the process to add these message handlers to `CInPlaceFrame`.

Edit the MFC ClassWizard template functions as follows (the `CMainframe` version is shown, the additions to the functions in `CInPlaceFrame` are identical):

```
     void CMainFrame::OnViewCameraTbar()
     {
➜       ShowControlBar(&m_wndCamToolBar,
➜           (m_wndCamToolBar.GetStyle() & WS_VISIBLE) == 0, FALSE);
     }


     void CMainFrame::OnUpdateViewCameraTbar(CCmdUI* pCmdUI)
     {
➜       pCmdUI->SetCheck(m_wndCamToolBar.GetStyle() & WS_VISIBLE);
     }
```

This is only one method for controlling visibility of the camera toolbar. If there are additional toolbars, it may be appropriate to have a toolbar dialogue such as the one in MS Visual C++.

When the application starts, the toolbars are stacked at the upper left of the frame. You may want the camera toolbar to originally appear either at the left, right, or bottom of the frame (check the `DockControlBars` member function). As the application is running, you can pull the camera toolbar over to the right and move it onto the same line as, and next to, the application toolbar (if the application toolbar is not too large).

It is often desirable to have a menu that reflects the selections available on the toolbar (in the event that the toolbar is not currently visible or, just as a matter of convenience). Here, we add a <u>C</u>amera pulldown menu to the application menus for camera control. The addition of this camera menu will show you how to access the message ID's that affect *JOEY* camera operations. You may want to relocate some of these menu items for consistency within your application menus. Also, your application may want to check and/or change the state of some of these controls automatically for some operations.

♦   Add a pulldown menu item, <u>C</u>amera, after the <u>V</u>iew pulldown menu items for the SDI main menu (`IDR_MAINFRAME` in an SDI application), or the document object menu (`IDR_3D_GEOTYPE` in an MDI application). In OLE server applications, add the same item to the item server menus (`IDR_3D_GEOTYPE_SRVR_EMB` and `IDR_3D_GEOTYPE_SRVR_IP` in an MDI OLE server enabled application, and `IDR_SRVR_EMBEDDED` and `IDR_SRVR_INPLACE` in an SDI OLE server enabled application).

Within the camera pulldown, add camera control menu items using the predefined *JOEY* IDs:

ID:	Caption:
IDM_CAM_TRANS	&Translate
IDM_CAM_ZOOM	&Zoom
IDM_CAM_ROTATE	&Rotate
IDM_CAM_ORBIT	&Orbit
IDM_CAM_APPROACH	&Approach
IDM_CAM_WALK	&Walk
IDM_CAM_LOOK	&Look
separator	
IDM_CAM_RESET	&Reset
separator	
IDM_CAM_LEFT_MOUSE	On Left &Mouse
separator	
IDM_CAM_DIALOGUE	&Camera Dialogue
IDM_GRID_DIALOGUE	&Grid Dialogue

The IDs used in this menu are provided by *JOEY* with the corresponding message handlers, menu status handlers, menu/tool tips for display on the status bar, and context sensitive help. Each menu entry corresponds to one of the buttons on the *JOEY* camera toolbar.

The application can now be built and run. The camera toolbar will appear on the screen although none of the cameras are yet loaded.

1.2.3 Adding Status Bar Camera Feedback

JOEY provides user feedback about both the camera projection that is currently active in a 3D view and the camera interaction paradigm (on the application status bar). The camera projection is not always immediately obvious, and correct interpretation of the graphic is dependent upon knowing the camera projection. It could be encoded into the titlebar of a window, however, the titlebar is more important for other details. In addition to the camera projection, it is important to know how the camera is manipulated. Some manipulations are axis aligned (plan, front, right, etc.) while others present unique paradigms for manipulating both camera position and orientation.

Providing camera projection and move paradigm feedback requires setting aside two panes on the status bar for that feedback and informing *JOEY* that these panes have been reserved for *JOEY*'s use.

♦ To implement this, add strings to your resources that identify the projection and move paradigm status bar panes. We used `ID_INDICATOR_CAM_PROJ` and `ID_INDICATOR_CAM_MOVE` as the IDs with the strings set to *proj* and *move* respectively.[7]

♦ Now, add these identifiers to the application status bar initialisation table and inform *JOEY* in the application frame. We elected to make the camera type indicator the last pane on the status bar and the modifications to the *mainfrm.cpp* are as follows:

```
static UINT BASED_CODE indicators[] =
{
    ID_SEPARATOR,           // status line indicator
➜   //ID_INDICATOR_CAPS,    // usually not for 3D apps
➜   //ID_INDICATOR_NUM,     // usually not for 3D apps
➜   //ID_INDICATOR_SCRL,    // usually not for 3D apps
➜   ID_INDICATOR_CAM_PROJ,
➜   ID_INDICATOR_CAM_MOVE
};

    •
    •

int CMainFrame::OnCreate(LPCREATESTRUCT lpCreateStruct)
{
    •
    •

    // additions for JOEY camera ToolBar

➜   // setup camera type feedback
➜   JoeyConfig->CamTypeStatus(&m_wndStatusBar,
➜       ID_INDICATOR_CAM_PROJ, ID_INDICATOR_CAM_MOVE);

    return 0;
}
```

From this point on, the current camera type for the active window will be displayed in the last two panes of the status bar. If the application is an MDI application and not all of the windows are *JOEY* windows, then the last two panes of the status bar will be blanked when non-*JOEY* windows are active.

1.2.4 Revising the View

JOEY provides a view class that serves as the base class from which you derive your application views. To adjust the view provided by the MFC AppWizard,

---

[7] It really doesn't matter what the strings are. *JOEY* re-sizes each pane to the largest string that will ever be displayed in that pane.

change the derivation from MFC `CView` class to the *JOEY* `CJoeyView` class, then make a few function modifications. This affects the include (*.h*) and implementation (*.cpp*) files for the application view class (*objview.h* and *objview.cpp*). The sequence of changes is described below. In most cases, the changes are performed using global substitute, or using the MFC ClassWizard. In the accompanying code samples, lines changed using global substitute or the MFC ClassWizard are noted with a lighter arrow, →, than the lines requiring hand editing, ➔. Complete changes are provided in the application templates.

◆ In both *objview.h* and *objview.cpp*, change every reference to the MFC `CView` class to a reference to the *JOEY* `CJoeyView` class. Global substitution works fine for this.

◆ The changes described above invalidate the MFC ClassWizard database for the project. To rebuild this database, delete the existing ClassWizard database, *viewit3d.clw*. Then, from within Microsoft Visual C++, open the *viewit3d.rc* file for editing. Select the ClassWizard icon from the toolbar. A dialogue will notify you that the ClassWizard database is missing and ask if you wish to create it. Select **Yes** in this dialogue. A project files dialogue will provide an opportunity to select files that are to be used in creating the MFC ClassWizard database. The project files are included in this list by default and are, in this case, sufficient. Select **OK** and the database will be recreated and the MFC ClassWizard dialogue will then appear.

◆ Use the MFC ClassWizard to add message handling to the application view, `CObjView`, for the `WM_MOUSEMOVE`, `WM_LBUTTONDOWN`, `WM_LBUTTONUP`, and `WM_LBUTTONDBLCLK` messages. Edit the MFC ClassWizard created `OnCreate`, `OnMouseMove`, `OnLButtonDown`, `OnLButtonUp`, and `OnLButtonDblClk` message handling member functions as shown below:

```
void CObjView::OnMouseMove(UINT nFlags, CPoint point)
{
    // allow JOEY to handle camera tracking
    if (IsCamTracking()) {
        CJoeyView::OnMouseMove(nFlags,point);
        return;
    }
    // TODO: Add your message handler code here
}

void CObjView::OnLButtonDown(UINT nFlags, CPoint point)
{
    if (IsCamLeft()) {
        CJoeyView::OnMButtonDown(nFlags, point);
        return;
    }
    // TODO: Add your message handler code here
```

```
→   }

→   void CObjView::OnLButtonUp(UINT nFlags, CPoint point)
→   {
→       if (IsCamLeft()) {
→           CJoeyView::OnMButtonUp(nFlags, point);
→           return;
→       }
→       // TODO: Add your message handler code here
→   }

→   void CObjView::OnLButtonDblClk(UINT nFlags, CPoint point)
→   {
→       if (IsCamLeft()) {
→           CJoeyView::OnMButtonDblClk(nFlags, point);
→           return;
→       }
→       // TODO: Add your message handler code here
→   }
```

The additions to the `OnMouseMove` message handler assure that the *JOEY* view receives this message during interactive camera movement. Failure to make these additions to the `OnMouseMove` message handler will result in the application mouse tracking overriding any *JOEY* mouse tracking.

The additions to the left mouse button message handling functions, `OnLButtonDown`, `OnLButtonUp`, and `OnLButtonDblClk`, immediately pass control to the *JOEY* middle mouse button handlers when the left mouse button is used for camera control. By default, *JOEY* uses the middle mouse button for camera control. The option for left button camera control is provided in the event that the user does not have a three button mouse, or for viewing applications that have no other use for the left mouse button. Failure to make these additions to the left mouse button handlers results in a lack of left button camera control.[8]

◆   Make additions to the `OnDraw` message handler as shown below. This defers drawing to `OnDraw`, which performs camera and renderer setup in preparation for the data draw then calls the document `OnDraw` function for data drawing.

```
    void CObjView::OnDraw(CDC* pDC)
    {
        CObjDoc* pDoc = GetDocument();
        ASSERT_VALID(pDoc);
→       CJoeyView::OnDraw(pDC);    // defer control of display to JOEY
    }
```

---

[8] The toolbar button for left mouse button camera control will still remain, however, which will be most confusing for the user.

1.2.5 Revising the Document

JOEY provides document classes that serve as the base class from which you derive your application documents. To adjust the document provided in the MFC AppWizard, change the derivation of the document from CDocument or COleServerDoc class to the *JOEY* CJoeyDoc or CJoeyOleServerDoc class, respectively. This affects the include *(.h)* and implementation *(.cpp)* files for the application document files (*objdoc.h* and *objdoc.cpp*). The changes are shown below. In most cases, the changes are performed using global substitute or using the MFC ClassWizard. In the accompanying code samples, lines changed using global substitute or the MFC ClassWizard are noted with a lighter arrow, →, than the lines requiring hand editing,➔. The complete changes are provided in the application templates.

◆ In both *objdoc.h* and *objdoc.cpp*, change every reference to the MFC COleServerDoc class to a reference to the *JOEY* CJoeyOleServerDoc class. Global substitution works fine for this. Note that if you are not creating an OLE server, the document is derived from the MFC CDocument class and you would change this to the *JOEY* CJoeyDoc class.

◆ The changes described above invalidate the MFC ClassWizard database for the project. To rebuild this database, delete the existing ClassWizard database, *viewit3d.clw*. Then, from within Microsoft Visual C++, open the *viewit3d.rc* file for editing. Select the ClassWizard icon from the toolbar. A dialogue will notify you that the ClassWizard database is missing and ask if you wish to create it. Select <u>Yes</u> in this dialogue. A project files dialogue will provide an opportunity to select files that are to be used in creating the MFC ClassWizard database. The project files are included in this list by default and are, in this case, sufficient. Select OK and the database will be re-created and the MFC ClassWizard dialogue will then appear.

◆ In *objdoc.h*, add a member function OnDraw, and in *objdoc.cpp*, add the body of this member function as shown below. In the *objdoc.h* header file, add the following:

```
        // objdoc.h : interface of the CObjDoc class
        •
        •
        // Operations
        public:
➔           virtual void OnDraw(PIRenderDevX,CJoeyView const *) const;
```

In the *objdoc.cpp* implementation file, add the ObjDoc::OnDraw member function as follows:

```
        // objdoc.cpp : implementation of the CObjDoc class
        •
```

     ♦

```
➔   /////////////////////////////////////////////////////////////
➔   // CObjDoc operations
➔   void CObjDoc::OnDraw(PIRenderDevX pRD,
➔       CJoeyView const *pJView) const
➔   {
➔       //TODO - add application drawing code here
➔   }
    /////////////////////////////////////////////////////////////
    // CObjDoc commands
```

♦ Add a call to the `CJoeyOleServerDoc::Serialize` function within the application document's `Serialize` member function in *objdoc.cpp:*

```
    void CObjDoc::Serialize(CArchive& ar)
    {
        if (ar.IsStoring())
        {
            // TODO: add storing code here
        }
        else
        {
    // TODO: add loading code here
        }
➔       CJoeyOleServerDoc::Serialize(ar);
    }
```

This completes the basic changes to the view and document class. The framework can be re-compiled and run as a stand-alone application.

1.2.6 Revising the OLE Server Item

This section applies to OLE Server applications only. *JOEY* provides an OLE server item class that serves as the base class from which you derive your application OLE server items. To adjust the OLE server item provided by the MFC AppWizard, change the derivation from MFC `COleServerItem` class to the `CJoeyOleServerItem` class, then make a few function modifications. This affects the include (*.h*) and implementation (*.cpp*) files for the application view class (*objsrvr.h* and *objsrvr.cpp*). The changes are described below. In most cases, the changes are performed using global substitute. The complete changes are provided in the application templates.

♦ In *objsrvr.cpp* and *objsrvr.h*, globally replace every reference to the MFC `COleServerItem` class with a reference to the *JOEY* `CJoeyOleServerItem` class.

♦ In *objsrvr.cpp* and *objsrvr.h*, remove the `OnGetExtent` member function. The functionality of `OnGetExtent` is handled entirely by *JOEY*.

♦ Remove the second argument passed to the `CJoeyOleServerItem` constructor in the `CObjSrvrItem` constructor.

```
    CObjSrvrItem::CObjSrvrItem(CObjDoc* pContainerDoc)
→       : CJoeyOleServerItem(pContainerDoc)
    {
        // TODO: add one-time construction code here
        //   (eg, adding additional clipboard formats ... source)
    }
```

♦ Replace the body of the `OnDraw` member function in *objsrvr.cpp*:

```
    BOOL CObjSrvrItem::OnDraw(CDC* pDC, CSize& rSize)
    {
        CObjDoc* pDoc = GetDocument();
        ASSERT_VALID(pDoc);
→       CJoeyOleServerItem::OnDraw(pDC,rSize);
        return TRUE;
    }
```

The basic interactive 3D functionality now exists both for stand-alone and OLE server operation. If you have created the *contain* application described in the MFC tutorial, you can experiment with running the framework as an OLE server within the *contain* application. You can also use a container application (e.g., MS Word[9]) to experiment with *viewit3d*.

1.2.7 Adding Context Sensitive Help for *JOEY*

MFC AppWizard has already created a help template for the project as a result of asking for Context Sensitive Help during project creation. To add context sensitive help to *JOEY*, it is necessary to augment this template with *JOEY* specific information. Help for MFC is implemented through template files in both rich text format (**.rtf*) and bitmap (**.bmp*) format, and through help map files (**.hm*). Adding help for *JOEY* is simply a matter of copying *JOEY* help template files into the project *hlp* subdirectory, and adding references to the *JOEY* help template file and map file in the help project file (**.hpj*) created by the MFC AppWizard.

In the case of the sample application, *viewit3d*, the help project file is *viewit3d.hpj*. MFC AppWizard has created a *hlp* subdirectory in the project subdirectory and copied all of the required MFC help templates into this directory.

---

[9] Version 6.0 or later.

♦ Copy all of the *JOEY* help template files from the **$(JOEY_DIR)***hlp_tmpl* directory into the project *hlp* directory.

♦ Add the references to the *JOEY* help template file and the *JOEY* help map file in the *viewit3d.hpj* help project file as noted below.

```
    [OPTIONS]
    •
    •
    [FILES]
    hlp\afxcore.rtf
    hlp\afxprint.rtf
    hlp\afxolesv.rtf
→   hlp\joey.rtf

    [BITMAPS]
    •
    •
    [MAP]
    #include <D:\MSVC20\MFC\include\afxhelp.hm>
→   #include <$(JOEY_DIR)\include\joey.hm>
    #include <hlp\viewit3d.hm>
```

♦ From the MS-DOS prompt in the project directory, run *makehelp.bat*. The help file will be created and copied into both the *WinDebug* and *WinRel* project subdirectories.

At this point, you can rebuild the application framework and Help will be available for the standard MFC application menu. It will also be available for all of the *JOEY* functionality including the *JOEY* toolbar and *JOEY* dialogue boxes.

1.2.8 Build and Test the Framework

The framework for an interactive 3D application is now complete. The following functionality has been added in Section 1.2:

Camera toolbar	A dockable camera toolbar has been added with tooltips, context sensitive help, and control for toolbar visibility.
Status bar feedback	Status bar feedback for the camera type in the current view has been added.
3D views and documents	A view/document template for 3D data has been added to the framework so that the default application document and view support 3D data display and manipulation.

3D camera control	Any 3D view has interactive camera control (though this is hard to see without data). The middle mouse button is used for camera control, and when depressed, the cursor will change to an icon describing camera move mode. A camera dialogue is available for dialogue entry of camera type and positioning data. It can be invoked by the last button of the toolbar.
3D grids and axis	Grid systems and axis systems can be displayed, and used for hit testing and positioning. The grid dialogue can be invoked by the next-to-last button of the toolbar.
Context sensitive help	Context sensitive help is available for all JOEY toolbar buttons and dialogue boxes. The help text is in template files that can be customised for the application.

All of this functionality can be exercised now, both in stand-alone operation or in the context of an embedded, in-place activated OLE server application. The framework is self registering (the system registration database is updated with application information when the application is run in stand-alone mode[10]). When the framework is run as an OLE in-place server, it is launched by the system. The **$(JOEY_DIR)***bin* directory (containing *joey.dll* and other *.dll* files) must be in the system path to be found during the launching of *viewit3d* as an OLE server application.[11]

1.3 Adding Application Read and Draw

Now, we start with the newly created framework and add functionality for a simple application that reads and displays 3D data. The reader and display for an *.a3d* (ASCII 3D) format file to the cObjDoc class are added. The editing for this is confined to the cObjDoc header and implementation files *objdoc.h* and *objdoc.cpp* respectively. First, we describe the format of the object data and then describe the code modifications required for reading and display.

---

[10] The registration database can be reviewed using *windows\system32\regedt32.exe* on a normal Windows NT 3.5 installation. It may be helpful to add a program item for this along with your other development tools as you may review the registration database frequently during development.

[11] This is done in NT using the system applet from the control panel, and in Windows 95 by an addition to the *autoexec.bat* file.

1.3.1 Object Data Definition

A simple ASCII data file will be used for objects that can be viewed by the sample application, *viewit3d*. These files are given a *.a3d* extension. Since *viewit3d* only has read and display capability at this point, data needs to be created outside of *viewit3d*. The ASCII format makes it possible (though painful) to create simple objects with a text editor. A collection of objects has been supplied in the **$(JOEY_DIR)***data* directory.

It is necessary to introduce a few graphic concepts here. They will be discussed in more detail later in the text. The default axis system used for graphics data representation is a left handed axis system oriented by *JOEY* as shown in Figure P-3.[12] The objects we create are defined by points (vertices) in the 3D space of this axis system and by the connection of points into planar faces. Faces have an inside and outside, defined by the direction of vertex ordering, either clockwise or counter-clockwise. When you are looking at the outside of the face, the vertices are ordered clockwise.

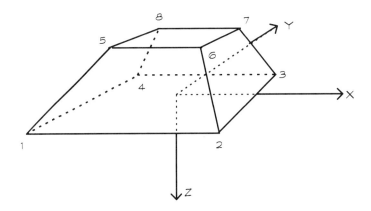

Figure P-3: Object with Axis System used for Graphics Data Representation

Vertices are entered in the file as a "v" followed by the X, Y, and Z coordinates of the vertex. The vertices are implicitly numbered in the order they appear in the file, and the numbering starts at 1. Faces are entered as an "f" followed by a list of vertex indices. The end of the file is indicated by the line "end".

---

[12] It is inevitable that this choice of default axis system will not match the way that you normally define data. See Section 3.1.1.2 for details about how to tell *JOEY* to adjust to your way of thinking.

Comment lines begin with a "#". Review the truncated pyramid object in Figure P-3, whose size is 4x4 units at the base. The data file for this object is:[13]

```
# base vertices
v -2.0 -2.0  0.0
v  2.0 -2.0  0.0
v  2.0  2.0  0.0
v -2.0  2.0  0.0
#top vertices
v -1.0 -1.0 -1.0
v  1.0 -1.0 -1.0
v  1.0  1.0 -1.0
v -1.0  1.0 -1.0
#base
f 1 2 3 4
#sides
f 1 5 6 2
f 2 6 7 3
f 3 7 8 4
f 4 8 5 1
#top
f 5 8 7 6
end
```

1.3.2 Adding Read and Draw

The implementation of the object database is not particularly brilliant. It declares a static vertex array of some maximum size, a static face array of some maximum size, and some other rather arbitrarily defined limits. If the limits are exceeded by the object, then a failure message for object loading is issued. This sounds like a step back into FORTRAN, but it makes it easier to write the code for the sample in a very straight-forward fashion. Since this is only a reader, the `Serialize` function for the `CObjDoc` will only process the reading of an *.a3d* file at this time.

The first step is to add the database for the geometric object to the `CObjDoc` class. The database will consist of an array of 3D points (vertices) and a linked list of faces. Each of the faces is a vertex count and a list of pointers to the vertices that define it.

◆   Add the following database definition to the *objdoc.h* header file:

```
// objdoc.h : interface of the CObjDoc class
//
/////////////////////////////////////////////////////////////

➜   #define MAX_OBJ_PTS    5000      // maximum vertices
➜   #define MAX_OBJ_FACES 10000      // maximum faces
```

---

[13] This data file is supplied in **$(JOEY_DIR)** \ *data* \ *pyra.a3d*.

```
→   typedef struct {
→       CPoint3f**      pts;
→       int             ptCt;
→   } FACE;

    class CObjSrvrItem;

    class CObjDoc : public CJoeyOleServerDoc
    {
→       CPoint3f        m_pts[MAX_OBJ_PTS];      // the vertex array
→       int             m_ptCt;                  // the point count
→       FACE            m_faces[MAX_OBJ_FACES];  // the face array
→       int             m_faceCt;                // the face count
→       int             m_maxFacePts;            // max pts in a face

    protected: // create from serialization only
        ♦
        ♦
    };
    //////////////////////////////////////////////////////////////
```

♦ Add initialisation information in the CObjDoc::CObjDoc constructor. Here,
   we initialise the object data:

```
    CObjDoc::CObjDoc()
    {
→       m_ptCt = 0;
→       m_faceCt = 0;
→       m_maxFacePts = 0;

        EnableAutomation();

        AfxOleLockApp();
    }
```

♦ Use the ClassWizard to add the DeleteContents function to the CObjDoc
   class. In the CObjDoc implementation, make the following changes:

```
→   void CObjDoc::DeleteContents()
→   {
→       m_ptCt = 0;    // reset the vertex count
→       // loop through faces, delete vertex buffers
→       while (--m_faceCt >= 0) {
→           if (NULL != m_faces[m_faceCt].pts)
→               free((void*)m_faces[m_faceCt].pts);
→       }
→       m_faceCt = 0;  // reset the face count
→       m_maxFacePts = 0;

→       CJoeyOleServerDoc::DeleteContents();
```

♦ Add object reading code to the `CObjDoc::Serialize` function. A library of useful helper functions with complete source code is provided in *vit3dlib.dll*. This includes some reading and parsing functions for ASCII data files that are used. Use the Project, Files... dialogue to add **$(JOEY_DIR)** \ *lib* \ *vit3dlib.dll* to the project files list. Add the include file at the beginning of *objdoc.cpp* as follows:

```
// objdoc.cpp : implementation of the CObjDoc class
//

#include "stdafx.h"
#include "viewit3d.h"
#include "objdoc.h"
#include "objsrvr.h"
```

➔   `#include <vit3dlib.h>`

♦ Add the reader for the ASCII *.a3d* file to the `CObjDoc::Serialize` function as follows. This is a lot to type, and you may just want to copy this from the sample code file.

```
//////////////////////////////////////////////////////////
// CObjDoc serialization
```
➔ `#define MAX_TOKEN_CT        50`
➔ `#define IN_BUFF_LEN         512`
```

```
➔ `#define OBJ_END_FILE    0`
➔ `#define OBJ_VERTEX      1`
➔ `#define OBJ_FACE        2`
```

```
➔ `static char*    s_strObjCmd[] = {"end",    "v",    "f",};`
➔ `static int      s_ctObjCmd = sizeof(s_strObjCmd)/sizeof(char*);`
```
void CObjDoc::Serialize(CArchive& ar)
{
```
➔ `    int     lineCt = 0;`
```

    if (ar.IsStoring())
    {
        // TODO: add storing code here
    }
    else
    {
```
➔ `        char    strIn[IN_BUFF_LEN];`
➔ `        char*   lpToken[MAX_TOKEN_CT];`
➔ `        int     ii, nCmd, ptInd, tokenCt;`
➔ `        float   fDataSpace = 1.0f;`
➔ `        // read lines in the file and parse into the database`
➔ `        while (V3dGetString(ar,strIn,IN_BUFF_LEN)) {`
➔ `            lineCt++;`
➔ `            if ((tokenCt = V3dParse(strIn,lpToken,`
➔ `                MAX_TOKEN_CT)) <= 0) continue;`
```
```

```
                    for (nCmd = 0; nCmd < s_ctObjCmd; nCmd++)
                        if (strcmp(s_strObjCmd[nCmd],lpToken[0]) == 0)
                            break;
                    switch (nCmd) {
                        case OBJ_END_FILE:
                            goto end_of_obj_data;
                        case OBJ_VERTEX:
                            if (m_ptCt >= MAX_OBJ_PTS) {
                                AfxMessageBox(IDS_EXCEED_PT_BUFF);
                                DeleteContents();
                                return;
                            }
                            if (tokenCt < 4) goto bad_format;
                            // load the vertex and update the dataspace
                            for (ii= PT_x; ii<=PT_z; ii++) {
                                m_pts[m_ptCt][ii] =
                                    (float)atof(lpToken[ii+1]);
                                if (m_pts[m_ptCt][ii] > fDataSpace)
                                    fDataSpace = m_pts[m_ptCt][ii];
                                else if ((-m_pts[m_ptCt][ii]) > fDataSpace)
                                    fDataSpace = -m_pts[m_ptCt][ii];
                            }
                            m_ptCt++;
                            break;
                        case OBJ_FACE:
                            if (m_faceCt >= MAX_OBJ_FACES) {
                                AfxMessageBox(IDS_EXCEED_FACE_BUFF);
                                DeleteContents();
                                return;
                            }
                            if (tokenCt < 4) goto bad_format; // 3 verts min
                            // allocate the vertex pointer list
                            if ( NULL == (m_faces[m_faceCt].pts=(CPoint3f**)
                                    malloc((tokenCt-1)*sizeof(CPoint3f*)))) {
                                AfxThrowMemoryException();
                                DeleteContents();
                                return;
                            }
                            // fill the vertex pointer list
                            m_faces[m_faceCt].ptCt = tokenCt-1;
                            if (m_maxFacePts < m_faces[m_faceCt].ptCt)
                                m_maxFacePts = m_faces[m_faceCt].ptCt;
                            for (ii = 1; ii < tokenCt; ii++) {
                                if ( ((ptInd = atoi(lpToken[ii])-1) < 0) ||
                                        (ptInd >= m_ptCt) ) goto bad_format;
                                m_faces[m_faceCt].pts[ii-1] = m_pts + ptInd;
                            }
                            m_faceCt++;
                            break;
                        default:
                            // not a meaningful line
                            break;
                    }
```

```
➜              }
➜     end_of_obj_data:
➜              //At 2.0 * dataspace, we fill the whole screen width
➜              RE()->DataSpace(fDataSpace*3.0f,TRUE,TRUE,FALSE);
         }
         CJoeyOleServerDoc::Serialize(ar);
➜     return;

➜     bad_format:
➜         {   TCHAR       lpstrLine[16];
➜             CString     cStr;
➜             _stprintf(lpstrLine,_TEXT("%d"),lineCt);
➜             AfxFormatString1(cStr,IDS_INVALID_FORMAT,lpstrLine);
➜             AfxMessageBox(cStr);
➜             DeleteContents();
➜         }
         }
```

♦ Add the body of the OnDraw function. We are using a simple wireframe
  drawing mode at this time. Later in the text, we explore the use of more
  sophisticated rendering techniques in the display.

```
      /////////////////////////////////////////////////////////
      // CObjDoc operations
      void CObjDoc::OnDraw(PIRenderDev pRD,
         CJoeyView const *pJView) const
      {
➜     CPoint3f**      ppPts = NULL;
➜     int             ii, jj;

➜     if ((0 == m_faceCt) || (0 == m_maxFacePts)) return;
➜     if (NULL == (ppPts = new PPoint3f[m_maxFacePts])) return;
➜     for (ii=0; ii<m_faceCt; ii++) {
➜         for (jj=0; jj<m_faces[ii].ptCt; jj++)
➜             ppPts[jj] = m_faces[ii].pts[jj];
➜         ppPts[jj] = m_faces[ii].pts[0];   // to close the polygon
➜         pRD->Draw3dPolyline(m_faces[ii].ptCt + 1,ppPts);
➜     }
➜     delete ppPts;
      }
```

♦ Use ClassWizard to add the OnOpenDocument function. Add user feedback
  to confirm that the object was read:

```
➜     BOOL CObjDoc::OnOpenDocument(LPCTSTR lpszPathName)
➜     {
➜         if (!CJoeyOleServerDoc::OnOpenDocument(lpszPathName))
➜             return FALSE;
➜         // provide feedback that the object was read
➜         CString     cstrFmt, cstr;
➜         cstrFmt.LoadString(IDS_OPEN_OBJECT);
➜         cstr.Format(cstrFmt,lpszPathName,m_ptCt,m_faceCt);
```

```
→        AfxMessageBox(cstr,MB_OK | MB_ICONINFORMATION);
→        return TRUE;
→   }
```

◆   Add the following strings to the project resources (*viewit3d.rc*) so that error messaging will work and the compiler will not complain about undeclared symbols.

ID	CAPTION
IDS_EXCEED_PT_BUFF	Vertex buffer length exceeded!!
IDS_EXCEED_FACE_BUFF	Face buffer length exceeded!!
IDS_INVALID_FORMAT	Invalid input format, line %1
IDS_OPEN_OBJECT	Read %s with %d vertices and %d faces

◆   Rebuild and run *viewit3d*. You can read the *.a3d* files supplied with *JOEY* and test the operation of the cameras, grids, etc. The context sensitive help explains camera and grid operation.

You have now created an interactive 3D graphics application!!

2. Integrating Graphic Applications Into Windows

Integrating an application into Windows requires both a consistent look and feel with other Windows applications and the capability to communicate data between applications. The last chapter combined MFC and *JOEY* to bring us a long way toward achieving the first objective. This section concentrates on the second objective; facilitating communication and data sharing between your application and other Windows applications. *JOEY* and MFC work together to facilitate this integration but some of the work is left to the application developer.

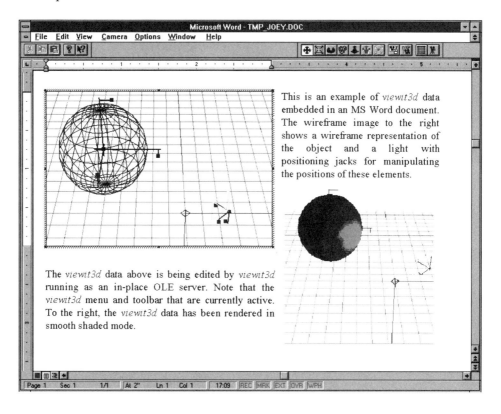

Figure P-4: *Viewit3d* running as an OLE server inside MS Word.

2.1 OLE Server Capabilities - Linking and Embedding

We start by making *viewit3d* an OLE server. First, we use this sample application to find out how an OLE server works when its data is linked or embedded into an OLE container. Then, armed with a cursory understanding of some of the mechanics of OLE operation in the MFC framework, we upgrade *viewit3d* to be an OLE server.

2.1.1 Investigating the workings of OLE

The *viewit3d* application is nearly a server in its present form simply because we asked for a server when creating the MFC framework in AppWizard. There are a few simple tests that can be made to help understand what it takes to complete the task. We temporarily add some message box feedback so that we can trace some of the things that are happening when a server operates.

Before trying to use *viewit3d* as a server, it is important to add some handling for storage of data to the `CObjDoc::Serialize` function. OLE will exercise both data saving and reading when *viewit3d* is used as an OLE server, and it is expected that a save will create data that can be read. In *objdoc.cpp*, add the following lines to write an empty object data file if a data save is requested:

```
    void CObjDoc::Serialize(CArchive& ar)
    {
        int     lineCt = 0;

        if (ar.IsStoring())
        {
➜           char    strOut[IN_BUFF_LEN];
➜           // write the data end
➜           sprintf(strOut,"%s\n",s_strObjCmd[OBJ_END_FILE]);
➜           ar.Write((void*)strOut,strlen(strOut));
        }
        •
        •
    }
```

Try running *viewit3d* as a server without making any more changes. Use a container application, such as MS Word 6.0 or *contain* (from the MS Visual C++ Tutorial), to test the server functionality. Try the following:

1. Embed by creating data in-place.

2. Embed and link from data files.

These can be done by either using *contain* or MS Word as follows:[14]

♦   Creating in-place:
In MS Word, select Insert, Object. In the Object dialogue that appears, use the Create New panel and select ASCII 3D Geometry (.a3d) as the Object Type. A small *viewit3d* window will appear with *viewit3d* running as an in-place server. The toolbars will change to the *viewit3d* toolbars. Since *viewit3d* cannot create any data, there will be nothing in the window. If you click outside the *viewit3d* window, the normal MS Word user interface will return and the *viewit3d* background colour square will be drawn.

♦   Embedding from a file:
In MS Word, select Insert, Object. In the Object dialogue that appears, use the Create from File panel and select *hand.a3d* as the File Name. A small *viewit3d* window will appear containing nothing but the background colour for *viewit3d*. Double click on this square to start *viewit3d* running as an in-place server. The toolbars will change to the *viewit3d* toolbars. Again, no data is displayed in the window.

♦   Linking from a file:
In MS Word, select Insert, Object. In the Object dialogue that appears, use the Create from File panel and select hand.a3d as the File Name. A small *viewit3d* window will appear with *hand.a3d* object displayed. Double-click on this box and the *viewit3d* application will be started. Though it is not running as an in-place server, there is communication between *viewit3d* and the container. Changes made in *viewit3d* will appear in the container.

Linking appears to work correctly while embedding does not. In order to understand what is happening, we need feedback from *viewit3d* while it is being run. Make the following changes to *viewit3d* for this investigation:

♦   Add message box feedback in the `CObjDoc::Serialize` function in *objdoc.cpp* as follows:

```
        void CObjDoc::Serialize(CArchive& ar)
        {
            int     lineCt = 0;

➔           TCHAR   outBuff[64];
➔           _stprintf(outBuff,_TEXT("CObjDoc::Serialize: %d"),
➔               ar.IsStoring());
```

---

[14] In MS Word, Shift F9 can be used to switch from the graphic representation of linked and embedded data to a textual description of what it is that is linked or embedded in the document.

```
➜          AfxMessageBox(outBuff,MB_OK | MB_ICONINFORMATION);

           if (ar.IsStoring())
              •
    }
```

♦ Add message box feedback in the `CObjView::OnDraw` function in *objview.cpp* as follows:

```
    void CObjView::OnDraw(CDC* pDC)
    {
        CObjDoc* pDoc = GetDocument();
➜       AfxMessageBox(_TEXT("CObjView::OnDraw"),
➜          MB_OK | MB_ICONINFORMATION);
        ASSERT_VALID(pDoc);
        CJoeyView::OnDraw(pDC);// defer control of display to Joey
    }
```

♦ Add message box feedback in the `CObjSrvrItem::OnDraw` function in *objsrvr.cpp* as follows:

```
    BOOL CObjSrvrItem::OnDraw(CDC* pDC, CSize& rSize)
    {
        CObjDoc* pDoc = GetDocument();
➜       AfxMessageBox(_TEXT("CObjSrvrItem::OnDraw"),
➜          MB_OK | MB_ICONINFORMATION);
        ASSERT_VALID(pDoc);
        CJoeyOleServerItem::OnDraw(pDC,rSize);
        return TRUE;
    }
```

Repeat the exercises of embedding and linking. DO NOT try to do any interactive camera manipulation with this version of *viewit3d* (mouse ownership gets confused by the message box displayed by `CObjView::OnDraw`, and system reboot may be required to resolve the problem).[15] To experiment with what happens if the linked or embedded object is edited, change the camera with the camera dialogue box.

The results of these experiments as well as additional discussion are found in **Implementation**. The important observation from these experiments is that data is always embedded into a container using the document `Serialize` member function once to read the data file and a second time to write the data file. Data is never embedded by simply copying the data file into the document.

---

[15] You may also encounter problems with the interaction between the message box and MS Word or *contain*. We suggest that you move the container so that the centre of the screen is relatively clear. Also remember that you can use *pView* (the process viewer) to kill processes that are out of control.

2.1.2 Completing the Implementation as an OLE Server

The main task to finish making *viewit3d* an OLE server is to complete the implementation of the CObjDoc::Serialize function and to remove the messaging added in the last section.

♦ Remove the feedback message boxes added in the last section (these are commented out in the sample source code provided with this book).

♦ Remove the object read feedback box in the CObjDoc::OnOpenDocument function, file *objdoc.cpp* (this message is particularly annoying when it shows up in a container while an embedded object is being read):

```
BOOL CObjDoc::OnOpenDocument(LPCTSTR lpszPathName)
{
    ♦

    // provide feedback that the object was read
    //CString       cstrFmt, cstr;
    //cstrFmt.LoadString(IDS_OPEN_OBJECT);
    //cstr.Format(cstrFmt,lpszPathName,m_ptCt,m_faceCt);
    //AfxMessageBox(cstr,MB_OK | MB_ICONINFORMATION);

    return TRUE;
}
```

♦ Add the serialisation code for writing to the ObjDoc::Serialize member function in *objdoc.cpp*:

```
void CObjDoc::Serialize(CArchive& ar)
{
    int     lineCt = 0;

    if (ar.IsStoring())
    {
        char    strOut[IN_BUFF_LEN];
        char    strIndx[16];
        int     ii, jj;

        // write the vertices
        for (ii = 0; ii< m_ptCt; ii++) {
            sprintf(strOut,"%s %.3f %.3f %.3f\n",
                s_strObjCmd[OBJ_VERTEX], m_pts[ii].x,
                m_pts[ii].y, m_pts[ii].z);
            ar.Write((void*)strOut,strlen(strOut));
        }
        // write the faces
        for (ii = 0; ii< m_faceCt; ii++) {
            sprintf(strOut,"%s", s_strObjCmd[OBJ_FACE]);
            for (jj = 0; jj < m_faces[ii].ptCt; jj++)  {
                sprintf(strIndx," %d",
                    (m_faces[ii].pts[jj] - m_pts) + 1);
```

```
→                       strcat(strOut,strIndx);
→                }
→                strcat(strOut,"\n");
→                ar.Write((void*)strOut,strlen(strOut));
→          }
          // write the data end
          sprintf(strOut,"%s\n",s_strObjCmd[OBJ_END_FILE]);
          ar.Write((void*)strOut,strlen(strOut));
     }
     else
        •
        •
        •
  }
```

Rebuild the *viewit3d* sample application and test it as a server application. You should be able to repeat all of the linking and embedding exercises at this time with a server that performs as you would expect.

2.2 Clipboards, Files, and 3D Viewers

Suppose you create some data within a 3D application and you wish to discuss this data with a colleague. There are currently two options; send the colleague the data files (which means that the colleague also needs to have licensed the 3D application that you used to create the data) or convert the views of the data to bitmaps or metafiles. Requiring your colleague to have a copy of the application just to look at data seems like overkill[16] and 2D views in metafiles and bitmaps may require multiple images to provide a good description of the data.

It is obvious that there is a missing standard format for application independent data transfer between applications (the equivalent of a 3D metafile). Accompanying this format, a viewer (similar to the current clipboard viewer) is required so that people can examine this 3D data and convert it to 2D metafile and/or bitmap representation. The *JOEY* 3D metafile (*.j3d* format) and *JOEY* 3D Viewers are provided to satisfy this need. Conceptually, this alters the application integration (with other Windows applications), Figure P-5.

---

[16] Especially in applications like technical documentation where a CAD or other model needs to be included in the documentation but it is not practical (for software licensing, data integrity and learning curve reasons) to have the documentor actually use the design application.

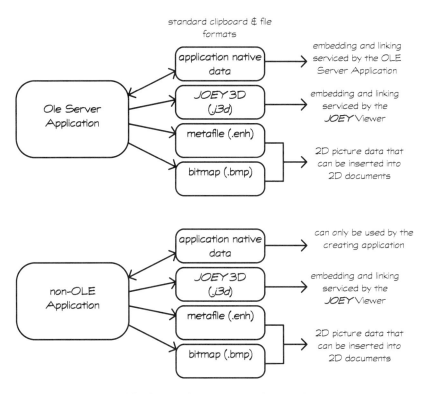

Figure P-5: Standard clipboard and file formats for integration of OLE and non-OLE applications in the Windows environment.

Now, we enable *viewit3d* to transfer data in application native, *JOEY* 3D, enhanced metafile, or bitmap formats using either the clipboard or data files. This provides the greatest opportunity to make the data available to other applications in the most useful form for the next operation that needs to be performed on that data.

2.2.1 Enabling Special Clipboard Copy Formats

JOEY works in conjunction with MFC to provide clipboard services. Normally, an application uses the clipboard as a place for keeping application specific data and data in standard formats that can be transferred between applications. This data finds its way to the clipboard through user selection of data followed by cut or copy operations. Standard clipboard formats are used for transferring data between applications. Here, we demonstrate how to put the data that you draw in a window onto the clipboard in a variety of formats so that it can be used by other applications.[17]

Enabling clipboard transfer of application native, *JOEY* 3D, enhanced metafile and bitmap data through *JOEY* is done by providing a source for the generation of an IDM_EDIT_COPY_SPECIAL command that is sent to a *JOEY* view.

♦   Edit the project resource file, *viewit3d.rc*, using AppStudio to add an separator and a Copy Special... menu item to the bottom of the Edit pulldown. In the IDR_3D_GEOTYPE menu Edit pulldown after Paste, add a separator entry, then a Copy Special... entry with the pre-defined ID: IDM_EDIT_COPY_SPECIAL, and Caption: *Copy &Special...* (the prompt string is picked up from the *JOEY* resources). Copy this newly created menu item to the Edit pulldowns in IDR_3D_GEOTYPE_SRVR_EMB and IDR_3D_GEOTYPE_SRVR_IP.

2.2.2 Enabling Special File Save Formats

In addition to copying data onto the clipboard for pasting into applications, we want to be able to send the data (as files) to other users. Reading and writing of native data is part of every application and is already implemented in *viewit3d*. We add a Save Special command to the Files menu for special data formats. We refer to these as Special because they are one-way data transfers. These special forms cannot be read back into the application in any meaningful way.

Like the special clipboard formats, special file formats are enabled by providing a source for the generation of an IDM_FILE_SAVE_SPECIAL command that is sent to the *JOEY* view.

♦   Edit the project resource file, *viewit3d.rc*, using AppStudio to add an separator and a Save Special... menu item to the bottom of the File pulldown. In the IDR_3D_GEOTYPE menu File pulldown after Save As..., add a separator entry, then a Save Special... entry with the pre-defined ID: IDM_FILE_SAVE_SPECIAL, and Caption: *Save &Special...* (the prompt string is picked up from the *JOEY* resources). Copy this newly created menu item to the File pulldowns in DR_3D_GEOTYPE_SRVR_EMB and IDR_3D_GEOTYPE_SRVR_IP.

---

[17] Though this discussion focuses on moving all of the application data, most of the formats are implemented through the document OnDraw function. This means that the OnDraw function can be used to filter only parts of the database for inclusion in the clipboard transfer if desired.

2.2.3 **Playing with the Clipboard and Files**

We can now rebuild and run a version of *viewit3d* that
supports the special clipboard and file formats. We investigate
them in order from that preserving the greatest data integrity
to that preserving the least:

1. OLE Embedding and linking of native application data

2. *JOEY* 3D data and the *JOEY* viewer

3. Enhanced metafiles

4. Bitmaps

2.2.3.1 **Native Application Data**

We have explored linking and embedding from the data files used by the
application. Now, we focus on the clipboard.

♦   In order to embed from the clipboard, run *viewit3d* and load an object such
    as *ball.a3d*. Select Edit, Copy Special... A Copy Special dialogue box will
    appear. It will allow you to specify the width and height for the graphic to
    appear when pasted into the container. The default format for the Copy
    Special... is the application native format. Select OK to initiate the copying
    of the application data to the clipboard.

♦   In MS Word, select Edit, Paste Special... The resulting Paste Special
    dialogue will allow you to select ASCII 3D Geometry Object or Picture as
    the type of data to paste. Select ASCII 3D Geometry Object to embed the
    data from the clipboard into the document. If you are using *contain*, it will
    paste the 3D geometry without offering a choice. The Picture format posted
    to the clipboard is the metafile representation which is cached for display
    when the 3D geometry object is not activated. After the object has been
    embedded, behaviour is the same as embedding from a file.

♦   When linking from the clipboard, the steps followed are the same as those
    in embedding, except in MS Word. Select Paste Link: in the Paste Special
    dialogue. In *contain*, select Paste Link from the Edit pulldown menu.

2.2.3.2 *JOEY* **3D Data**

Now, we create *JOEY* 3D formats on the clipboard and in files for linking and
embedding.

Embedding from the Clipboard:

♦ To copy *JOEY* 3D to the clipboard, run *viewit3d* and load a geometry object. Select Edit, Copy Special... In the Copy Special dialogue, select JOEY 3D Viewer as the format. Again, the height and width can be set. Only the embed form is put on the clipboard since there is no *JOEY* 3D file for linking.

♦ In MS Word, select Edit, Paste Special. The resulting Paste Special dialogue will allow you to select JOEY 3D Viewer object or Picture as the type of data to paste. Select JOEY 3D Viewer object to embed the data from the clipboard. The Picture format posted to the clipboard is the metafile representation which is cached for display when the *JOEY* 3D object is not activated.

Linking and Embedding from a File:

♦ To create *JOEY* 3D files, run *viewit3d* and load a geometry object. Select File, Save Special... In the Save Special dialogue, accept the default format selection JOEY 3D Viewer (.j3d) and select OK. A file selection dialogue will appear for selection of a name for saving the file.

♦ Embedding and Linking the *JOEY* 3D data files is done in the same way that embedding and linking *viewit3d* native data files was done except that you will select *.j3d files. When you activate the object, the *JOEY* viewer will run for in-place editing. The *JOEY* viewer can also be run as a stand-alone application for data viewing.

You may notice that there does not seem to be much difference between the functionality of *viewit3d* and that of the *JOEY* 3D Viewer. There is not much difference because, at this point in its implementation, *viewit3d* is primarily a viewer. The differences will be significant as you continue to add functionality to *viewit3d*.

2.2.3.3 Metafiles and Bitmaps

Copying a bitmap or metafile to the clipboard or writing a bitmap or metafile to a file is similar to copying *JOEY* 3D data to the clipboard or writing *JOEY* 3D data to a file except that the bitmap or metafile needs to be selected in the *viewit3d* Copy Special or Save Special Dialogues.

Rendered images are almost always bitmaps so there is little difference between bitmap and metafile data except that the size and resolution (when pasted into a document) can be controlled in metafile representations. See Section 3.1.2 and Section 2.2.3.3 in **Theory** for more discussion about metafiles and bitmaps.

2.2.4 The *JOEY* Viewer

The *JOEY* Viewer is simply a *JOEY* application whose native data is the *JOEY* 3D (*.j3d*) format. The Viewer is an editor for the camera and the render environment that is contained in the *.j3d* file. This allows for data examination, editing the camera, editing of materials, lighting and render type.

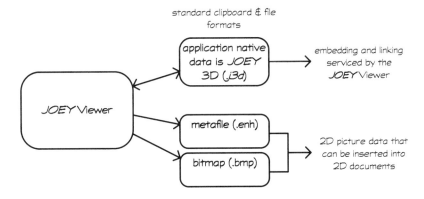

Figure P-6: Standard Clipboard and File Formats for the *JOEY* Viewer

The *JOEY* Viewer can be freely distributed with *JOEY* 3D data files and should be available for data viewing on any machine.

2.3 OLE Automation

OLE automation is a way to expose programmable objects to other applications. The programmable objects are called "automation servers" and the applications that manipulate them are called "automation clients". Almost all of the *JOEY* classes expose OLE Automation interfaces.

If you have not already done so, please go through the OLE Automation tutorial that creates *Autoclik* in the Introducing Visual C++ manual. This will familiarise you with concepts and tools that you will need to make sense of this section.

2.3.1 OLE Automation within *JOEY* Classes

Almost all *JOEY* classes are accessible (to some extent) through OLE Automation.[18] Some *JOEY* classes use *joey.dll* as the in-process server, while others can only be obtained from a running application. An application may be completely unaware that the *joey.dll* it is using is busy creating objects that are being used elsewhere. An example of this is the `CJoeyCamera` class.

What do you need to do to use one of these classes? Well, almost nothing except have an automation client laying around that wants to use the object. In this case, the *camdriv* project has been included in the *\chpt2_4* sample code directory in order to provide an automation client for a `CJoeyCamera` object. *Camdriv.mak* is a Visual Basic project file that can be run through *disptest.exe* (the Microsoft Disp Test program supplied with Visual C++). If you have not installed it as a part of MS Visual C++, you may want to include it now as a program item icon in the Visual C++ group.

Open *disptest.exe* and from within *disptest.exe*, open the *camdriv.mak* file. Select <u>R</u>un, <u>S</u>tart from the *disptest* menu and a Joey.Camera test drive dialogue will pop onto the screen, Figure P-7.

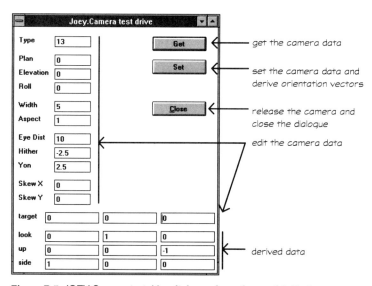

Figure P-7: JOEY.Camera test drive dialogue from the *camdriv* Project.

---

[18] Refer to the *JOEY* programmer's documentation for specific OLE Automation information about each class.

This dialogue is connected to a `CJoeyCamera` object. You can set camera parameters with this dialogue by typing a new value and clicking the Set button. The look, up, and side vectors for the camera are derived from the plan, elevation, and roll angles, and cannot be set directly. If you try to do something that is illegal for the camera type, you will probably get an **Assertion Failed!** message box since you are running a debug version of *JOEY*. These assertion failures can be simply ignored because the `CJoeyCamera` class has internal error handling to prevent problems in the event that this were a release version being badly treated by an automation client.

The camera types that are used in this demonstration are summarised in the table below:

number	move paradigm	axis aligned	projection
1	JOEY_CAM_PLAN	X	JOEY_PROJ_PERSPECTIVE
2	JOEY_CAM_BOTTOM	X	
3	JOEY_CAM_FRONT	X	
4	JOEY_CAM_BACK	X	
5	JOEY_CAM_LEFT	X	
6	JOEY_CAM_RIGHT	X	
7	JOEY_CAM_LOOK		
8	JOEY_CAM_LOOK_CTR		
9	JOEY_CAM_WALK		
10	JOEY_CAM_TBALL		
11	JOEY_CAM_PLAN	X	JOEY_PROJ_ORTHOGRAPHIC
12	JOEY_CAM_BOTTOM	X	
13	JOEY_CAM_FRONT	X	
14	JOEY_CAM_BACK	X	
15	JOEY_CAM_LEFT	X	
16	JOEY_CAM_RIGHT	X	
17	JOEY_CAM_LOOK		
18	JOEY_CAM_LOOK_CTR		
19	JOEY_CAM_WALK		
20	JOEY_CAM_TBALL		
21	JOEY_CAM_ISOMETRIC	X	

22	JOEY_CAM_PLAN	X	JOEY_PROJ_OBLIQUE
23	JOEY_CAM_BOTTOM	X	
24	JOEY_CAM_FRONT	X	
25	JOEY_CAM_BACK	X	
26	JOEY_CAM_LEFT	X	
27	JOEY_CAM_RIGHT	X	
28	JOEY_CAM_LOOK		
29	JOEY_CAM_LOOK_CTR		
10	JOEY_CAM_WALK		
31	JOEY_CAM_TBALL		
32	JOEY_CAM_AXONOMETRIC	X[19]	

The axis aligned cameras do not let you set the plan, elevation, and roll angles, and that even though you have set the X and Y skew for oblique projections, they are always returned as 0 for non-oblique projections.

If you have any questions about how the camera class works that are not covered in the *JOEY* programmer's documentation, you can probably discover the answer to those questions by using this example.

Your response to this has probably been "yeah, so?" (it was our initial response, too). To try to answer this, let us take a closer look at what is happening. If you run the process viewer, you have will notice that the *joey.dll* was started by *viewit3d* which is running in a hidden window. The *joey.dll* was loaded by *viewit3d* in response to *camdriv* requesting a `Joey.Camera` (the external OLE automation reference for the `CJoeyCamera`) object in the following code:

```
Sub Form_Load ()
    Set camera = CreateObject("Joey.Camera")
    GetAll_Click
End Sub
```

The instance of *viewit3d* stops running as soon as the camera is released. You also notice (in looking at the code for the target point and camera orientation) vector value edit boxes in *camdriv*. The dispatch interfaces for both points and vectors are being used. These objects have self-registered during previous tests using *viewit3d* which is why *viewit3d* is running as the server. You can check the system registry and you will notice that each of the *JOEY* classes registered under both a name and a CLSID. Under the CLSID, *viewit3d* is registered as the local server.

---

[19] The axonometric camera always has an elevation angle of 90º.

One answer to "yeah, so?" is that we can very simply write tools to manipulate these objects so that we can edit them from outside of an application and better understand how they work without a lot of programming and debugging. Once having these tools, we can start to manipulate the objects while they are in the context of an application.

2.3.2 OLE Automation in *JOEY* Applications

Now that we can get a camera, let's set properties and give it to an application to use in displaying an object. With a little work, we can do some simple animation.

It will reduce complications if we have an SDI rather than an MDI application to work with.[20] To build an SDI version of *viewit3d*, run AppWizard to create the basic framework as was done for the MDI version (except Step 4 of AppWizard). Use the File Type ID: of *ASCII3D.sdi* to differentiate the SDI version from the MDI version. Copy all of the SDI template files except the *viewit3d.rc*, and *viewit3d.cpp* files into this new project. Copy the *viewit3d* changes to the *viewit3d.rc* file from the chapter 2.1 version of *viewit3d* (some slight customisations are required for the SDI menu structure) and copy the *objdoc.cpp* and *objdoc.h* files from the chapter 2.1 version. You can now build and test a running SDI version of *viewit3d*. This will update the system registry.

Since *viewit3d* was setup for OLE automation (in MFC AppWizard you selected Yes, Please under OLE Automation) all we need to do is add three methods to the *viewit3d* document class, CObjDoc, dispatch interface:

GetJoeyDoc	Gets the dispatch interface to the CJoeyOleServerDoc the object document (CObjDoc) was derived from.
ShowWindow	Shows the *viewit3d* window, which is normally hidden when *viewit3d* is launched as an OLE automation server.
CloseWindow	Closes the *viewit3d* application which was launched by the OLE automation client.

---

[20] This example can be done with the existing MDI version of *viewit3d*. However, when the automation client starts a document window in *viewit3d*, you will get a window without an object and you will not be able to read an object into that window.

Add these three methods as follows:

♦   Open ClassWizard. Select the OLE Automation tab. In the Class Name: box, select CObjDoc. Choose Add Property... In the Add Property dialogue box, set the External Name: to *JoeyDoc*. In Implementation, select Get/Set Methods. Delete the Set Function: name (the `CJoeyOleServerDoc` the `CObjDoc` is derived from cannot be set). Leave the Get Function: as `GetJoeyDoc` and select LDISPATCH as the Type: of property to get. Select OK to finish adding the `GetJoeyDoc` method.

Select Edit Code to go to the ClassWizard created `GetJoeyDoc` member function and fill it in as follows:

```
    LPDISPATCH CObjDoc::GetJoeyDoc()
    {
→       // add a reference count so the document does not get
→       // deleted when released on the outside
→       return CJoeyOleServerDoc::GetIDispatch(TRUE);
    }
```

♦   Open ClassWizard. Select the OLE Automation tab. In the Class Name: box, select CObjDoc. Choose Add Method... In the Add Method dialogue box, set the External Name: to *ShowWindow*. Select void as the Return Type:. Select OK to finish adding the `ShowWindow` method.

Select Edit Code to go to the ClassWizard created `ShowWindow` member function and fill it in as follows:

```
    void CObjDoc::ShowWindow()
    {
→       POSITION    pos = GetFirstViewPosition();
→       CView*      pView = GetNextView(pos);
→       if (NULL != pView) {
→           CFrameWnd* pFrameWnd = pView->GetParentFrame();
→           pFrameWnd->ActivateFrame(SW_SHOW);
→           pFrameWnd = pFrameWnd->GetParentFrame();
→           if (pFrameWnd != NULL)
→               pFrameWnd->ActivateFrame(SW_SHOW);
→       }
    }
```

♦   Open ClassWizard. Select the OLE Automation tab. In the Class Name: box, select CObjDoc. Choose Add Method... In the Add Method dialogue box, set the External Name: to *CloseWindow*. Select void as the Return Type:. Select OK to finish adding the `CloseWindow` method.

Select <u>E</u>dit Code to go to the ClassWizard created `CloseWindow` member function and fill in:

```
void CObjDoc::CloseWindow()
{
    AfxGetMainWnd()->PostMessage(WM_CLOSE);
}
```

You can now rebuild *viewit3d*. It will run exactly the same as it did before these additions. The disptest project *v3ddriv* is provided in the *chpt2_4* sample code directory in order to test the *viewit3d* automation server which you have just created.[21] This project makes some interesting additions to initialisation and termination of the automation client as shown in the following code:

```
Sub Form_Load ()
    Set viewit3d = CreateObject("ASCII3D.sdi")
    Rem Set viewit3d = CreateObject("ASCII3D.mdi")
    Set camera = CreateObject("Joey.Camera")
    Set rgb_back = CreateObject("Joey.Color")
    viewit3d.ShowWindow
    GetAll_Click
    get_bkg_click
End Sub

Sub Close_Click ()
    viewit3d.CloseWindow
    Set viewit3d = Nothing
    Set camera = Nothing
    Set rgb_back = Nothing
    End
End Sub
```

The first `CreateObject` call starts the server for the `ASCII3D.sdi` object. You can look in the registry and see that this maps to the *viewit3d* application. The second `CreateObject` call starts a camera object. Both the camera and the *viewit3d* objects exist until *v3ddriv* is closed. The Get Camera function is also interesting for reviewing the process of working through the application document and *JOEY* to get the current camera for the active view:

```
Sub GetAll_Click ()
    Set joey_doc = viewit3d.JoeyDoc
    Set joey_view = joey_doc.ActiveView
    Set camTmp = joey_view.CurrentCamera
```

---

[21] If you have worked through this example on your MDI version of *viewit3d*, review the `Form_Load()` client code. Un-comment the creation to the MDI object and comment the creation of the SDI object.

```
    camera.CamType = 128
    camera.PlanAngle = camTmp.PlanAngle
    camera.ElevationAngle = camTmp.ElevationAngle
    camera.RollAngle = camTmp.RollAngle
    camera.Width = camTmp.Width
    camera.Aspect = camTmp.Aspect
    camera.Hither = camTmp.Hither
    camera.Yon = camTmp.Yon
    camera.EyeDistance = camTmp.EyeDistance
    camera.SkewX = camTmp.SkewX
    camera.SkewY = camTmp.SkewY
    Set pt_target = camTmp.Target
    Set camera.Target = pt_target

    SetCamera
End Sub
```

The first line gets the `CJoeyOleServerDoc` from the `CObjDoc` which is derived from it. The second line gets the active `CJoeyView` attached to the `CJoeyOleServerDoc`. The third line gets the current camera for the `CJoeyView`. The next collection of lines sets the `camera` object held by *v3ddriv* to the camera of the current view, and the last line calls the routine that displays the data for the camera.

You can interact with *viewit3d* in the normal way, however, at any time the client can **Get Camera** to get the current camera data from *viewit3d* or **Set Camera** to set the current camera data in *viewit3d*. The **Animate Camera** button plays a short animation sequence by setting different plan, elevation, and roll angles. It is most exciting if you read an object into *viewit3d* before you start the animation. You will observe similar interactions for the **Get Background**, **Set Background** and **Animate Background** functions.

3. Graphic Display and Interaction

This chapter concentrates on the construction of the actual application. The previous sections have addressed the problem of creating the framework for a Windows integrated application (the syntax for the application). It is now time to address data display and editing (semantics of the application).

The sections in this chapter:

♦ Provide a practical overview of the graphics subsystem.

♦ Provide a sampling of ways to represent graphic data.

♦ Introduce and explore methods for data manipulation.

♦ Explore methods to handle hardware performance issues that interfere with data manipulation.

♦ Explore using grids.

3.1 Graphic Elements

In order to proceed, it is necessary to provide an overview of graphic elements and how they are used by *JOEY*. While there is a brief description of some graphic principles, this text does not attempt to be a graphics reference text.

3.1.1 Axis Systems

In computer graphics, we generally refer to three frames of reference; world, camera, and object. Each frame of reference has an associated axis system, Figure P-8 (Upstill 1990). The world axis is the universal frame of reference in which object and camera axis systems are located. The camera frame of reference considers the camera to be the origin and, by the conventions of computer graphics, defines an axis system with the view direction being in the +Z direction, up being in the +Y direction, and the +X direction being to the right side.[22] The camera axis system is attached to the camera and moves with the camera through space. Objects are generally defined with respect to a local

---

[22] This is a left handed axis system in contrast to the right handed axis system that is used in engineering.

axis system. When the object is moved with respect to the world axis system, its local object axis system travels with it.[23]

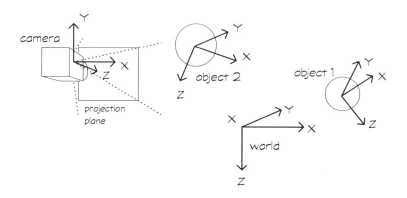

Figure P-8: Common axis system rotation in computer graphics

It really doesn't matter which axis system we consider to be the fixed axis system. Nor does it matter how we define the locations of the other axes. It is very simple to transform from one system to another (and the relative relationships are the same regardless of which system we pick as the reference). In many cases, the distinction between world and object axis system is not apparent. If there is only one simple object in a scene, its axis system is usually left coincident with the world axis system.

Computer graphics has traditionally been based on a left-handed axis system, while engineering typically uses a right-handed axis system. Other complications arise from different conventions for which axis pair describes the ground plane and which axis is the up direction in the world axis system.

---

[23] These axis systems are used in the definition of 3D data. There are also several coordinate systems used for mapping 3D data into the 2D window. These are the normalized camera coordinates, the device or window coordinates, and the screen coordinates. We defer discussion of these until Theory Section 3.11. At this point it is sufficient to say that *JOEY* and the graphic subsystem handle getting from the camera axis system to the window.

3.1.1.1 Camera Projections and Conventions

Camera projections are the methods for representing 3D data in a 2D drawing. When the camera projection is applied to geometric object data, the 3D data is projected onto the camera XY projection plane. This projection is, in turn, displayed in a window on the screen. The cameras available in *JOEY* include standard projections used in engineering and architecture. All cameras in *JOEY* are handled by CJoeyCamera. A wide variety of projection techniques have been invented for reasons ranging from realism, to scalability of drawings, to showing the most information with a single drawing. The camera projections supported by *JOEY* are orthographic, oblique and perspective, Figure P-9. They are described briefly below:

Orthographic Projection (JOEY_PROJ_ORTHOGRAPHIC)
   Orthographic projections are standard drafting views and often provide the best view of relationships between object components. All points are projected to the viewing plane are perpendicular to that plane. There is no projection distortion, so the drawings are scaleable, i.e. measurement on the drawing corresponds directly to real dimensions (for lines in space that are parallel to the projection plane).

Oblique projection (JOEY_PROJ_OBLIQUE)
   Oblique projections are similar to orthographic projections with the exception that the projection direction is not perpendicular to the viewing plane. These projections are used to add three dimensionality to the presentation of data while maintaining the scalability of lines parallel to the projection plane. Lines perpendicular to the viewing plane are also scaleable and are some fraction of their true length (1/2 is the default used by *JOEY*). A common concern with oblique projections is that they suffer from the Necker cube illusion which makes it difficult to distinguish front from back unless hidden surface removal is used in rendering, Figure P-9.

Perspective Projection (JOEY_PROJ_PERSPECTIVE)
   Perspective views are what we think of as realistic views. Projection is done by intersecting rays between object points and the eye with a projection plane perpendicular to the view direction. This is analogous to what happens when a scene is projected into film to take a photograph. While perspective provides the most realistic view, there is a distortion associated with perspective that makes it extremely difficult to visualise relationships during object placement (Wanger 1992).

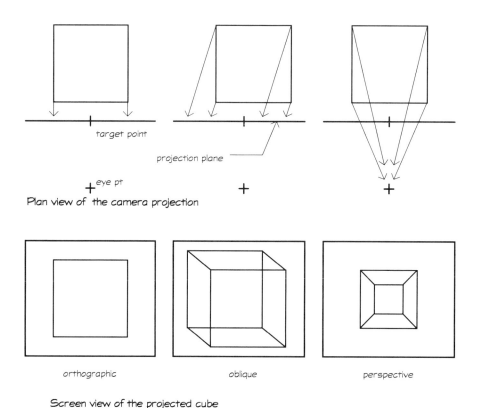

target point

projection plane

eye pt

Plan view of the camera projection

orthographic   oblique   perspective

Screen view of the projected cube

Figure P-9: Orthographic, oblique, and perspective camera projections.

The second aspect of the camera axis system relates to camera positioning or camera interaction. The camera move modes provide controlled and predictable ways of orienting the camera in world space regardless of the camera projection. There are six axis-aligned move modes that are constrained to look parallel to one of the world axis system axes, Figure P-10; generalised move modes that look in any direction; and some projection-specific move modes. In more detail, the move modes are:

Plan (JOEY_CAM_PLAN)
   "Plan" cameras look at the XY plane in the -Z direction (viewer at +Z), +Y is up.

Bottom (JOEY_CAM_BOTTOM)

"Bottom" cameras look at the XY plane in the +Z direction (viewer at -Z), -Y is up.

Front (JOEY_CAM_FRONT)

"Front" cameras look at the XY plane in the +Y direction (viewer at -Y), -Z is up.

Back (JOEY_CAM_BACK)

"Back" cameras look at the XY plane in the -Y direction (viewer at +Y), -Z is up.

Right (JOEY_CAM_RIGHT)

"Right" cameras look at the YZ plane in the -X direction (viewer at +X), -Z is up.

Left (JOEY_CAM_LEFT)

"Left" cameras looks at the YZ plane in the +X direction (viewer at -X), -Z is up.

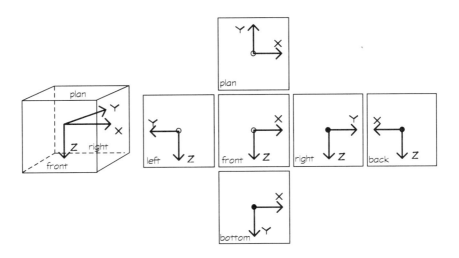

Figure P-10: Axis-aligned views of the data.

Look At (JOEY_CAM_LOOK)

"Look at" cameras look from any direction. The interaction is as though you are holding the object in front of you and moving the object. The camera position is given by a plan angle measured from the front view (or the bearing of the camera if +Y is north), an elevation angle above the XY plane, and a roll angle. The origin for rotating the object is the target point (rotation is always around a point fixed with respect to the camera).

Look At Centered (JOEY_CAM_LOOK_CTR)

The interaction is similar to the "Look at" camera except that the centre of rotation is fixed with respect to the object.

Walking (JOEY_CAM_WALK)

The interaction is as though you are holding the camera and walking through the object. This is different from all the other move modes in that it "feels" like the camera is being moved through the object as opposed to the object being moved in front of the camera.

Trackball (JOEY_CAM_ORTHO_TBALL)

The interaction is as though the object is inside a trackball. Unlike the other cameras, the up direction is not fixed with respect to the world axis during interactive camera manipulation.

Projection Specific Move Modes:

Isometric (JOEY_CAM_ISOMETRIC)

The isometric view is specific to orthographic projections. The view looks along the diagonal of a quadrant. The view direction can be the diagonal of any of the eight quadrants. The main advantage of this view is that all three axis are scaleable in a 1:1:1 relationship and that the 3D drawing appears reasonably undistorted.

Axonometric (JOEY_CAM_AXONOMETRIC)

Axonometric is a name given to a large family of projection techniques. The implemented axonometric is one that is commonly used in architecture and 3D mapping and is specific to oblique projections. The projection is a rotated plan view with a vertical (screen Y) displacement on the drawing corresponding to the Z dimension (or height). Since the basis is a plan, plan dimensions are scaleable. The Z offset is scaled by a factor so that XYZ measurement is in the ratio 1:1:z-scale.

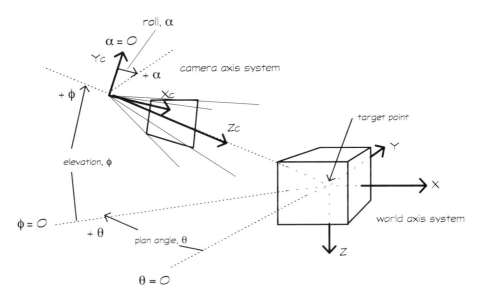

Figure P-11: *JOEY* conventions for camera position specification.

The camera convention used by *JOEY* is that the ground plane is the world axis system XY plane. The camera interaction methods are based largely around the notion of moving a camera through a world with a ground plane, Figure P-11. This poses problems if the native definition of the object(s) in your discipline does not match this convention.

3.1.1.2 World Axis System and Axis Mapping

The world axis system is, by conventions in computer graphics, a left-handed coordinate system. By *JOEY* convention, the XY plane is the ground plane for camera view specification and manipulation. What do you do if your data does not follow these conventions? In the past, the answer would be to adjust your data to match the graphics conventions, or to play with transformations until you found one that mapped your data into the graphic convention.

JOEY provides a facility for world axis mapping. Instead of worrying about how to get your data into a form that matches the world axis conventions of computer graphics and *JOEY*, simply define how the orthographic plan camera is oriented in your data axis system. It is not necessary that all of your data follow the same convention.

We now add a dialogue to set the world axis mapping in *viewit3d*. Normally, you would set this mapping once at the beginning of the application. Any data created by the application would then follow the conventions of this mapping. Adding the dialogue code is a bit tedious; you may just want to copy it from the sample code directory.

Axis mapping is particularly useful in the sample application since it is unclear which conventions were used for creating some of the object data provided with the *JOEY* Toolkit.

◆ Edit the project resource file, *viewit3d.rc*, using AppStudio to add an <u>O</u>ptions pulldown in the `IDR_3D_GEOTYPE` to the right of the existing <u>C</u>amera pulldown menu. Add a <u>W</u>orld <u>A</u>xis <u>M</u>ap entry with the <u>I</u>D: *ID_OPTIONS_AXISMAP*, <u>C</u>aption: *&World Axis Map*, and <u>P</u>ro<u>m</u>pt: *Examine or edit the world axis map\nworld axis map*, to the <u>O</u>ptions menu. Copy the newly created <u>O</u>ptions pulldown menu into the `IDR_3D_GEOTYPE_SRVR_EMB` and `IDR_3D_GEOTYPE_SRVR_IP` menus.

◆ Continue editing the project resource file, *viewit3d.rc*, to add an axis mapping dialogue box with <u>I</u>D: *IDD_AXIS_MAP* and <u>C</u>aption: *Camera Axis Map*. Create this dialogue with three combo boxes of <u>T</u>ype: *Drop List* with S<u>o</u>rt disabled and <u>I</u>D:s of `IDC_CMB_AXISMAP_LOOK`, `IDC_CMB_AXISMAP_UP`, and `IDC_CMB_AXISMAP_SIDE`, Figure P-12.

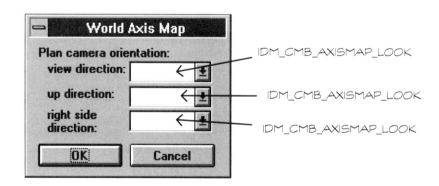

Figure P-12: World Axis Mapping Dialogue Box.

♦ Add a class to manage this dialogue using ClassWizard, Add Class... with Class Name: *CAxisMapDlg*, Class Type: *CDialog*, Header File: *axismap.h*, Implementation File: *axismap.cpp*, and Dialog: *IDD_AXIS_MAP*. Add message handling functions for the WM_INITDIALOG message of CAxisMapDlg, and for the BN_CLICKED message of IDOK.

♦ Add member variables for the current axis map and indices into the axis map orientation tables to the header file, *axismap.h*:

```
// axismap.h : header file
   •
// Dialog Data
   //{{AFX_DATA(CAxisMapDlg)
   enum { IDD = IDD_AXIS_MAP };
       // NOTE: the ClassWizard will add data members here
   //}}AFX_DATA
   CUnitV3    m_uvAxisMap[3];
   int        m_iDir[3];

// Overrides
   •
};
```

♦ Add a table of axis vectors and the body for the message handlers in the implementation file, *axismap.cpp*:

```
//////////////////////////////////////////////////////////////
// CAxisMapDlg message handlers

static int      s_iAxisTxt[6] = {
    IDS_AXIS_PX, IDS_AXIS_NX, IDS_AXIS_PY,
    IDS_AXIS_NY, IDS_AXIS_PZ, IDS_AXIS_NZ
};
static CUnitV3 s_uvAxis[6] = {
    CUnitV3( 1.0f, 0.0f, 0.0f),CUnitV3(-1.0f, 0.0f, 0.0f),
    CUnitV3( 0.0f, 1.0f, 0.0f),CUnitV3( 0.0f,-1.0f, 0.0f),
    CUnitV3( 0.0f, 0.0f, 1.0f),CUnitV3( 0.0f, 0.0f,-1.0f)
};

BOOL CAxisMapDlg::OnInitDialog()
{
    CComboBox* ccb[3];
    int        ii, jj, iItem;
    CString    cStr;

    CDialog::OnInitDialog();

    // load the dialog lists
    ccb[CAM_side] =
        (CComboBox*)GetDlgItem(IDC_CMB_AXISMAP_SIDE);
    ccb[CAM_up] =
```

```
→           (CComboBox*)GetDlgItem(IDC_CMB_AXISMAP_UP);
→       ccb[CAM_look] =
→           (CComboBox*)GetDlgItem(IDC_CMB_AXISMAP_LOOK);
→       for (ii=CAM_side; ii<=CAM_look; ii++)
→           ccb[ii]->ResetContent();
→       for (ii = 0; ii < 6; ii++) {
→           cStr.LoadString(s_iAxisTxt[ii]);
→           for (jj = CAM_side; jj <= CAM_look; jj++)  {
→               iItem = ccb[jj]->AddString(cStr);
→               ccb[jj]->SetItemData(iItem,(DWORD)ii);
→               if ( (s_uvAxis[ii][VEC_i] == m_uvAxisMap[jj][VEC_i]) &&
→                    (s_uvAxis[ii][VEC_j] == m_uvAxisMap[jj][VEC_j]) &&
→                    (s_uvAxis[ii][VEC_k] == m_uvAxisMap[jj][VEC_k]) )
→                   m_iDir[jj] = ii;
→           }
→       }
→       // set the selections to the current values
→       for (jj = CAM_side; jj <= CAM_look; jj++)  {
→           cStr.LoadString(s_iAxisTxt[m_iDir[jj]]);
→           ccb[jj]->SelectString(-1,cStr);
→       }
        return TRUE;
    }

    void CAxisMapDlg::OnOK()
    {
→       // read selections and make sure the choice is valid
→       CComboBox* ccb[3];
→       int        ii, jj, iItem;
→
→       // get the choice indices
→       ccb[CAM_side] =
→           (CComboBox*)GetDlgItem(IDC_CMB_AXISMAP_SIDE);
→       ccb[CAM_up] =
→           (CComboBox*)GetDlgItem(IDC_CMB_AXISMAP_UP);
→       ccb[CAM_look] =
→           (CComboBox*)GetDlgItem(IDC_CMB_AXISMAP_LOOK);
→       for (jj = CAM_side; jj <= CAM_look; jj++)  {
→           if (CB_ERR != (iItem = ccb[jj]->GetCurSel()))
→               m_iDir[jj] = (int)ccb[jj]->GetItemData(iItem);
→       }
→       // check for orthogonality
→       for (ii = VEC_i; ii <= VEC_k; ii++) {
→           if (0.0f == (s_uvAxis[m_iDir[CAM_side]][ii] +
→                        s_uvAxis[m_iDir[CAM_up]][ii] +
→                        s_uvAxis[m_iDir[CAM_look]][ii])) {
→               CString    cStr;
→               cStr.LoadString(IDS_AXIS_NOT_ORTHO);
→               AfxMessageBox(cStr,MB_OK | MB_ICONINFORMATION);
→               return;
→           }
→       }
→       // set map field to the selections
```

```
→        for (jj = CAM_side; jj <= CAM_look; jj++)
→            m_uvAxisMap[jj] = s_uvAxis[m_iDir[jj]];
         CDialog::OnOK();
     }
```

◆   Add strings to the string table in the project resource file, *viewit3d.rc*:

ID	CAPTION

<u>ID</u>	<u>CAPTION</u>
IDS_AXIS_PX	+1 0 0
IDS_AXIS_NX	-1 0 0
IDS_AXIS_PY	0 +1 0
IDS_AXIS_NY	0 -1 0
IDS_AXIS_PZ	0 0 +1
IDS_AXIS_NZ	0 0 -1
IDS_AXIS_NOT_ORTHO	This camera orientation is not orthogonal, Please adjust it.

◆   Use ClassWizard to add a message handler to CObjView to handle the **COMMAND** message for ID_OPTIONS_AXISMAP. Add a reference to the CAxisMapDlg header file and modify the OnOptionsAxismap function that ClassWizard adds to the implementation file, *objview.cpp*:

```
     // objview.cpp : implementation of the CObjView class
     //
     •
     #include "objview.h"
→    #include "axismap.h"
     •
     •
     void CObjView::OnOptionsAxismap()
     {
→        CAxisMapDlg    dlg;
→        const CUnitV3* pAxisMap =
→            ((CObjDoc*)GetDocument())->RE()->AxisMap();
→        int            ii;
→        // setup the axis mapping rotation
→        for (ii=CAM_side; ii<=CAM_look; ii++)
→            dlg.m_uvAxisMap[ii] = pAxisMap[ii];
→        // do the dialog and reset the axis if requested
→        if (IDOK == dlg.DoModal()) {
→            ((CObjDoc*)GetDocument())->RE()->AxisMap
→            (dlg.m_uvAxisMap);GetDocument()->UpdateAllViews(NULL);
→        }
     }
```

You can now build and test *viewit3d* to see how axis mapping really works. A good model to use is *hand.a3d*. This model is oriented so that the thumb points down the +X axis, the index finger points down the +Y axis, and the fingers curl in the direction of the +Z axis. In this default axis mapping, the hand is a left hand with the palm facing down. You can pick any  default orientation for the hand by using the axis mapping dialogue. The axis map is saved as part of the model, so everything will work correctly when *viewit3d* is used as an OLE server. A change to the axis map is considered a change to the model.

3.1.1.3 Object Axis Systems and Transformation Stacks

Viewit3d draws an object relative to the world axis. If you turn on the *JOEY* grid and examine the objects that you have drawn relative to the grid, the points are exactly where you specified that they should be located. Suppose you would like to put the object somewhere else or you want to draw the same object twice (side-by-side). Your could add some offset to all of the points of an object in order to shift it somewhere else. That would be quite a bit of work. Or, you could use transformations in the render device to move the object. The *JOEY* class `CXfm4x4f` provides transformations and transformation manipulation.

Although we have been using the render device for every example in this text, the only place it has been evident is the `CObjDoc::OnDraw` function. All that has been done so far is to draw the outlines of the polygons in the object. The default setup of the render device has been satisfactory to familiarise you with graphics without worrying about how the graphics was actually working. Now it is time to get into the details.

We will now use the transformation stack to do positioning. There are many parts of the `IRenderDevX` interface, not related to positioning, that we use in this example. This may be a bit confusing and may raise questions that will be answered as we proceed.

In this example, we position an object using a positioning jack (Bier 1987). We use one that provides translation (changing the origin) and rotation (changing the orientation) of the object. This is our first excursion into interactive manipulation of the data. The positioning jack is shown in Figure P-13.

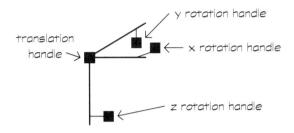

Figure P-13: Positioning Jack.

To use the jack, position the cursor over the handle, depress the left mouse button to grab it, then drag it until the button is released.

Before starting the example, we need to provide some background on transformations. When we draw points to the screen through the `IRenderDevX` interface, they go through a few steps, Figure P-14.

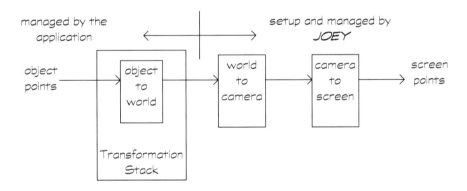

Figure P-14: Graphic Transformation Pipeline.

The etiquette for drawing an object is to save the object-to-world transformation state, set the object-to-world transform, draw the object, then restore the transform state. The transformation stack aids in saving and restoring the transformation state. You save the state by pushing a transform and restore the state by popping the transform. Pushing a transform simply means adding one to the top of the stack and loading it with the transformation that was at the top. Then you manipulate the transformation that you pushed on the stack. It is bad form for an object to manipulate or to pop a transform that it did not push.

In this example, we use one transformation for drawing the positioning jack and a second transformation for drawing the object. The separate transformation for the object lets it have a different axis map than the world axis map. The position of the object is described relative to the world coordinate system. We use some utilities in the *vit3dlib.dll* library to handle the drawing and manipulation of the jack.

We start the example by adding manipulation of the object and then fill in the details that demonstrate other functionality and insure that *viewit3d* will still work with other Windows programs. We continue to work with the MDI version of *viewit3d* as it was completed at the end of Section 2.2.

◆   The original implementation of *viewit3d* referenced the *vit3dlib.dll* functionality only in the application document. We now use the functionality of this library in several areas. Cut out the include of *vit3dlib.h* at the beginning of *objdoc.cpp* and paste it into *stdafx.h* after the include for *joey.h*:

```
        ◆
        ◆

        #include <joey.h>
➔       #include <vit3dlib.h>

        __declspec(dllimport) extern CJoeyConfig* JoeyConfig;
```

◆   Make additions to *objdoc.h* to add the data for the object transformation and the positioning jack. Also, add functions for accessing and manipulating this data.

```
        ◆
        ◆
        class CObjDoc : public CJoeyOleServerDoc
        {
            CPoint3f    m_pts[MAX_OBJ_PTS];      // the vertex array
            int         m_ptCt;                  // the point count
            FACE        m_faces[MAX_OBJ_FACES];  // the face array
            int         m_faceCt;                // the face count
            int         m_maxFacePts;            // maximum pts in a face

➔           CXfm4x4f    m_xfmObj;                // object transformation
➔           CUnitV3f    m_uvObjAxisMap[3];       // object axis map

➔           CV3dJack    m_jack;                  // the manipulator jack
```

```
→        CJoeyMaterial const* m_pMtlJack;        // the jack material

    protected: // create from serialisation only
    •
    •
    // Attributes
    public:
        CObjSrvrItem* GetEmbeddedItem() { return
            (CObjSrvrItem*)CJoeyOleServerDoc::GetEmbeddedItem(); }

→        CUnitV3f const*     ObjAxisMap() const {return m_uvObjAxisMap;}
→        void                ObjAxisMap(const CUnitV3f[3]);
→        CXfm4x4f const&     ObjectTransform()  {return m_xfmObj;}
→        void                ObjectTransform(CXfm4x4f const&);
→        CV3dJack&           ObjectJack()        {return m_jack;}

    // Operations
    •
    •
```

The access functions `ObjAxisMap`, `ObjectTransform`, and `ObjectJack` get or set object data. When the object transformation is set, the object modified flag is set and all views are updated (re-drawn).

◆   Add initialisation of the added data in the document constructor in
    objdoc.cpp:

```
    CObjDoc::CObjDoc()
    {
→        CString         cstr;
→        CJoeyMaterial   mtl;

        m_ptCt = 0;
        m_faceCt = 0;
        m_maxFacePts = 0;

→        // create the manipulator jack material -
→        // this is not very robust - you should do a way better job
→        // checking in a real app.
→        VERIFY(m_pMtlJack = RE()->MaterialNew("manipulator jack"));
→        mtl.Flags(JOEY_MTL_POINT_RGB | JOEY_MTL_POINT_SIZE |
→            JOEY_MTL_LINE_RGB | JOEY_MTL_LINE_WIDTH |
→            JOEY_MTL_LINE_STYLE);
→        mtl.PointColor(CRGBf(0.0f,0.0f,1.0f));
→        mtl.PointSize(6.0f);
→        mtl.LineColor(CRGBf(0.0f,0.0f,1.0f));
→        mtl.LineStyle(0);
→        mtl.LineWidth(2.0f);
→        RE()->MaterialSet("manipulator jack",mtl);

        EnableAutomation();
```

```
AfxOleLockApp();
    }
```

There are a few new things here that should not be cause for alarm. We
have created a material for the jack. Materials will be covered in detail in
Section 3.1.3. The distressing comment, "this is not very robust," before
creating the positioning jack material is a reminder that you should check
for the existence of a material before you try to create it. In this case we
knew this would be a valid material and we are rather sloppy in error
avoidance and error checking.

♦   Add cleanup code in the document destructor in *objdoc.cpp*. In this case, the
    only required cleanup is releasing the positioning jack material as follows:

```
      CObjDoc::~CObjDoc()
      {
→         if (NULL != m_pMtlJack) m_pMtlJack->Release();
          AfxOleUnlockApp();
      }
```

♦   Add the transformation and the positioning jack to the document OnDraw
    function in *objdoc.cpp*. As we have previously described, you will find a
    transformation pushed and used to describe the position of the object. The
    jack and the object are drawn within this pushed transformation. A second
    transformation is pushed within the first, specifically for the axis mapping
    of the object. Make changes to the OnDraw function as follows:

```
      void CObjDoc::OnDraw(PIRenderDevX pRD,
          CJoeyView const *pJView) const
      {
          CPoint3f**      ppPts = NULL;
          int             ii, jj;

→         // position in world space
→         pRD->XfmPush();
→         pRD->XfmConcat(m_xfmObj);
→         m_jack.OnDraw(pRD,m_pMtlJack);
→         // draw the object
→         pRD->XfmPushDataDef(m_uvObjAxisMap,
→             RENDER_DATADEF_CLOCKWISE | RENDER_DATADEF_CAN_CULL);

→         if ( (0 == m_faceCt) || (0 == m_maxFacePts) ||
→             (ppPts = new PPoint3f[m_maxFacePts]) ) goto obj_draw_done;
          for (ii=0; ii<m_faceCt; ii++) {
              for (jj=0; jj<m_faces[ii].ptCt; jj++)
                  ppPts[jj] = m_faces[ii].pts[jj];
              ppPts[jj] = m_faces[ii].pts[0];   // close the polygon
              pRD->Draw3dPolyline(m_faces[ii].ptCt + 1,ppPts);
          }
          delete ppPts;
```

```
→   obj_draw_done:

→       pRD->XfmPop();
→       // pop the world space positioning transform
→       pRD->XfmPop();
    }
```

◆ In *objdoc.cpp*, add the `ObjAxisMap` function that sets a new object axis map. We added this right after the `OnDraw` function:

```
→   void CObjDoc::ObjAxisMap(const CUnitV3f uvAxisMap[3])
→   {
→       int     ii;
→       for (ii = CAM_side; ii <= CAM_look; ii++)
→           m_uvObjAxisMap[ii] = uvAxisMap[ii];
→       SetModifiedFlag();
→       if (IsEmbedded()) NotifyChanged();
→       UpdateAllViews(NULL);
→   }
```

An important thing is happening here, and in other functions that set object properties; the modified flag is being set and the container is being notified of the change if the data is embedded.

◆ In *objdoc.cpp*, add the `ObjectTransform` function that sets a new object axis map. We added this right after the `OnAxisMap` function:

```
→   void CObjDoc::ObjectTransform(CXfm4x4f const& xfm)
→   {
→       m_xfmObj = xfm;
→       SetModifiedFlag();
→       if (IsEmbedded()) NotifyChanged();
→       UpdateAllViews(NULL);
→   }
```

◆ In the `Serialize` function, add code to save and restore the object position and the axis map as part of the ASCII data for the object. This requires adding some new keywords to the file definition with the associated serialization code. The object transformation is broken down into the translation of the origin and the x, y, and z rotations to orient the object. A library function in *vit3dlib.all* decomposes the transformation into rotations.

```
        /////////////////////////////////////////////////////////
        // CObjDoc serialization
        #define MAX_TOKEN_CT   50
        #define IN_BUFF_LEN    512

        #define OBJ_END_FILE   0
        #define OBJ_VERTEX     1
        #define OBJ_FACE       2
→       #define OBJ_TRANSLATE  3
```

```
→    #define OBJ_ROTATE      4
→    #define OBJ_AXISMAP     5

→    static char*    s_strObjCmd[] = {"end",          "v",     "f",
→        "translate", "rotate", "axismap"};
     static int      s_ctObjCmd = sizeof(s_strObjCmd)/sizeof(char*);
     void CObjDoc::Serialize(CArchive& ar)
     {
                  ·
                  ·
→        // write the location (translate, rotate, and axismap)
→        sprintf(strOut,"%s %.3f %.3f %.3f\n",
→            s_strObjCmd[OBJ_TRANSLATE],
→            m_xfmObj[3][0], m_xfmObj[3][1], m_xfmObj[3][2]);
→        ar.Write((void*)strOut,strlen(strOut));
→        V3dDecomposeRotation(m_xfmObj,fRotX,fRotY,fRotZ);
→        sprintf(strOut,"%s %.3f %.3f %.3f\n",
→            s_strObjCmd[OBJ_ROTATE], fRotX, fRotY, fRotZ);
→        ar.Write((void*)strOut,strlen(strOut));
→        sprintf(strOut,
→            "%s %.3f %.3f %.3f %.3f %.3f %.3f %.3f %.3f %.3f\n",
→            s_strObjCmd[OBJ_AXISMAP],m_uvObjAxisMap[0][0],
→            m_uvObjAxisMap[0][1],m_uvObjAxisMap[0][2],
→            m_uvObjAxisMap[1][0],m_uvObjAxisMap[1][1],
→            m_uvObjAxisMap[1][2],m_uvObjAxisMap[2][0],
→            m_uvObjAxisMap[2][1],m_uvObjAxisMap[2][2]);
→        ar.Write((void*)strOut,strlen(strOut));
         // write the data end
         sprintf(strOut,"%s\n",s_strObjCmd[OBJ_END_FILE]);
         ar.Write((void*)strOut,strlen(strOut));
     }
     else
     {
→        CPoint3f    ptObjCtr;
         char        strIn[IN_BUFF_LEN];
         char*       lpToken[MAX_TOKEN_CT];
→        int         ii, jj, kk, nCmd, ptInd, tokenCt;
                  ·
                  ·
             switch (nCmd) {
                  ·
                  ·
             case OBJ_FACE:
                  ·
                  ·
                 break;
→            case OBJ_TRANSLATE:
→                if (tokenCt < 4) goto bad_format;
→                for (ii = PT_x; ii <= PT_z; ii++)
→                    ptObjCtr[ii] = (float)atof(lpToken[1+ii]);
→                break;
→            case OBJ_ROTATE:
→                if (tokenCt < 4) goto bad_format;
→                m_xfmObj.Identity();
```

```
→                              for (ii = AXIS_x; ii <= AXIS_z; ii++)
→                                  m_xfmObj.Rotate(ii,CAngle(ANGLE_DEGREE,
→                                      (float)atof(lpToken[1+ii])));
→                              break;
→                          case OBJ_AXISMAP:
→                              if (tokenCt < 10) goto bad_format;
→                              for (ii=CAM_side,kk=1; ii <= CAM_look; ii++)
→                                  for (jj = VEC_i; jj <= VEC_k; jj++, kk++)
→                                      m_uvObjAxisMap[ii][jj] =
→                                          (float)atof(lpToken[kk]);
→                              break;
                          default:
                              // not a meaningful line
                              break;
                      }
                  }
      end_of_obj_data:
→             // make the jack 30% larger than the data
→             m_jack.Resize(fDataSpace * 1.3f);
→             // make the dataspace 3x the size of the object
→             RE()->DataSpace(fDataSpace*6.0f,TRUE,TRUE,FALSE);
→             // add the centre into the object transformation
→             m_xfmObj.Translate(ptObjCtr.x,ptObjCtr.y,ptObjCtr.z);
          }
          CJoeyOleServerDoc::Serialize(ar);
          return;
              •
              •
      }
```

After the object has been read, the dataspace and the positioning jack are re-sized to fit the object.

♦   Make changes in the DeleteContents function to initialise the object transformation to the identity transformation, the object axis map to an identity axis map, and to reset the size of the positioning jack. We set the initial object transformation to the identity transformation, so that the object will remain at the origin. In the setup of the positioning jack, we assigned an initial size which is much smaller than the dataspace so that there is room to move it around. These are done after the DeleteContents function of the CJoeyOleServerDoc so that the dataspace has been re-set before the positioning jack is re-sized.

```
      void CObjDoc::DeleteContents()
      {
          •
          •
          CJoeyOleServerDoc::DeleteContents();

→         // the default object position and placement
→         m_xfmObj.Identity();
```

```
→        m_uvObjAxisMap[CAM_side] = CUnitV3f(1.0f,0.0f,0.0f);
→        m_uvObjAxisMap[CAM_up]  = CUnitV3f(0.0f,1.0f,0.0f);
→        m_uvObjAxisMap[CAM_look] = CUnitV3f(0.0f,0.0f,1.0f);
→        m_jack.Resize(RE()->DataSpace() * 0.25f);
    }
```

You can now rebuild and run *viewit3d*. There is little to see
other than a blue positioning jack which is be displayed along
with the object. If you do save an object, you will see
additional data in the file and notice that the translation is
0,0,0, the rotations are 0,0,0, and an identity axis map is being
used for the object.

The next step is enabling the manipulation of the jack and the setting of the axis
map for the object. You will make modifications to the view to enable
interaction with the positioning jack and to provide a dialogue for controlling
the axis map of the object.

♦ Add a test in the left mouse button down message processing (for the view)
   to see if one of the positioning jack handles was hit. Start tracking if it was.
   Make changes in the OnLButtonDown member function in *objview*:

```
    void CObjView::OnLButtonDown(UINT nFlags, CPoint point)
    {
→       CJoeyMouse      mouse(point);
→       CObjDoc*        pDoc = GetDocument();
→       float           fDist;
→       int             nEditID;

        if (IsCamLeft()) {
            CJoeyView::OnMButtonDown(nFlags, point);
            return;
        }
→       // test for a hit on the jack handles.  if hit, start the jack
→       //  manipulation (the jack selects the closest hit).
→       PrepareMouse (mouse,MOUSE_WORLD_TOL);
→       if ((pDoc->ObjectJack()).Hit(pDoc->ObjectTransform(),mouse,
→               fDist,nEditID)) {
→           pDoc->ObjectTransform((pDoc->ObjectJack()).TrackStart(
→               pDoc->ObjectTransform(),mouse,fDist,nEditID));
→           SetCapture();
→       }
    }
```

The PrepareMouse function gets the requested information about the
current mouse position, in this case, a hit frustum sized for the current hit
tolerance. This information is passed on to the jack for hit testing against the
handles. The jack tells you if a handle was hit, and how far the hit was from

the eye. This is useful in helping you decide which jack to activate if there are multiple jacks that overlap each other.

♦ Add a test in the mouse move message handling to see if the jack is in tracking mode. If it is, pass mouse information to the jack for processing. The jack returns a revised object transformation if the processing is successful. The new transformation is loaded into the object. In the OnMouseMove message handler in *objview.cpp*, make the following additions:

```
    void CObjView::OnMouseMove(UINT nFlags, CPoint point)
    {
➜       CObjDoc*        pDoc = GetDocument();

        // allow JOEY to handle camera tracking
        if (IsCamTracking()) {
           CJoeyView::OnMouseMove(nFlags,point);
           return;
        }
➜       if ((pDoc->ObjectJack()).IsTracking()) {
➜          CJoeyMouse      mouse(point);
➜          PrepareMouse(mouse,MOUSE_WORLD);
➜          pDoc->ObjectTransform((pDoc->ObjectJack()).Track(mouse));
➜       }
    }
```

♦ Add a test in the left button up processing to see if the jack is in tracking mode. If it is, then end tracking mode. The jack TrackEnd function updates the transformation to the last mouse position and terminates tracking. In the OnLButtonUp message handler in *objview.cpp*, make the following additions:

```
    void CObjView::OnLButtonUp(UINT nFlags, CPoint point)
    {
➜       CObjDoc*        pDoc = GetDocument();

        if (IsCamLeft()) {
           CJoeyView::OnMButtonUp(nFlags, point);
           return;
        }
➜       if ((pDoc->ObjectJack()).IsTracking()) {
➜          CJoeyMouse      mouse(point);
➜          PrepareMouse(mouse,MOUSE_WORLD);
➜          pDoc->ObjectTransform(
➜              (pDoc->ObjectJack()).TrackEnd(mouse));
➜          ReleaseCapture();
➜       }
    }
```

♦ Edit the project resource file, *viewit3d.rc,* using AppStudio (to add menu access to object axis map control). In the IDR_3D_GEOTYPE menu Options pulldown after the <u>W</u>orld Axis Map entry, add an <u>O</u>bject Axis Map entry with the <u>I</u>D: *IDM_OPTIONS_OBJ_AXISMAP*, <u>C</u>aption: *&Object Axis Map*, and Pro<u>m</u>pt: *Examine or edit the object axis map\nobject axis map dialogue.* Copy this newly created menu item to the Options pulldowns in `IDR_3D_GEOTYPE_SRVR_EMB` and `IDR_3D_GEOTYPE_SRVR_IP` menus.

◆ While still editing the resource file in AppStudio, add an entry to the string table with an <u>I</u>D: *IDS_DLG_OBJ_AXIS_MAP* and a <u>C</u>aption: *Object Axis Map*. This will be the title for the axis map dialogue created in the last section (when it is used to edit the object axis map).

◆ In the header file for the axis map dialogue, *axismap.h*, add a flag to note whether this is an object axis map:

```
        class CAxisMapDlg : public CDialog
        {
            ◆
            ◆
→           BOOL        m_bIsObject;
            CUnitV3f    m_uvAxisMap[3];
            int         m_iDir[3];
            ◆
            ◆
        };
```

◆ In the constructor for the `CAxisMapDlg` in *axismap.cpp*, add initialisation for the `m_bIsObject` flag:

```
        CAxisMapDlg::CAxisMapDlg(CWnd* pParent /*=NULL*/)
            : CDialog(CAxisMapDlg::IDD, pParent)
        {
→           m_bIsObject = FALSE;
            //{{AFX_DATA_INIT(CAxisMapDlg)
                // NOTE: the ClassWizard will add member initialisation
            //}}AFX_DATA_INIT
        }
```

◆ In the initialisation function for the axis map dialogue, `OnInitDialog` in *axismap.cpp*, correct the dialogue title if the axis map is for an object:

```
        BOOL CAxisMapDlg::OnInitDialog()
        {

            ◆
            ◆
            CDialog::OnInitDialog();
→           // reset title for the object dialogue
→           if (m_bIsObject) {
→               cStr.LoadString(IDS_DLG_OBJ_AXIS_MAP);
→               SetWindowText(cStr);
→           }
```

```
        •
        •
        •
    return TRUE;
    }
```

♦ Use ClassWizard to add a message handler to CObjView to handle the
   COMMAND message for IDS_DLG_OBJ_AXIS_MAP. We are using the same
   axis mapping dialogue as we used for world axis mapping, and the message
   handler is very similar to the OnOptionsAxisMap handler added in the last
   section. Fill in the body of the OnOptionsObjAxismap function that
   ClassWizard adds to the implementation file, *objview.cpp*:

```
    void CObjView::OnOptionsObjAxismap()
    {
→       CAxisMapDlg        dlg;
→       const CUnitV3f*        pAxisMap;
→       int                ii;
→       // setup the axis mapping rotation
→       pAxisMap = ((CObjDoc*)GetDocument())->ObjAxisMap();
→       for (ii=CAM_side; ii<=CAM_look; ii++)
→           dlg.m_uvAxisMap[ii] = pAxisMap[ii];
→       dlg.m_bIsObject = TRUE;   // for correct dialogue title
→       // do the dialog
→       if (IDOK == dlg.DoModal())
→           ((CObjDoc*)GetDocument())->ObjAxisMap(dlg.m_uvAxisMap);
    }
```

You can now rebuild and run *viewit3d*. The positioning jack
can be used to move and spin the object relative to the world
axis. You may notice that it becomes difficult to keep track of
the object with only one view. Try opening different views
and using different camera types and grid settings to clarify
the position. You may also notice that the interactivity is not
what you were hoping for. We will address both positioning confusion and
slow interaction in later sections.

**Congratulations, you have just finished interacting with data in your 3D
graphics application !!**

3.1.2 Rendering

The term "rendering" is used in many ways to mean many things. When we use the term, we are referring to the process of taking 3D data and turning it into a 2D image. The last section showed how geometry gets to the renderer, and future sections talk about how materials and lights get to the renderer. Here, we explore what happens when the geometric data gets there.

Up to this point, we have used the default setup of the renderer and the default rendering material. The result has been wireframe drawings (because we only have drawn line elements). We now work with filled polygons and lighting and augment *viewit3d* to have four selectable levels of realism in rendering:

Realism level	*Description*
Wireframe	Only the edges of the polygons are drawn. Depth buffer is turned off.
Unshaded	The polygons are drawn in a single colour with the edges highlighted in a different colour. There is no lighting or smoothing of the polygons.
Flat Shaded	The polygons are lit but they are shaded as a collection of flat surfaces. This gives a faceted appearance but does provide lighting effects.
Smooth Shaded	The polygons are lit and blended together as though they were part of a smooth surface. This will provide the most realistic appearance for most objects.

The appearance is controlled by the rendering style that has been set, the material properties, and the lighting. There are two important observations from this example; different representations work better for different tasks (more realistic is not necessarily better), and rendering speed is significantly affected by the choice of rendering styles.

We use materials and lights in this example. Detailed discussions are in Section 3.1.3 and Section 3.1.4.

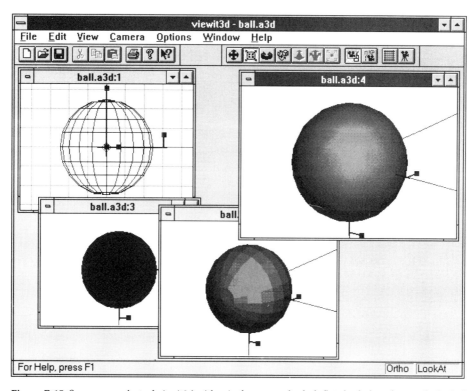

Figure P-15: Screen snapshot of *viewit3d* with wireframe, unshaded, flat shaded, and smooth shaded views.

We now create four different drawing functions, one for each rendering style, and a dialogue to control which is used in the object. The rendering style will be saved as a part of the object database. Each view can have a different rendering style. We use a separate material for each rendering style so that it is very clear what is important about the material properties as they relate to the final rendering. We start with changes to the document and then move on to the view and the rendering style dialogue.

♦ Revise the document header in *objdoc.h* to include the additional material data, light data, geometric information, and drawing functions as follows:

```
•
•
typedef struct {
    CPoint3f**    pts;
```

```
➜      CUnitV3f**    uvs;
➜      CUnitV3f      uvFace;
       int           ptCt;
   } FACE;

   class CObjSrvrItem;

➜  #define DRAW_WIREFRAME     0
➜  #define DRAW_UNSHADED      1
➜  #define DRAW_FLAT_SHADED   2
➜  #define DRAW_SMOOTH_SHADED 3

   class CObjDoc : public CJoeyOleServerDoc
   {
       CPoint3f      m_pts[MAX_OBJ_PTS];     // the vertex array
➜      CUnitV3f      m_uvs[MAX_OBJ_PTS];     // vertex normals
       int           m_ptCt;                 // the point count
       FACE          m_faces[MAX_OBJ_FACES];   // the face array
       int           m_faceCt;               // the face count
       int           m_maxFacePts;           // maximum pts in a face

       CXfm4x4f      m_xfmObj;               // object transformation
       CUnitV3f      m_uvObjAxisMap[3];      // object axis map

       CV3dJack      m_jack;                 // the manipulator jack
       CJoeyMaterial const* m_pMtlJack;      // the jack material

➜      int           m_nRenderStyle;         // default render style
➜      CJoeyMaterial const* m_pMtlWire;      // wireframe matl
➜      CJoeyMaterial const* m_pMtlUnshaded;  // unshaded matl
➜      CJoeyMaterial const* m_pMtlFlat;      // flat shaded matl
➜      CJoeyMaterial const* m_pMtlSmooth;    // smooth shaded matl

➜      CJoeyLight const* m_pLight;           // a light

   protected: // create from serialization only
       CObjDoc();
       DECLARE_DYNCREATE(CObjDoc)

➜      void DrawWireframe(PIRenderDevX,CJoeyView const *) const;
➜      void DrawUnshaded(PIRenderDevX,CJoeyView const *) const;
➜      void DrawFlatShaded(PIRenderDevX,CJoeyView const *) const;
➜      void DrawSmoothShaded(PIRenderDevX,CJoeyView const *) const;

   // Attributes
   public:
       CObjSrvrItem* GetEmbeddedItem() { return
           CObjSrvrItem*)CJoeyOleServerDoc::GetEmbeddedItem(); }
➜      void              InitMaterialAndLight();
➜      void              InitNormals();

       CUnitV3f const*   ObjAxisMap() const {return m_uvObjAxisMap;}
       •
```

```
      ◆
      CV3dJack&      ObjectJack()      {return m_jack;}
→     int            RenderStyle() const {return m_nRenderStyle;}
→     void           RenderStyle(int, BOOL =FALSE);

  // Operations
      ◆
      ◆
```

There are a few interesting additions here. Most of the additions are self-explanatory and directly associated with providing the functions for drawing the four rendering styles with a unique material for each. The odd additions to the FACE structure are for an array of pointers to vertex normals and for a face normal. The normal is perpendicular to the surface and provides surface orientation information that is required for lighting computations.

When the faces are flat shaded, the face normal is used to compute a single colour for the face. When the faces are smooth shaded, the vertex normals are used to compute a colour at each vertex and then these colours are interpolated (smoothly blended) across the face.

♦   Add initialisation for the added data in the document constructor on *objdoc.cpp* as follows:

```
    CObjDoc::CObjDoc()
    {
        ◆
        ◆
→       // create the drawing materials and light
→       VERIFY(m_pMtlWire = RE()->MaterialNew("wireframe"));
→       VERIFY(m_pMtlUnshaded = RE()->MaterialNew("unshaded"));
→       VERIFY(m_pMtlFlat = RE()->MaterialNew("flat shaded"));
→       VERIFY(m_pMtlSmooth = RE()->MaterialNew("smooth shaded"));
→       VERIFY(m_pLight = RE()->LightNew("test light"));
→       m_nRenderStyle = DRAW_WIREFRAME;

        EnableAutomation();

        AfxOleLockApp();
    }
```

Why are we getting materials and lights from the rendering environment? Why don't we just declare static material and light classes in the document header and be done with it? It would work fine in the context of this example but not in all cases. We use the rendering environment to keep track of materials and lights because it provides handy editing functionality for our application and the viewer (if the materials and lights are registered with it). We will make use of this in future sections.

♦ Add cleanup code in the document destructor in *objdoc.cpp*. In this case, we need to release the materials and lights we are using:

```
CObjDoc::~CObjDoc()
{
    if (NULL != m_pMtlJack) m_pMtlJack->Release();
→   if (NULL != m_pMtlWire) m_pMtlWire->Release();
→   if (NULL != m_pMtlUnshaded) m_pMtlUnshaded->Release();
→   if (NULL != m_pMtlFlat) m_pMtlFlat->Release();
→   if (NULL != m_pMtlSmooth) m_pMtlSmooth->Release();
→   if (NULL != m_pLight) m_pLight->Release();
    AfxOleUnlockApp();
}
```

♦ Add initialisation for the drawing materials and the light. The initialisation function, `InitMaterialAndLight`, was previously declared in the document header. This function should be added in *objdoc.cpp*:

```
→  void CObjDoc::InitMaterialAndLight()
→  {
→      CJoeyMaterial  mtl;
→      CJoeyLight     lgt;
→      // set the line style for wireframe
→      mtl.Flags(JOEY_MTL_LINE_RGB | JOEY_MTL_LINE_WIDTH |
→          JOEY_MTL_LINE_STYLE);
→      mtl.LineColor(CRGBf(0.0f,0.0f,0.0f));
→      mtl.LineWidth(1.0f);
→      mtl.LineStyle(0);
→      RE()->MaterialSet("wireframe",mtl);
→      // add the face properties for unshaded
→      mtl.Flags(JOEY_MTL_LINE_RGB | JOEY_MTL_LINE_WIDTH |
→          JOEY_MTL_LINE_STYLE | JOEY_MTL_FACE_RGB |
→          JOEY_MTL_FACE_STYLE);
→      mtl.FaceColor(CRGBf(0.0f,0.5f,0.0f));
→      mtl.FaceStyle(
→          JOEY_FACE_STYLE_FILL | JOEY_FACE_STYLE_EDGE |
→          JOEY_FACE_STYLE_DRAW | JOEY_FACE_STYLE_FLAT |
→          JOEY_FACE_STYLE_CULL);
→      RE()->MaterialSet("unshaded",mtl);
→      // add rendering properties for flat shaded
→      mtl.Flags(JOEY_MTL_FACE_STYLE | JOEY_MTL_AMBIENT_CLR |
→          JOEY_MTL_DIFFUSE_CLR | JOEY_MTL_SPECULAR_CLR);
→      mtl.Ambient(CRGBf(0.0f,0.8f,0.0f));
→      mtl.Diffuse(CRGBf(0.0f,0.8f,0.0f));
→      mtl.Specular(CRGBf(0.0f,0.8f,0.0f));
→      mtl.FaceStyle(
→          JOEY_FACE_STYLE_FILL | JOEY_FACE_STYLE_CULL |
→          JOEY_FACE_STYLE_SHADE | JOEY_FACE_STYLE_FLAT);
→      RE()->MaterialSet("flat shaded",mtl);
```

```
→      // just change the face style to smooth for smooth shaded
→      mtl.FaceStyle(
→          JOEY_FACE_STYLE_FILL | JOEY_FACE_STYLE_CULL |
→          JOEY_FACE_STYLE_SHADE | JOEY_FACE_STYLE_SMOOTH);
→      RE()->MaterialSet("smooth shaded",mtl);
→      // set a directional light from over your right shoulder
→      // in the front view
→      lgt.Flags(JOEY_LIGHT_TYPE | JOEY_LIGHT_INTENSITY |
→          JOEY_LIGHT_DIRECTION);
→      lgt.Type(JOEY_LIGHT_TYPE_DIRECTIONAL);
→      lgt.Intensity(CRGBf(1.0f,1.0f,1.0f));
→      RE()->LightSet("test light",lgt);
→  }
```

In each material, we are setting only the properties that are relevant to the rendering style that will be used. This is discussed in detail in the next section. Note that all of the material specification is encapsulated in the CJoeyMaterial class; you need only specify the items that you are interested in, and use the flag member to describe the information that should be used by the MaterialSet function. This encapsulation provides a mechanism for you to extend these classes if your application has specific needs not addressed in the default implementation of the material. Lights, grids, and cameras work in a similar fashion.

♦ In the serialisation function, add code to save and restore the rendering style for the document. Also, make additions so that face and vertex normals are computed after an object is loaded. Make changes to *objdoc.cpp*:

```
////////////////////////////////////////////////////////////////////
// CObjDoc serialization
     ♦
     ♦
#define OBJ_AXISMAP    5
→ #define OBJ_RENDER     6

static char*   s_strObjCmd[] = {"end",        "v",    "f",
→     "translate", "rotate", "axismap", "render"};
static int     s_ctObjCmd = sizeof(s_strObjCmd)/sizeof(char*);
void CObjDoc::Serialize(CArchive& ar)
{
          ♦
          ♦
→          // rendering style
→          sprintf(strOut,"%s %d\n",s_strObjCmd[OBJ_RENDER],
→              m_nRenderStyle);
→          ar.Write((void*)strOut,strlen(strOut));
           // write the data end
           sprintf(strOut,"%s\n",s_strObjCmd[OBJ_END_FILE]);
           ar.Write((void*)strOut,strlen(strOut));
     }
     else
```

```
      {
          CPoint3f    ptObjCtr;
➜         int         nRenderStyle = m_nRenderStyle;
                .
                .
              switch (nCmd) {
                  .
                  .
              case OBJ_FACE:
                  if (m_faceCt >= MAX_OBJ_FACES) {
                      AfxMessageBox(IDS_EXCEED_FACE_BUFF);
                      DeleteContents();
                      return;
                  }
                  if (tokenCt < 4) goto bad_format; // 3 vertices min
                      // allocate vertex and vertex normal ptr list
➜                     if ((NULL==(m_faces[m_faceCt].pts=(CPoint3f**)
➜                          malloc((tokenCt-1)*sizeof(CPoint3f*)))) ||
➜                         (NULL==(m_faces[m_faceCt].uvs=(CUnitV3f**)
➜                          malloc((tokenCt-1)*sizeof(CUnitV3f*)))))) {
                      AfxThrowMemoryException();
                      DeleteContents();
                      return;
                  }
                  // fill vertex and vertex normal pointer list
                  m_faces[m_faceCt].ptCt = tokenCt-1;
                  if (m_maxFacePts < m_faces[m_faceCt].ptCt)
                      m_maxFacePts = m_faces[m_faceCt].ptCt;
                  for (ii = 1; ii < tokenCt; ii++) {
                      if ( ((ptInd = atoi(lpToken[ii])-1) < 0) ||
                          (ptInd >= m_ptCt) ) goto bad_format;
                      m_faces[m_faceCt].pts[ii-1] = m_pts + ptInd;
➜                     m_faces[m_faceCt].uvs[ii-1] = m_uvs + ptInd;
                  }
                  m_faceCt++;
                  break;
              case OBJ_TRANSLATE:
                  .
                  .
                  break;
➜             case OBJ_RENDER:
➜                 if (tokenCt < 2) goto bad_format;
➜                 nRenderStyle = atoi(lpToken[1]);
➜                 break;
              default:
                  // not a meaningful line
                  break;
              }
          }
  end_of_obj_data:
➜         // compute the vertex normals
➜         InitNormals();
➜         // set the render style
➜         RenderStyle(nRenderStyle,TRUE);
```

```
                        // make the jack 30% larger than the data
                        .
                        .
                }
                CJoeyOleServerDoc::Serialize(ar);
                return;
                .
                .

        }
```

♦ Add an initialisation function for face and vertex normals. This function is called at the end of serialisation to prepare the object for drawing. Face normals are computed from the face vertices. Vertex normals are approximated by averaging the normals of the faces that use the vertex. While this approximation method works reasonably well, it is no substitute for using the actual normals if they are available.

```
→   void CObjDoc::InitNormals()
→   {
→       int         ii, jj;
→       // create vertex normals for smooth shading.
→       // zero the vertex normals
→       for (ii = 0; ii < m_ptCt; ii++)
→           m_uvs[ii] = CUnitV3f(0.0f,0.0f,0.0f);
→       // add the polygon normals into each vertex normal
→       for (ii = 0; ii < m_faceCt; ii++) {
→           m_faces[ii].uvFace.Polygon(m_faces[ii].ptCt,
→               m_faces[ii].pts);
→           for (jj = 0; jj < m_faces[ii].ptCt; jj++)
→               *(m_faces[ii].uvs[jj]) += m_faces[ii].uvFace;
→       }
→       // normalise the vertex normals
→       for (ii =0; ii < m_ptCt; ii++)
→           m_uvs[ii].Normalize();
→   }
```

We are using utility functions in the CUnitV3f class to do the gnarly work of computing and averaging face normals. The geometric classes, CUnitV3f, CPoint3f, CLine3f, and CPlane3f provide many of the commonly used geometric utility functions. Review the *JOEY* programmer's help for details.

♦ Add the body of the document RenderStyle function to set the render style for the document in *objdoc.cpp*. This function is used both to set the style for the document and to revise all of the views to the same rendering style. We have commented the call to the view function that sets render style for the view to allow for testing. We added the RenderStyle function after the ObjAxisMap function:

```
→   void CObjDoc::RenderStyle(int nRenderStyle, BOOL bSetViews)
→   {
```

```
➜         // set the document rendering style
➜         if (m_nRenderStyle != nRenderStyle) {
➜             m_nRenderStyle = nRenderStyle;
➜             SetModifiedFlag();
➜             if (IsEmbedded()) NotifyChanged();
➜         }
➜         // set the rendering style for the views
➜         if (bSetViews) {
➜             POSITION   pos = GetFirstViewPosition();
➜             while (pos != NULL) {
➜                 CObjView* pView = (CObjView*)GetNextView(pos);
➜                 //pView->RenderStyle(nRenderStyle);
➜             }
➜         }
➜     }
```

♦   Update the document `DeleteContents` function to free the face vertex normal pointer lists and to reset the materials, lights, and render style:

```
    void CObjDoc::DeleteContents()
    {
        m_ptCt = 0;      // reset the vertex count
        // loop through faces, delete vertex buffers
        while (--m_faceCt >= 0) {
            if (NULL != m_faces[m_faceCt].pts)
                free((void*)m_faces[m_faceCt].pts);
➜           if (NULL != m_faces[m_faceCt].uvs)
➜               free((void*)m_faces[m_faceCt].uvs);
        }
        •
        •
➜       // set the lights and the render style
➜       InitMaterialAndLight();
➜       RenderStyle(DRAW_WIREFRAME,TRUE);
    }
```

You may wonder about why we devote so much attention to window reset in the `DeleteContents` function. In the context of an MDI application, we get a new window whenever we open a new file, and the object windows close when the object is closed. Most of this could just be located in the document constructor. In an MDI application, we are indulging in overkill. However, if you were writing an SDI application, the document is cleared and re-used whenever you open a new file. The changes we have made are not MDI specific; you could have used the SDI version of *viewit3d* for these examples, and it would behave as expected.

♦   The next step is to add new drawing functions. We have made quite a few changes at this point, so we will compile and run *viewit3d* after we add each function so we can examine what is really happening. Make changes to the document `OnDraw` and move the wireframe drawing functionality to the `DrawWireframe` function in *objdoc.cpp*:

```
     void CObjDoc::OnDraw(PIRenderDevX pRD,
        CJoeyView const *pJView) const
     {
➔        int    nRenderStyle = m_nRenderStyle;

➔        // get the rendering style
➔        //if (NULL != pJView)
➔            //nRenderStyle = ((CObjView*)pJView)->RenderStyle();
➔        // draw the light if required
➔        if (nRenderStyle >= DRAW_FLAT_SHADED)
➔            pRD->LightSet(*m_pLight);
➔        // position in world space
         pRD->XfmPush();
         pRD->XfmConcat(m_xfmObj);
         m_jack.OnDraw(pRD,m_pMtlJack);
         // draw the object
         pRD->XfmPushDataDef(m_uvObjAxisMap,
            RENDER_DATADEF_CLOCKWISE | RENDER_DATADEF_CAN_CULL);
➔        if (DRAW_WIREFRAME == nRenderStyle)
➔            DrawWireframe(pRD,pJView);
➔        else if (DRAW_UNSHADED == nRenderStyle)
➔            DrawUnshaded(pRD,pJView);
➔        else if (DRAW_FLAT_SHADED == nRenderStyle)
➔            DrawFlatShaded(pRD,pJView);
➔        else if (DRAW_SMOOTH_SHADED == nRenderStyle)
➔            DrawSmoothShaded(pRD,pJView);
         pRD->XfmPop();
         // pop the world space positioning transform
         pRD->XfmPop();
     }

➔   void CObjDoc::DrawWireframe(PIRenderDevX pRD,
➔        CJoeyView const *pJView) const
➔   {
➔        CPoint3f**    ppPts = NULL;
➔        int           ii, jj;

➔        if ((0 == m_faceCt) || (0 == m_maxFacePts)) return;
➔        if (NULL == (ppPts = new PPoint3f[m_maxFacePts])) return;
➔        pRD->MaterialPush(m_pMtlWire);
➔        for (ii=0; ii<m_faceCt; ii++) {
➔            for (jj=0; jj<m_faces[ii].ptCt; jj++)
➔                ppPts[jj] = m_faces[ii].pts[jj];
➔            ppPts[jj] = m_faces[ii].pts[0];   // to close the polygon
➔            pRD->Draw3dPolyline(m_faces[ii].ptCt + 1,ppPts);
➔        }
➔        pRD->MaterialPop();
➔        delete ppPts;
➔   }
```

```
→   void CObjDoc::DrawUnshaded(PIRenderDevX pRD,
→       CJoeyView const *pJView) const
→   {
→   }

→   void CObjDoc::DrawFlatShaded(PIRenderDevX pRD,
→       CJoeyView const *pJView) const
→   {
→   }

→   void CObjDoc::DrawSmoothShaded(PIRenderDevX pRD,
→       CJoeyView const *pJView) const
→   {
→   }
```

We have just moved the wireframe drawing into its own function. The stub functions for drawing unshaded, flat shaded, and smooth shaded models have been added so that we can rebuild and run *viewit3d*. Near the beginning of the draw, we set the render style to the document render style and then replace it with the view render style  if the draw has been called from a view. This supports multiple views with different rendering styles, yet deals with the case when the document is being drawn to something other than a *JOEY* view (e.g., when it is being drawn to the OLE container). The reset to the view render style is commented out for testing. We will un-comment it later in this example. You can now build and run *viewit3d*. There should be no observable difference in operation at this time.

One new thing in the DrawWireframe function is the push, set, and pop of the wireframe material around the drawing of the lines. Like transformations, the push and pop provide a mechanism for saving and restoring the material state. If you refer back to the InitMaterialAndLight function, you will notice that the only properties we have set for the wireframe material are line drawing properties (since we are only using this material to draw lines).

♦   Fill in the body of the document DrawUnshaded function in *objdoc.cpp*:

```
    void CObjDoc::DrawUnshaded(PIRenderDevX pRD,
        CJoeyView const *pJView) const
    {
→       int             ii;

→       if ((0 == m_faceCt) || (0 == m_maxFacePts)) return;
→       pRD->MaterialPush(m_pMtlUnshaded);
→       for (ii=0; ii<m_faceCt; ii++)
→           pRD->Draw3dPolygon(m_faces[ii].ptCt,m_faces[ii].pts);
→       pRD->MaterialPop();
```

```
}
```

In the `DeleteContents` function, set the render style to unshaded (the change is in bold):

```
RenderStyle(DRAW_UNSHADED,TRUE);
```

You can now rebuild and run *viewit3d* and you will have objects that are solid, coloured green, and have outlines around the polygons. We are now using the rendering device's `Draw3dPolygon` function to draw the faces. The data this function needs happens to be in the same form as the object database so the draw is very straightforward.
You may notice that the edge lines of the polygons do not look very solid, and that unshaded drawing without the polygon edges may not be useful in all situations.

The loss of solidity in the edges is a z-buffer artifact that is renderer specific. In OpenGL, the polygons are actually drawn twice by the render device, once for the filled polygon and once for the edges. Since they are both at exactly the same depth or Z value from the eye, the algorithm gets confused about which should be in front.

The usefulness of shading without edges can be explored by removing the `JOEY_FACE_STYLE_EDGE` flag from the face style for the unshaded material in the `InitMaterialAndLight` function. When an object is made of unshaded polygons of the same colour, there is no difference between faces and it just becomes a blob of colour on the screen.

◆ Fill in the body of the document `DrawFlatShaded` function in *objdoc.cpp*:

```
    void CObjDoc::DrawFlatShaded(PIRenderDevX pRD,
        CJoeyView const *pJView) const
    {
➜       int         ii;
➜       CUnitV3f    uv;
➜       CUnitV3f*   pUv[2] = {&uv,NULL};

➜       if ((0 == m_faceCt) || (0 == m_maxFacePts)) return;
➜       pRD->MaterialPush(m_pMtlFlat);
➜       for (ii=0; ii<m_faceCt; ii++) {
➜           uv = m_faces[ii].uvFace;
➜           pRD->Draw3dPolygon(m_faces[ii].ptCt,m_faces[ii].pts,
➜               NULL,pUv);
➜       }
```

```
→        pRD->MaterialPop();
    }
```

In the `DeleteContents` function, set the render style to flat shaded (the change is in bold):

```
RenderStyle(DRAW_FLAT_SHADED,TRUE);
```

You can now rebuild and run *viewit3d*, and you will have objects that are green, and lit by a light that appears to come from the left. The faces appear to be flat, and the light moves with the world axis system (if you move the camera, the light stays fixed relative to the world axis system). There are a few new things needed to draw flat shaded objects First, a light is required; second, surface orientations are required, and third, a different set of material properties must be specified.

The light was initialised as a directional light (a light infinitely far away, such as the sun), and was set before the object was drawn. We set the light in the `OnDraw` function so that it would be in world space before any transformations were pushed onto the stack. It must also be specified before the geometry (that should be lit) is drawn.[24]

The surface orientation is specified in the `Draw3dPolygon` function. This function expects that when normals are specified, there is either a NULL terminated normal list, or a list equal containing a normal for each vertex. If there is only one normal on the list, it is used as the face normal.

Materials have both drawing and shading properties. In this example, we could actually use a single material in either draw or shaded mode to get most of the rendering styles we are demonstrating, but for demonstration and explanation purposes we have kept them separate.

◆   Fill in the body of the document `DrawSmoothShaded` function in *objdoc.cpp*:

```
    void CObjDoc::DrawSmoothShaded(PIRenderDevX pRD,
        CJoeyView const *pJView) const
    {
→        int            ii;

→        if ((0 == m_faceCt) || (0 == m_maxFacePts)) return;
→        pRD->MaterialPush(m_pMtlSmooth);
→        for (ii=0; ii<m_faceCt; ii++)
→            pRD->Draw3dPolygon(m_faces[ii].ptCt,m_faces[ii].pts,
```

---

[24] The requirement that lights be specified before the geometry is drawn is a function of the operation of z-buffer algorithms. Since the geometry is processed by the renderer as it is received and there is essentially no data caching, there is no opportunity to specify the whole environment before rendering starts. This can pose some strange problems when rendering complex environments. This is addressed in Section 3.1.4.

```
➜                NULL,m_faces[ii].uvs);
➜        pRD->MaterialPop();
     }
```

In the `DeleteContents` function, set the render style to smooth shaded (the change is in bold):

```
RenderStyle(DRAW_SMOOTH_SHADED,TRUE);
```

You can now rebuild and run *viewit3d*, and you will have objects that are green, lit by a light that appears to come from over your right shoulder, and apparently smooth surfaces. The faces appear to be blended together into a single surface. The only new thing required was the specification of smooth shading for the face style of the material, and a normal for every vertex. As you play with different objects, you will notice that the vertex averaging approximation works reasonably well with objects made of many small surfaces, like *ball.a3d*, but is dismal on objects made of just a few surfaces, like *pyra.a3d* or *hand.a3d*.

Now that the rendering styles are complete, we can build a dialogue to control the rendering style. This will be useful for exploration in the materials and lights sections of the text. It is also useful for exploring how an application should work when it is OLE enabled.

♦ Edit the project resource file, *viewit3d.rc* using AppStudio to add an Rendering Style menu item to the Options pulldown. In the `IDR_3D_GEOTYPE` menu Options pulldown after the Object Axis Map entry add an Rendering Style entry with the ID: *IDM_OPTIONS_RENDERING*, Caption: *&Rendering Style*, and Prompt: *Set the rendering style for a view\nView Render Style*. Copy this newly created menu item to the Options pulldowns in `IDR_3D_GEOTYPE_SRVR_EMB` and `IDR_3D_GEOTYPE_SRVR_IP` menus.

♦ Continue editing the project resource file, *viewit3d.rc*, to add a rendering style dialogue box with ID: *IDD_RENDERING* and Caption: *Rendering Style*. Create this dialogue with four radio buttons for the rendering styles, and a checkbox for saving the rendering style as the document default rendering style using the IDs noted, Figure P-16.

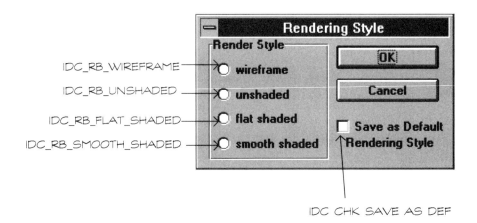

Figure P-16: Rendering Style dialogue box.

♦ Add a class to manage this dialogue using ClassWizard, Add Class... with Class Name: *CRenderStyleDlg*, Class Type: *CDialog*, Header File: *rend_dlg.h*, Implementation File: *rend_dlg.cpp*, and Dialog: *IDD_RENDERING*. Add message handling functions for the WM_INITDIALOG message of CRenderStyleDlg, and for the BN_CLICKED message of IDC_RB_WIREFRAME, IDC_RB_UNSHADED, IDC_RB_FLAT_SHADED, and IDC_RB_SMOOTH_SHADED. In the Member Variables property page of ClassWizard, select IDC_CHK_SAVE_AS_DEF, then click Add Variable.... In the Add Member Variable dialogue, set Member Variable Name: to *m_bSaveAsDef* , and accept the Category: *Value*, and Variable Type: *BOOL*. Select OK to complete the addition of the variable. Select OK again to complete the creation of the CRenderTypeDlg class.

♦ Add a member variable in the header file for CRenderStyleDlg, *rend_dlg.h*, to keep track of the rendering style:

```
class CRenderStyleDlg : public CDialog
{
    ♦
    ♦
// Dialog Data
    //{{AFX_DATA(CRenderStyleDlg)
    enum { IDD = IDD_RENDERING };
```

```
         BOOL     m_bSaveAsDef;
            //}}AFX_DATA
→        int      m_nRenderStyle;
            •
            •
         };
```

♦ In the implementation file for CRenderStyleDlg, *rend_dlg.cpp*, fill in the
  bodies of the message handling functions created by ClassWizard:

```
/////////////////////////////////////////////////////////////////
// CRenderStyleDlg message handlers
BOOL CRenderStyleDlg::OnInitDialog()
{
     CDialog::OnInitDialog();

→        // set the right radio button
→        if (DRAW_WIREFRAME == m_nRenderStyle)
→            ((CButton*)GetDlgItem(IDC_RB_WIREFRAME))->SetCheck(1);
→        else if (DRAW_UNSHADED == m_nRenderStyle)
→            ((CButton*)GetDlgItem(IDC_RB_UNSHADED))->SetCheck(1);
→        else if (DRAW_FLAT_SHADED == m_nRenderStyle)
→            ((CButton*)GetDlgItem(IDC_RB_FLAT_SHADED))->SetCheck(1);
→        else if (DRAW_SMOOTH_SHADED == m_nRenderStyle)
→            ((CButton*)GetDlgItem(IDC_RB_SMOOTH_SHADED))->SetCheck(1);

         return TRUE;  // return TRUE unless you set the focus to ...
                       // EXCEPTION: OCX Property Pages should ...
}

void CRenderStyleDlg::OnRbFlatShaded()
{
→    m_nRenderStyle = DRAW_FLAT_SHADED;
}

void CRenderStyleDlg::OnRbSmoothShaded()
{
→    m_nRenderStyle = DRAW_SMOOTH_SHADED;
}

void CRenderStyleDlg::OnRbUnshaded()
{
→    m_nRenderStyle = DRAW_UNSHADED;
}

void CRenderStyleDlg::OnRbWireframe()
{
→    m_nRenderStyle = DRAW_WIREFRAME;
}
```

♦ Use ClassWizard to add a message handler to CObjView to handle the
  COMMAND message for IDM_OPTIONS_RENDERING.

◆ In the header file for the *viewit3d* view, *objview.h*, add a member variable for the rendering style, and member functions to get and set the rendering style:

```
        class CObjView : public CJoeyView
        {
→           int     m_nRenderStyle;

        protected: // create from serialization only
            ♦
            ♦

        // Implementation
        public:
            virtual ~CObjView();
        #ifdef _DEBUG
            virtual void AssertValid() const;
            virtual void Dump(CDumpContext& dc) const;
        #endif
→           int         RenderStyle()  {return m_nRenderStyle;}
→           void        RenderStyle(int);
            ♦
            ♦
        };
```

◆ Add the RenderStyle member function to the *viewit3d* view in *objview.cpp*, fill in the body for the OnOptionsRendering message handler added by ClassWizard, and add an include for the CRenderStyleDlg header file:

```
        // objview.cpp : implementation of the CObjView class
        //
        ♦
        ♦
        #include "axismap.h"
→       #include "rend_dlg.h"
        ♦
        ♦
        //////////////////////////////////////////////////////////////
        // CObjView implementation
→       void CObjView::RenderStyle(int nRenderStyle)
→       {
→           m_nRenderStyle = nRenderStyle;
→           if (DRAW_WIREFRAME == nRenderStyle)
→               RendererType(RENDER_HIDSURF_NONE |
→                           RENDER_SHADE_NONE |
→                           RENDER_GLOBAL_NONE);
→           else RendererType(RENDER_HIDSURF_Z_BUFFER |
→                           RENDER_SHADE_GOURAUD |
→                           RENDER_GLOBAL_AMBIENT);
→           InvalidateRect(NULL);
→       }
        ♦
        ♦
```

```
void CObjView::OnOptionsRendering()
{
    CObjDoc*          pDoc = GetDocument();
    CRenderStyleDlg   dlg;
    if (pDoc->IsEmbedded())
        dlg.m_bSaveAsDef = TRUE;
    dlg.m_nRenderStyle = m_nRenderStyle;
    if (IDOK == dlg.DoModal()) {
        RenderStyle(dlg.m_nRenderStyle);
        if (dlg.m_bSaveAsDef)
            pDoc->RenderStyle(dlg.m_nRenderStyle);
    }
}
```

When the document is embedded, we set the m_bSaveAsDef flag to TRUE so the document render style is also updated when the view render style is set. This is so that the view drawn through the CJoeyOleServerItem (the cached view) has the same rendering style as the in-place editing window.

♦ Revise the document, *objdoc.cpp*, to reflect the desired default rendering style and to allow communication about rendering style between the view and the document. In DeleteContents, specify your desired default rendering style. We select wireframe as the default:

```
RenderStyle(DRAW_WIREFRAME,TRUE);
```

In the RenderStyle function, un-comment the call to the view RenderStyle function when the render style is being reset for all the views:

```
pView->RenderStyle(nRenderStyle);
```

In the OnDraw function, un-comment the two lines where the view render style overrides the document render style if it is a view that is requesting the draw:

```
// get the rendering style
if (NULL != pJView)
    nRenderStyle = ((CObjView*)pJView)->RenderStyle();
```

You can now rebuild and run *viewit3d*. We have now completed user selectable control for the rendering style. If you exercise the positioning jack to change the location of the object, you will probably note that the translation centre is obscured for all of the solid representations of the object. The best views for communicating information about the object to others (usually the flat or smooth shaded views) are not necessarily the best views for object editing and manipulation.

3.1.3 Materials

Moving from wireframe or unshaded imagery to shaded imagery (pictures with lighting effects) required additional information about surface geometry, surface materials and lighting. Now, we explore the relationship between material properties, rendering styles and geometric information.

Previously, we registered a material for each of the four rendering styles with the render environment. The render environment has limited database capabilities but it can keep a list of materials and provide access to the material editing services.

We make use of the editing services of the rendering environment by calling the rendering environment `MaterialDialogue` function. We add a <u>M</u>aterials... item in the Edit pulldown to access these services.

This is just an example; you do not need to access these services through the <u>E</u>dit pulldown or even to use the material registry in the render environment in your own application. There will be many cases where it makes more sense to use and edit materials without registering them. In this example, we access tools to facilitate our exploration of materials with little effort by using the render environment material database.

♦   Edit the project resource file, *viewit3d.rc*, using AppStudio to add menu access to material editing. In the `IDR_3D_GEOTYPE` menu <u>E</u>dit pulldown after the Copy <u>S</u>pecial..., add a separator entry, then a <u>M</u>aterials... entry with the pre-defined <u>I</u>D: `IDM_EDIT_MATERIALS`, and <u>C</u>aption: *&Materials...* (the prompt string is picked up from the *JOEY* resources). Copy this newly created menu item to the <u>E</u>dit pulldowns in the `IDR_3D_GEOTYPE_SRVR_EMB` and `IDR_3D_GEOTYPE_SRVR_IP` menus.

♦   Use ClassWizard to add a message handler to `CObjView` to handle the COMMAND message for `IDM_EDIT_MATERIALS`. Fill in the body of the message handler added by ClassWizard as follows:

```
        void CObjView::OnEditMaterials()
        {
→           CObjDoc*   pDoc = GetDocument();
→           if (pDoc->RE()->MaterialDialogue(
→                   JOEY_RB_DB_NO_CREATE | JOEY_RE_DB_NO_RENAME)) {
```

```
→            pDoc->SetModifiedFlag();
→            if (pDoc->IsEmbedded()) pDoc->NotifyChanged();
→            pDoc->UpdateAllViews(NULL);
→        }
    }
```

You can now rebuild *viewit3d* and use the material editor database editor that is part of the render environment to edit the materials for the document. Each object (document) that you are looking at in *viewit3d* has a render environment associated with it, and a unique set of materials. All of the views associated with a single object share the render environment that is owned by the document. There are four materials that are pre-defined by *JOEY*:

axis, world	The material used for the world axis system.
gridlines, major	The material used for drawing the major gridlines
gridlines, minor	The material used for drawing the minor gridlines
default	The material used for drawing things if a material has not been specified. *JOEY* loads the camera, draws the world axis and grids, and then loads the default material before calling the document OnDraw function.

You can select any of the materials used in rendering the object, jack, and grid and edit them as you please. We outline an exploration sequence below. You should not restrict yourself the these examples; just consider them a guide of some of the key points.

Use the wireframe rendering style and edit the "wireframe" material. The only properties that affect the image are line colour, line width and line style. Geometry is drawn as lines only in the DrawWireframe function.

Now, use the unshaded rendering style and edit the "unshaded" material. The face style has the greatest effect on the image. The unshaded style is drawn from polygons but no surface normal or lighting data is supplied during the draw. Though you can specify that you want the faces to be shaded, the lack of sufficient data results in an incomplete visual experience. It is interesting to play with a combinations of edge display, vertex display and fill to see if particular combinations will provide valuable information for your application.

Use the flat shaded rendering style and edit the "flat shaded" material. When you request shading, the colour is determined by the ambient, diffuse, specular and specular exponent properties and when shading is turned off, the appearance depends on the polygon and line colour. It makes no difference to request smoothing; the face normal is being sent to the polygon draw in flat shaded style. As a result, there is not enough geometric information to compute a different colour at each vertex of the polygon. In this case, the greatest degree of realism is limited by the geometric information that was provided to the rendering device.

Now, use the smooth shaded render style and edit the "smooth shaded" material. The `DrawSmoothShaded` function provides complete geometric information to the render device. In this case, the realism of the resulting image is limited by the material specification.

You may wonder whether you really need to use the material database in the render environment. You don't. The `CJoeyMaterial` class includes an editing dialogue which is used by the render environment (which you can use if your application maintains its own materials database). The advantage of using the material database is that it is serialized with the object and is available to the viewer to make it easier to edit the viewing of data in the *JOEY* 3D metafile format.

To appreciate the power of the render environment database (relative to the viewer), build a version of *viewit3d* where the materials are not referenced by pointers, but are declared in, and part of, the object database. You will need a menu to initiate editing (which calls the `MaterialDialogue` function). When the files are written to the viewer, there is no materials database in the rendering environment so the viewer is unable to edit the object appearance.

3.1.4 Lights

Lighting is the last part of the rendering process. In the last two sections, we were limited to a directional light.[25] Now, we provide access to the light editing services provided by `CJoeyLight` and `CJoeyRenderEnv` to explore how lighting relates to the generated imagery.

We make use of the editing services of the render environment by calling the rendering environment `LightDialogue` function. We add a Lights... item in the edit pulldown to provide access to these services.

---

[25] A light from a single direction that is of constant intensity.

Again, you are not required to use the render environment database or the editing services which it provides but by using them, the *JOEY* 3D metafile will have better information for viewing and you may save yourself some work in writing your application. We now add light editing to *viewit3d*:

◆ Edit the project resource file, *viewit3d.rc*, using AppStudio to menu access to light editing. In the IDR_3D_GEOTYPE menu <u>E</u>dit pulldown after the <u>M</u>aterials..., add a separator entry, then a <u>L</u>ights... entry with the pre-defined <u>I</u>D: IDM_EDIT_LIGHTS, and <u>C</u>aption: *&Lights...* (the prompt string is picked up from the *JOEY* resources). Copy this newly created menu item to the <u>E</u>dit pulldowns in the IDR_3D_GEOTYPE_SRVR_EMB and IDR_3D_GEOTYPE_SRVR_IP menus.

◆ Use ClassWizard to add a message handler to CObjView to handle the COMMAND message for IDM_EDIT_LIGHTS. Fill in the body of the message handler added by ClassWizard:

```
      void CObjView::OnEditLights()
      {
→        CObjDoc*   pDoc = GetDocument();
→        if (pDoc->RE()->LightDialogue(
→              JOEY_RB_DB_NO_CREATE | JOEY_RE_DB_NO_RENAME)) {
→            pDoc->SetModifiedFlag();
→            if (pDoc->IsEmbedded()) pDoc->NotifyChanged();
→            pDoc->UpdateAllViews(NULL);
         }
      }
```

This addition allows you to access the render environment editor to change the properties of the light. In order to make things more interesting, add a little mode code so that you can manipulate the position of the light. This will help teach you a little more about the different lights, transformations, and interacting with data.

First, we add data for positioning transformation, positioning jack, and material for the abstract representation of the light along with the functions that control access to this data in the document, CObjDoc. Then we add the mouse tracking control in the view mouse message functions.

◆ Make additions to *objdoc.h* to add data for the light transformation, material, and positioning jack, along with the functions to manipulate this data:

```
      class CObjDoc : public CJoeyOleServerDoc
      {
          •
          •
          CJoeyLight const*  m_pLight;          // a light
```

```
→      CV3dLgtJack         m_jackLight;         // manipulator forlight
→      CXfm4x4f            m_xfmLight;          // light transformation
→      CJoeyMaterial const* m_pMtlLight;        // light material
       ◆
       ◆
       CV3dJack&           ObjectJack()         {return m_jack;}
→      CXfm4x4f const&     LightTransform()     {return m_xfmLight;}
→      void                LightTransform(CXfm4x4f const&);
→      CV3dLgtJack&        LightJack()     {return m_jackLight;}
→      CJoeyLight const*   Light() const   {return m_pLight;}
       int                 RenderStyle() const {return m_nRenderStyle;}
       void                RenderStyle(int, BOOL =FALSE);
       ◆
       ◆
};
```

◆ Add initialisation of the added data in the document constructor in
   objdoc.cpp:

```
CObjDoc::CObjDoc()
{
       ◆
       ◆
       RE()->MaterialSet("manipulator jack",mtl);
→      VERIFY(m_pMtlLight = RE()->MaterialNew("light"));
→      mtl.PointColor(CRGBf(1.0f,1.0f,0.0f));
→      mtl.LineColor(CRGBf(1.0f,1.0f,0.0f));
→      RE()->MaterialSet("light",mtl);

       // create the drawing materials and light
       ◆
       ◆
}
```

The definition of the light to the rendering device does not provide any
physical form for the light, only a mathematical description of light
originating from some point in space. In order to make this situation a little
less abstract, we draw a light icon that is yellow (the colour set above) with
a positioning jack that is the same colour as the object positioning jack.

◆ Add cleanup code to the destructor in *objdoc.h* to release the light material
   when the document is destroyed:

```
CObjDoc::~CObjDoc()
{
       ◆
       ◆
→      if (NULL != m_pMtlLight) m_pMtlLight->Release();
       if (NULL != m_pLight) m_pLight->Release();
       AfxOleUnlockApp();
}
```

♦ Add the transformation and light positioning jack to the document `OnDraw`
function in *objdoc.cpp*. We were already displaying the effects of the light by
using the `LightSet` function. Now, we will add a geometry transformation
to position the light, and the drawing of the light icon and jack to support
manipulation of light type and direction. In *objdoc.cpp*, add the following to
the `OnDraw` function:

```
void CObjDoc::OnDraw(PIRenderDevX pRD,
    CJoeyView const *pJView) const
{
    int     nRenderStyle = m_nRenderStyle;

    // get the rendering style
    if (NULL != pJView)
        nRenderStyle = ((CObjView*)pJView)->RenderStyle();
    // draw the light if required - it is both set the
    //  render device as a light, and drawn as an object
    pRD->XfmPush();
    pRD->XfmConcat(m_xfmLight);
    if (nRenderStyle >= DRAW_FLAT_SHADED)
        pRD->LightSet(m_pLight);
    m_jackLight.OnDraw(pRD,m_pLight,m_pMtlLight,m_pMtlJack);
    pRD->XfmPop();
    // object position in world space
    ♦
    ♦
}
```

♦ In *objdoc.cpp*, add the `LightTransform` function that sets the light
transformation and performs the required drawing update and change
notification (added right after the `ObjectTransform` function):

```
void CObjDoc::LightTransform(CXfm4x4f const& xfm)
{
    m_xfmLight = xfm;
    SetModifiedFlag();
    if (IsEmbedded()) NotifyChanged();
    UpdateAllViews(NULL);
}
```

In addition to setting the modified flag, we notify the container of the
change if this is embedded data.

♦ Revise the document `Serialize` function in *objdoc.cpp* so that the position
of the light is part of the object data, and for sizing of the light icon and
positioning jack:

```
//////////////////////////////////////////////////////////
// CObjDoc serialization
    ♦
    ♦
```

```
    #define OBJ_RENDER     6
➜   #define LGT_TRANSLATE 7
➜   #define LGT_ROTATE     8

    static char*   s_strObjCmd[] = {"end",        "v",     "f",
➜       "translate", "rotate", "axismap", "render",
➜       "lgtTrans", "lgtRot"};
    static int     s_ctObjCmd = sizeof(s_strObjCmd)/sizeof(char*);
    void CObjDoc::Serialize(CArchive& ar)
    {
        •
        •
        if (ar.IsStoring())
        {
            •
            •
➜           // write light location (translate, rotate, and axismap)
➜           sprintf(strOut,"%s %.3f %.3f %.3f\n",
➜               s_strObjCmd[LGT_TRANSLATE],
➜               m_xfmLight[3][0], m_xfmLight[3][1], m_xfmLight[3][2]);
➜           ar.Write((void*)strOut,strlen(strOut));
➜           V3dDecomposeRotation(m_xfmLight,fRotX,fRotY,fRotZ);
➜           sprintf(strOut,"%s %.3f %.3f %.3f\n",
➜               s_strObjCmd[LGT_ROTATE],fRotX,fRotY,fRotZ);
➜           ar.Write((void*)strOut,strlen(strOut));
            // write the data end
            sprintf(strOut,"%s\n",s_strObjCmd[OBJ_END_FILE]);
            ar.Write((void*)strOut,strlen(strOut));
        }
        else
        {
➜           CPoint3f    ptObjCtr, ptLgtCtr;
            int         nRenderStyle = m_nRenderStyle;
                •
                •
            switch (nCmd) {
                •
                •
                case OBJ_RENDER:
                    •
                    •
                    break;
➜               case LGT_TRANSLATE:
➜                   if (tokenCt < 4) goto bad_format;
➜                   for (ii = PT_x; ii <= PT_z; ii++)
➜                       ptLgtCtr[ii] = (float)atof(lpToken[1+ii]);
➜                   break;
➜               case LGT_ROTATE:
➜                   if (tokenCt < 4) goto bad_format;
➜               m_xfmLight.Identity();
➜               for (ii = AXIS_x; ii <= AXIS_z; ii++)
➜                   m_xfmLight.Rotate(ii,CAngle(ANGLE_DEGREE,
➜                           (float)atof(lpToken[1+ii])));
➜                   break;
```

```
                    default:
                        // not a meaningful line
                        break;
                }
            }
    end_of_obj_data:
            •
            •
            m_jack.Resize(fDataSpace * 1.3f);
➔           m_jackLight.Resize(fDataSpace * 0.2f);
            // make the dataspace 3x the size of the object
            RE()->DataSpace(fDataSpace*6.0f,TRUE,TRUE,FALSE);
            // add the centre into the object transformation
            m_xfmObj.Translate(ptObjCtr.x,ptObjCtr.y,ptObjCtr.z);
➔           m_xfmLight.Translate(ptLgtCtr.x,ptLgtCtr.y,ptLgtCtr.z);
        }
        CJoeyOleServerDoc::Serialize(ar);
        return;
            •
            •
    }
```

When you begin to play with the example, you will notice that changes you
make to the light data are saved and restored even though you have not
explicitly saved the light. This is because the light has been loaded into the
render environment database. When the render environment database is
loaded, the light settings in the file overwrite the settings of the light that
was loaded and initialised into the document render environment database
in the document constructor and the `InitMaterialAndLight` function. The
render environment data is keyed by the light name. This is why the name
and existence of the lights are locked when the *JOEY* render environment
light editor is started.

◆   Revise the document `DeleteContents` function in *objdoc.cpp* so that the
    light transform is initialised and to set initial sizing of the camera icon and
    jack are set:

```
    void CObjDoc::DeleteContents()
    {
        •
        •
        m_jack.Resize(RE()->DataSpace() * 0.25f);
➔       m_xfmLight.Identity();
➔       m_jackLight.Resize(RE()->DataSpace() * 0.05f);
        // set the lights and the render style
        InitMaterialAndLight();
        RenderStyle(DRAW_WIREFRAME,TRUE);
    }
```

This completes the code changes that affect the document. The remaining changes are in the mouse message handling functions of the view. now that we have more than one object we are manipulating, there are many opportunities for conflict. For example, both the object and the light are initially located at the origin. When the user selects the translation handle, is the light or the object selected, or do they both move together? Our implementation simply gives the object precedence over the light.

♦ Add a test to the left mouse button down processing for the view to see if one of the light positioning jack handles was hit. Start light tracking if it was. Make changes in the OnLButtonDown member function of *objview.cpp* as follows:

```
    void CObjView::OnLButtonDown(UINT nFlags, CPoint point)
    {
        CJoeyMouse       mouse(point);
        ♦
        ♦
        PrepareMouse(mouse,MOUSE_WORLD_TOL);
        if ((pDoc->ObjectJack()).Hit(pDoc->ObjectTransform(),mouse,
                fDist,nEditID)) {
            ♦
            ♦
        } else if ((pDoc->LightJack()).Hit(pDoc->LightTransform(),
                mouse, pDoc->Light(),fDist,nEditID)) {
            pDoc->LightTransform((pDoc->LightJack()).TrackStart(
                pDoc->LightTransform(),mouse,
                pDoc->Light(),fDist,nEditID));
            SetCapture();
        }
    }
```

♦ Add a test in the mouse move message handling to check the light tracking status. If the light is tracking, pass mouse information to the light jack for processing. The jack returns a revised light transformation which is loaded into the document database. In the OnMouseMove message handler in *objview.cpp,* make the following additions:

```
    void CObjView::OnMouseMove(UINT nFlags, CPoint point)
    {
        CObjDoc*       pDoc = GetDocument();
        ♦
        ♦
        if ((pDoc->ObjectJack()).IsTracking()) {
            ♦
            ♦
        } else if ((pDoc->LightJack()).IsTracking()) {
```

```
→          CJoeyMouse        mouse(point);
→          PrepareMouse(mouse,MOUSE_WORLD);
→          pDoc->LightTransform((pDoc->LightJack()).Track(mouse));
→      }
   }
```

◆ Add a test in the left mouse button up message handling to check the light
   tracking status. If the light is tracking, pass mouse information to the light
   jack, end light tracking, and update the light transformation. In the
   OnLButtonUp message handler in *objview.cpp*, make the following additions:

```
void CObjView::OnLButtonUp(UINT nFlags, CPoint point)
{
    CObjDoc*        pDoc = GetDocument();
    •
    •

    if ((pDoc->ObjectJack()).IsTracking()) {
    •
    •
→   } else if ((pDoc->LightJack()).IsTracking()) {
→       CJoeyMouse        mouse(point);
→       PrepareMouse(mouse,MOUSE_WORLD);
→       pDoc->LightTransform(
→           (pDoc->LightJack()).TrackEnd(mouse));
→       ReleaseCapture();
→   }
   }
```

You can rebuild and run *viewit3d*. *Viewit3d* is now a
manipulator for an environment containing an object and a
light. You can edit the object material, the light type and
parameters, object and light position and orientation, and
rendering style.

You should play a bit with lighting types at this point. You
get a directional light (light of constant intensity coming from a fixed direction)
by default. Ambient light is non-directional light; it is equal in all directions and
provides an even level of lighting across the entire object. Local lights are lights
that have a position in the environment and radiate light equally in all
directions from the light. As you move a local light, you will see the lighting on
the object change as though you were moving an unshaded light bulb around
the object. The spot light has both location and direction, so you can position
and aim the spot light. The direction of the spot light is also the direction of the
directional light when the type is changed back to directional.

In addition to the lighting considerations of position and intensity, there is also an interaction of material colour and light colour that can be studied. The final colour of an object results from a multiplication of the light colour by the material colour factored for surface roughness, geometry, and other properties. If the material is white, the lighted colour will be the colour of the light. If the light is white, the lighted colour will be the colour of the material. If the colours are complementary (e.g. green (0,1,0) and magenta (1,0,1)), the lighted colour will be black.

The most realistic lighting will come from a combination of ambient light and at least one direct source, either directional, local, or spot light. Try adding additional lights to *viewit3d* to test the effects of multiple lights. To do this, you can just repeat the additions of this section for an additional light or two. This will give you some experience making the kind of interaction decisions that are required in a real application. For those of you who are more adventurous, you might consider a dialogue that lets you add or delete lights from the scene.[26]

3.2 Graphic Representations of Data

The changes to *viewit3d* in the last section provided several different ways to display data using different rendering styles. It also showed that different information is communicated with different rendering styles and the representation available to the user needs to be the one that makes it easiest to complete a given task. You have probably noticed that it is very difficult to pick the translation centre of the jack when the object is sold and hides the translation centre, and that it is difficult to set up lighting when you are using a wireframe rendering style. You have probably also noticed that it is very difficult to position objects once you have rotated the view.

We will not try to lay out principles for designing representations, but encourage you to experiment with *viewit3d* to try to better understand how to structure a display to provide better representation to the user. You may want to try multiple views with different cameras. A four view representation containing orthographic plan view, orthographic front view, orthographic side view, and a perspective or other view is often helpful in positioning data,

Figure P-17. The first three views provide good feedback for understanding position while the fourth view provides a more "realistic" view of the data for inspection. Ideally, there would be the equivalent of splitter windows for two or

---

[26] If you are using the OpenGL IRenderDevX driver, you are limited to a maximum of 8 lights.

four view representations. This is beyond the scope of the *JOEY* Toolkit. Since the `CJoeyView` can be used as a child window, you could easily implement a view that used several *JOEY* views as child windows.

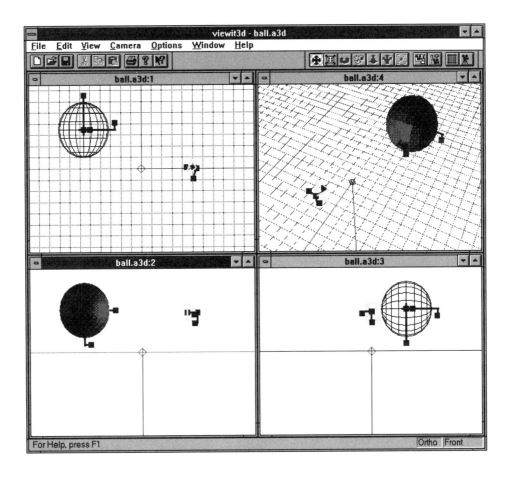

Figure P-17: Four views of an environment with object and light positioning.

If you do implement a two or four view window, there should be an option (probably the default operation) to couple cameras so that the centre is aligned between corresponding views. You may also want to fix the camera choices in the three orthographic views and allow camera selection in the fourth view, Figure P-18.

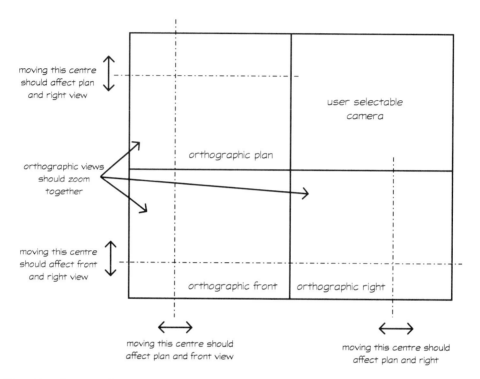

Figure P-18: Layout and camera interaction for a four view data display.

To encourage exploration, we add two more data representations in this section. The first is a vertex only point representation, and the second is a bounding volume.

♦   Revise the document header in *objdoc.h* to include data for the additional wireframe and vertex only representations and their associated drawing functions. This additional data is a min-max box corner vertex, the lines for drawing the min-max box, and an array of vertex pointers to hold the pointer array for the point draw function:

```
→    #define DRAW_MIN_MAX           0
→    #define DRAW_POINTS            1
→    #define DRAW_WIREFRAME         2
→    #define DRAW_UNSHADED          3
→    #define DRAW_FLAT_SHADED       4
→    #define DRAW_SMOOTH_SHADED     5

     class CObjDoc : public CJoeyOleServerDoc
     {
```

```
            CPoint3f        m_pts[MAX_OBJ_PTS];    // the vertex array
➜           CPoint3f**      m_ppPts;               // temp array ptr
➜           CPoint3f        m_ptMM[8];             // min-max verts
➜           CPoint3f*       m_pPtMM[4][4];         // min-box lines
            CUnitV3f        m_uvs[MAX_OBJ_PTS];    // vertex normals
              •
              •
➜           void DrawMinMax(PIRenderDevX,CJoeyView const *) const;
➜           void DrawPoints(PIRenderDevX,CJoeyView const *) const;
            void DrawWireframe(PIRenderDevX,CJoeyView const *) const;
              •
              •
      };
```

Rendering styles were re-numbered to keep the styles in a least detail to greatest detail organisation.

◆ Add initialisation for the vertex pointer array pointer in the document constructor in *objdoc.cpp*:

```
      CObjDoc::CObjDoc()
      {
            •
            •
            m_maxFacePts = 0;
➜           m_ppPts = NULL;
            •
            •
      }
```

◆ Add cleanup of the vertex pointer array in the document destructor and the `DeleteContents` function in *objdoc.cpp*:

```
      CObjDoc::~CObjDoc()
      {
            •
            •
            if (NULL != m_pLight) m_pLight->Release();
➜           if (NULL != m_ppPts) delete m_ppPts;
            AfxOleUnlockApp();
      }

      void CObjDoc::DeleteContents()
      {
            •
            •
            m_faceCt = 0;  // reset the face count
            m_maxFacePts = 0;
➜           if (NULL != m_ppPts) delete m_ppPts;
➜           m_ppPts = NULL;
            •
            •
      }
```

♦ The min-max box and vertex only representations use the same material as
   the wireframe representation. Add initialisation of the point colour and size
   for this material in the document function, `InitMaterialAndLight` in
   objdoc.cpp:

```
    void CObjDoc::InitMaterialAndLight()
    {
        ⬩
        // set the line style for wireframe
➜       mtl.Flags(JOEY_MTL_POINT_RGB | JOEY_MTL_POINT_SIZE |
➜           JOEY_MTL_LINE_RGB | JOEY_MTL_LINE_WIDTH |
            JOEY_MTL_LINE_STYLE);
➜       mtl.PointColor(CRGBf(0.0f,0.0f,0.0f));
➜       mtl.PointSize(2.0f);
        mtl.LineColor(CRGBf(0.0f,0.0f,0.0f));
        ⬩
        ⬩
    }
```

♦ Add the initialisation of the bounding box and vertex pointer array in the
   document `Serialize` function in *objdoc.cpp*:

```
    void CObjDoc::Serialize(CArchive& ar)
    {
        ⬩
        ⬩
        if (ar.IsStoring())
        {
            ⬩
            ⬩
        }
        else
        {
            ⬩
            ⬩
            float       fDataSpace = 1.0f;
➜           CPoint3f    ptMM[2];
➜           ptMM[PT_min] = CPoint3f((float)HUGE_VAL,
➜                       (float)HUGE_VAL,(float)HUGE_VAL);
➜           ptMM[PT_max] = CPoint3f((float)-HUGE_VAL,
➜                       (float)-HUGE_VAL,(float)-HUGE_VAL);
            // read the lines in the file and parse into the database
                ⬩
                ⬩
            case OBJ_VERTEX:
                ⬩
                ⬩
                // load the vertex and update the dataspace
                for (ii= PT_x; ii<=PT_z; ii++) {
                    m_pts[m_ptCt][ii] = (float)atof(lpToken[ii+1]);
                    if (m_pts[m_ptCt][ii] > fDataSpace)
                        fDataSpace = m_pts[m_ptCt][ii];
                    else if ((-m_pts[m_ptCt][ii]) > fDataSpace)
                        fDataSpace = -m_pts[m_ptCt][ii];
```

```
➔                          if (ptMM[PT_min][ii] > m_pts[m_ptCt][ii])
➔                              ptMM[PT_min][ii] = m_pts[m_ptCt][ii];
➔                          if (ptMM[PT_max][ii] < m_pts[m_ptCt][ii])
➔                              ptMM[PT_max][ii] = m_pts[m_ptCt][ii];
                        }
                        m_ptCt++;
                        break;
                    case OBJ_FACE:
            •
            •
    end_of_obj_data:
➔          // set min-max box
➔          V3dBuildMinMax(m_ptMM,m_pPtMM,ptMM);
➔          m_ppPts = new PPoint3f[m_ptCt];
➔          for (ii=0; ii<m_ptCt; ii++)   m_ppPts[ii] = m_pts + ii;
           // compute the vertex normals
            •
            •
    }
```

Start the computation of the min-max box by setting the minimum point to
the largest possible value and the maximum point to the smallest possible
value. As the vertices are read, the comparisons on the first vertex will
result in both minimum and maximum points being set equal to that vertex.
The box then expands from there. The V3dBuildMinMax function loads the
eight vertices of a rectangular box from the min-max points. It also loads the
vertex pointer arrays in preparation for drawing.

◆   Revise the document OnDraw function to recognise the two new
    representations and add draw functions for each in *objdoc.cpp*:

```
    void CObjDoc::OnDraw(PIRenderDevX pRD,
        CJoeyView const *pJView) const
    {
        •
        •
        // draw the object
        pRD->XfmPushDataDef(m_uvObjAxisMap,
        RENDER_DATADEF_CLOCKWISE | RENDER_DATADEF_CAN_CULL);
➔       if (DRAW_MIN_MAX == nRenderStyle)
➔           DrawMinMax(pRD,pJView);
➔       else if (DRAW_POINTS == nRenderStyle)
➔           DrawPoints(pRD,pJView);
➔       else if (DRAW_WIREFRAME == nRenderStyle)
            DrawWireframe(pRD,pJView);
        •
        •
    }

➔   void CObjDoc::DrawMinMax(PIRenderDevX pRD,
➔       CJoeyView const *pJView) const
```

```
➔  {
➔      int                ii;
➔      if (0 == m_ptCt) return;
➔      pRD->MaterialPush(m_pMtlWire);
➔      for (ii=0; ii<4; ii++)
➔          pRD->Draw3dPolyline(4,m_pPtMM[ii]);
➔      pRD->MaterialPop();
➔  }

➔  void CObjDoc::DrawPoints(PIRenderDevX pRD,
➔      CJoeyView const *pJView) const
➔  {
➔      if (0 == m_ptCt) return;
➔      pRD->MaterialPush(m_pMtlWire);
➔      pRD->Draw3dPoint(m_ptCt,m_ppPts);
➔      pRD->MaterialPop();
➔  }
```

♦   The changes to the document are now complete. The only thing left to do is
    augment the Rendering Style dialogue to include selections for these two
    representation styles. Edit the project resource file, *viewit3d.rc* using
    AppStudio to add selection buttons for min-max box and vertex only
    rendering styles. Give these radio button IDs of IDC_RB_MINMAX and
    IDC_RB_POINTS respectively.

♦   Using ClassWizard, add message handling to the CRenderStyleDlg class
    for   the   BN_CLICKED   message   of   IDC_RB_MINMAX   and
    IDC_RB_POINTS. Make additions to the OnInitDialog message handler
    for initialisation of the rendering style, and fill in the bodies of the new
    message handling functions added by ClassWizard.

```
BOOL CRenderStyleDlg::OnInitDialog()
{
        ♦
        // set the right radio button
➔       if (DRAW_MIN_MAX == m_nRenderStyle)
➔           ((CButton*)GetDlgItem(IDC_RB_MINMAX))->SetCheck(1);
➔       else if (DRAW_POINTS == m_nRenderStyle)
➔           ((CButton*)GetDlgItem(IDC_RB_POINTS))->SetCheck(1);
➔       else if (DRAW_WIREFRAME == m_nRenderStyle)
➔           ((CButton*)GetDlgItem(IDC_RB_WIREFRAME))->SetCheck(1);
➔       else if (DRAW_UNSHADED == m_nRenderStyle)
            ((CButton*)GetDlgItem(IDC_RB_UNSHADED))->SetCheck(1);
        ♦
        ♦
    }

    void CRenderStyleDlg::OnRbMinmax()
    {
➔       m_nRenderStyle = DRAW_MIN_MAX;
    }
```

```
      void CRenderStyleDlg::OnRbPoints()
      {
→          m_nRenderStyle = DRAW_POINTS;
      }
```

You have finished adding two additional object representations to *viewit3d*. You can rebuild and run *viewit3d* to test these representations.

We would be remiss if we did not also mention textual and diagrammatic representations. Though we will not implement any for *viewit3d*, it might be helpful to have textual listing of face and/or vertex information and properties, or diagrammatic representations of groupings or transformation hierarchies for use in selection, manipulation, or feedback. There is sufficient discussion of text based presentation and manipulation in other references that we felt we could add very little.

3.3 Manipulating Data

You are probably beginning to wonder how to do any meaningful work with tools that rely on data manipulations in 3D. We suspect that you are having a terrible time getting your object and light positioned and aimed so that they are where you wanted them to be. If you have been adventurous and augmented *viewit3d* so that there is more that one light and one object, the problem is compounded. The last section suggested part of the answer, presenting data representations and views that give the best visual feedback for the task that you are trying to accomplish. Another part of the answer is to provide manipulation methods that are intuitive and of sufficient accuracy for the task.

A number of interaction techniques are already in place in *viewit3d*. Now, we explore the nuances that you may not have been aware of, and suggest some other enhancements for *viewit3d* that should ease some of the manipulation problems.

3.3.1 Direct, Indirect, Immediate, and Delayed Interaction

What does it mean for something to be interactive? When we speak of interaction, we are talking about the graphic presentation changing in response to, and at the same time as, the actions of the user. This suggests that "interactive" includes an action on the part of the user, which changes the application data and, results in a change in the graphic. It also suggests that "interactive" includes an immediacy in the connection of the action with the visual change that confirms the results of the action.

Manipulation actions are often characterised as direct or indirect. Direct actions are applied directly to the data (like picking up an object with your hand in the real world), while indirect actions are applied through some control (like depressing the brake pedal to get your automobile to slow down). Some manipulations give an immediate result (like turning up the volume on the stereo), while in others, there is a delay (such as the time it takes from when you refill your hot tub until it reaches a usable temperature). A third dimension of the manipulation is absolute and relative control. A channel on a television is absolute, it locks on specified frequencies, while the accelerator pedal of an automobile is relative, controlling speed by continuous variation of power.

Controlling the temperature of water is a good example for thinking about what is, in fact, truly interactive. Once both the hot and cold water temperature have stabilised coming into a faucet (the room temperature water sitting in the lines has been flushed out), a kitchen faucet provides nearly immediate feedback (since the controls are at the faucet). A shower, on the other hand, experiences some time lag between when the valves are adjusted, and when the water makes it to the shower head. And for a hot tub, it may be hours between when you make a temperature adjustment, and the water temperature stabilises. All of these devices are interactive, the point here is that because of the time delay or the accuracy of the control device some interactions are far more likely to achieve the desired results quickly and efficiently than others.[27]

Now we return to the computer and examine interaction with the scrollbar. The scrollbar is an indirect manipulating device, however, if the movement of the text is closely coupled with the movement of the scroll bar, it "feels" like a direct manipulation of the screen position. The scrolltab provides absolute positioning, while the scroll arrows provide relative positioning. The positioning jack used by *viewit3d* is a direct manipulation device. Camera positioning in *JOEY* is absolute (default) or relative (control key depressed with the mouse button).

---

[27] "Quickly and efficiently" could mean many things in this context; the hot tub thermostat is an accurate control, so although we need to wait quite awhile for the desired result, it is very quick and efficient to set the control for a few degrees warmer and do something else. A shower, on the other hand, seems to require a lot of attention to stay at the desired temperature but that is OK because the activity of showering keeps us in close proximity to the control for the duration of the event.

The table below provides a summary of interaction methods:

	delayed	*immediate*
indirect absolute	A scroll tab that follows the cursor, but results in no motion of the text until the tab is released is indirect and delayed. It can quickly get to an approximate position, but often takes several tries to get within "scroll arrow" range of the desired position. Dialogues are an excellent example of very indirect, delayed, and usually absolute control.	When the text position follows the scroll tab, immediate feedback is provided that makes it possible to reach the desired position very quickly. The cursor when controlled by a digitising tablet is an excellent example of an indirect absolute manipulation.
indirect relative	Generally, indirect manipulation initiates an immediate action, but the steps may be very slow. An example is *JOEY* relative camera control in a complex environment.	The scroll arrow provides immediate motion of the text at some fixed speed for as long as the scroll arrow is depressed. The cursor, when controlled by a mouse is an excellent example of immediate indirect relative manipulation.
direct absolute	The positioning jack in *viewit3d* is a delayed direct manipulation when the system response is slow.	The positioning jack in *viewit3d* is a an immediate direct manipulation when the system response is fast.
direct relative	Direct manipulation and relative manipulation are mutually exclusive actions.	

When you think of applications that have worked well for you, generally, it is because you can get the desired result quickly, often using a combination of all of these methods.

The difficulty with writing good interactive applications is finding a balance between making it possible and easy for users to do what they want to do and making it reasonable to program. We cannot possibly hope to second guess users, instead, it seems to make more sense to have a wide array of tools available to the programmer that make it almost impossible not to produce an application that gives users incredible freedom in how they wish to have the data presented and how they wish to interact with the data.

Data entry is an interesting challenge because there are a multitude of methods for input of 3D data. The most natural method is highly debatable and depends on the training of the user, familiarity with the tool, and relationship of the tool to traditional methods of accomplishing the task. During the development of *JOEY*, we observed that although the direct methods are great for data inspection and presentation, the speed and control of the interaction is often slow and cumbersome during editing. Indirect methods can often provide very quick access to many basic manipulation needs. This is demonstrated in the operation of the *JOEY* camera interaction modes.

3.3.2 JOEY Camera Interaction

The use of direct, indirect, immediate, and delayed interaction modes in *JOEY* cameras is summarised below. In *JOEY*, all camera interaction modes are attached to the middle mouse button so that they can be accessed immediately without a separate mode selection. The interaction modes are optionally also attached to the left mouse button using the camera toolbar 🔲 button.

indirect delayed absolute (dialogue box)
> A camera dialogue box can be started from the camera toolbar. It provides precise positioning input, inspection of positioning and access to information and editing capabilities that are not available through other interaction methods.

indirect delayed absolute/relative (shift - middle/left button) -
> Single click - centre the graphic at the point the cursor is over when the button is clicked (absolute control).

> Double click - centre the graphic at the point the cursor is over when the button is double-clicked and pull back (zoom out) by a factor of 2 (absolute and relative control).

> Single click and move - define a zoom-in box centered where the cursor was located at button down and defined in size by where the button was released. A sizing rectangle is displayed during this operation that maintains the aspect ratio of the screen to that the user knows exactly what will fill the screen when the view changes (absolute control).

direct immediate absolute (middle/left button) -

Select the camera move type from the camera toolbar. Grab the object at button down and push/pull it to the desired position. The object does not move unless the cursor is moved while the middle button is down.

indirect immediate relative(control - middle/left button)

Select the camera move type from the camera toolbar. Button down with the cursor shifted from the centre of the view in the direction you want the object to go. The further from the screen centre, the faster the object moves. The object moves as long as the button is down. The reset button is often important when working in relative mode because it is easy to send the object off-screen and lose it.

It is useful to keep this range of camera interaction techniques in mind when designing the methods for manipulating application data.

3.3.3 Dialogue Interaction

In this section, we augment the positioning jacks in *viewit3d* with positioning dialogues. Dialogues are a very common method for indirect delayed interaction. Though they do not provide the immediate feedback of interactive manipulation, they do provide a means for very precise specification of data. In many cases, the user knows what the desired position or destination is, and dialogue specification is vastly superior to other forms of manipulation.

To present the user with the widest range of options, we have found it helpful for the dialogues to provide a keypad/calculator alternative so that attention can focus on the screen and computations are easily possible during data entry. Data editing controls (with a button on the right that invokes a popup calculator/keypad) have been used in *JOEY* and they provide a data entry alternatives with little dialogue box real estate overhead, Figure P-19.[28]

---

[28] It has been pointed out to us that plopping a keypad button at each edit box adds quite a bit of clutter to a dialogue and that we should be able to easily drag-and-drop values from our favourite calculators into the dialogue in a component software environment. This is an extremely valid point. Another possible implementation could be to use a double click In the editing area to make our favourite calculator the top, active window.

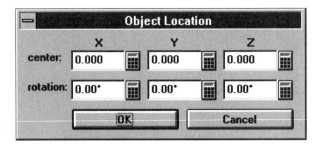

Figure P-19: The object positioning dialogue for *viewit3d* showing linear dimensions, angular dimensions, and keypad entry buttons.

In this example, we add dialogue controls for the positioning jacks in *viewit3d*. This is simple because the jack in the *vit3dlib.dll* library includes a dialogue interaction method, so we just need to provide access to it. Two methods of access, that are consistent with the MS style guidelines, are menu access and a double-click on the element to be changed. We provide both in the next example.

♦   Add tests in the left mouse button double-click message handler to see if the double-click occurred with the cursor located over either an object or light positioning jack handle. If it did, call the jack `Dialogue` function to bring up the positioning dialogue. In the `OnLButtonDblClk` message handler in *objview.cpp*, make the following additions:

```
      void CObjView::OnLButtonDblClk(UINT nFlags, CPoint point)
      {
→         CJoeyMouse      mouse(point);
→         CObjDoc*        pDoc = GetDocument();
→         float           fDist;
→         int             nEditID;

          if (IsCamLeft()) {
              CJoeyView::OnMButtonDblClk(nFlags, point);
              return;
          }

→         PrepareMouse(mouse,MOUSE_WORLD_TOL);
→         if ((pDoc->ObjectJack()).Hit(pDoc->ObjectTransform(),mouse,
→             fDist,nEditID)) {
→             pDoc->ObjectTransform(
→                 (pDoc->ObjectJack()).Dialogue(
→                 pDoc->ObjectTransform(),pDoc->LinearIn(),
→                 pDoc->LinearOut(),pDoc->LinearKeypad()));
→         }else if((pDoc->LightJack()).Hit(pDoc->LightTransform(),mouse,
→             pDoc->Light(),fDist,nEditID)) {
→             pDoc->LightTransform(
```

```
→                    (pDoc->LightJack()).Dialogue(
→                    pDoc->LightTransform(),pDoc->Light(),pDoc->LinearIn(),
→                    pDoc->LinearOut(),pDoc->LinearKeypad()));
→       }
        }
```

If the *JOEY* camera is not processing left mouse actions, the cursor position is mapped into a *JOEY* mouse and passed to the jacks for hit-testing. If a hit occurs, the jack `Dialogue` function is called. The dialogue makes no assumptions about the formatting of angular and positional dimensions. Functions for formatting, input interpretation , and keypad entry of data are passed to the dialogue from the document.

◆ Edit the project resource file, *viewit3d.rc* using AppStudio to add menu access to the jack dialogues for the object and the light. In the `IDR_3D_GEOTYPE` menu, add a <u>P</u>osition pulldown between the <u>E</u>dit and <u>V</u>iew pulldowns. Add an <u>O</u>bject menu item with the ID: *IDM_POSITION_OBJECT*, <u>C</u>aption: *&Object*, and Pro<u>m</u>pt: *Start object positioning dialogue\nobject dialog.* Add a second menu item, <u>L</u>ight, with the ID: *IDM_POSITION_LIGHT*, <u>C</u>aption: *&Light*, and Pro<u>m</u>pt: *Start light positioning dialogue\nlight dialog.* Copy this newly created pulldown and its contents to the `IDR_3D_GEOTYPE_SRVR_EMB` and `IDR_3DGEOTYPE_SRVR_IP` menus.

◆ Use ClassWizard to add message handling functions to `CObjView` to handle the **COMMAND** message for `IDM_POSITION_OBJECT`, and the **COMMAND** and **UPDATE_COMMAND_UI** messages for `IDM_POSITION_LIGHT`. The object position is always editable while the light position is only editable for some light types. Menu selectability for light editing is set according to the light type. Fill in the bodies of the message handlers added in *objview.cpp* by ClassWizard:

```
    void CObjView::OnPositionObject()
    {
→       CObjDoc*        pDoc = GetDocument();
→       pDoc->ObjectTransform(
→          (pDoc->ObjectJack()).Dialogue(
→          pDoc->ObjectTransform(),pDoc->LinearIn(),
→          pDoc->LinearOut(),pDoc->LinearKeypad()));
    }

    void CObjView::OnPositionLight()
    {
→       CObjDoc*        pDoc = GetDocument();
→       pDoc->LightTransform(
→          (pDoc->LightJack()).Dialogue(
→          pDoc->LightTransform(),pDoc->Light(),pDoc->LinearIn(),
→          pDoc->LinearOut(),pDoc->LinearKeypad()));
```

```
          }

          void CObjView::OnUpdatePositionLight(CCmdUI* pCmdUI)
          {
→             CObjDoc*          pDoc = GetDocument();
→             pCmdUI->Enable(
→                 (pDoc->LightJack()).CanDialogue(pDoc->Light()));
          }
```

You have finished adding dialogue positioning of the object and light to *viewit3d*. You can rebuild and test this dialogue. There has been relatively little work to do in order to add light and object interaction because of the encapsulation of both interactive position and dialogue control in the positioning jack. We encourage similar encapsulation of interface tool  functionality so that you can maintain a constant look and feel with minimal work during development and on-going maintenance of your application.

There are some nuances of the dialogue itself that we think are worth investigation. Though MFC and ClassWizard provide great tools for creating dialogues, there are some subtleties in working with floating point numbers that are not well addressed. Also, there are a collection of services provided by *JOEY* that help with consistent formatting for linear dimensions and angles.

We have used ClassWizard to create all of the *JOEY* dialogues and the dialogues for the *viewit3d* example. The data exchange handling between the member variables of the class managing the dialogue and the controls of the dialogue is fine in many instances, but poses round-off problems for floating point parameters, and delayed invalid value error feedback if not treated carefully.

The data exchange expects to load the edit fields and set states on other controls at the initialisation of the dialogue, and to read all of the edit fields and controls at the end of the dialogue, when the OK button is clicked. Every value using this mechanism is loaded, and then later read. With floating point parameters, loading these into the edit fields results in round off depending upon the formatting of the field. At the termination of the dialogue, a different value may be read back into the parameter even though the user has not performed any editing.

The dialogues for the positioning jack use the data exchange structure, but flag the data items that have changed, and read only those data items back from the dialogue box. The read is performed immediately after the edit is complete and the user is shifting focus to another edit control. This provides an opportunity for immediate feedback if an invalid entry has been entered.

In implementing the positioning jack dialogue, we have also used *JOEY* facilities for formatting angles and linear dimensions. The advantages of this will become apparent when we discuss dimensioning in a future section. To illustrate the use of the formatting facilities and data exchange handling, review the `DoDataExchange` function in the sample code file *vit3dlib\jack_dlg.cpp*:

```
void CJackDlg::DoDataExchange(CDataExchange* pDX)
{
    CDialog::DoDataExchange(pDX);
    //{{AFX_DATA_MAP(CJackDlg)
        // NOTE: the ClassWizard will add DDX and DDV calls here
    //}}AFX_DATA_MAP
    if ((!pDX->m_bSaveAndValidate) || (m_usChanged & CHG_CTR_X))
        V3dLinearDDX(pDX, IDC_EDT_CTR_X, m_fTx,  m_fncIn, m_fncOut);
    if ((!pDX->m_bSaveAndValidate) || (m_usChanged & CHG_CTR_Y))
        V3dLinearDDX(pDX, IDC_EDT_CTR_Y, m_fTy,  m_fncIn, m_fncOut);
    if ((!pDX->m_bSaveAndValidate) || (m_usChanged & CHG_CTR_Z))
        V3dLinearDDX(pDX, IDC_EDT_CTR_Z, m_fTz,  m_fncIn, m_fncOut);

    if ((!pDX->m_bSaveAndValidate) || (m_usChanged & CHG_ROT_X))
        m_aRotX.DDX(pDX, IDC_EDT_ROT_X);
    if ((!pDX->m_bSaveAndValidate) || (m_usChanged & CHG_CTR_X))
        m_aRotY.DDX(pDX, IDC_EDT_ROT_Y);
    if ((!pDX->m_bSaveAndValidate) || (m_usChanged & CHG_CTR_X))
        m_aRotZ.DDX(pDX, IDC_EDT_ROT_Z);

    // update the changed flag for the dialogue
    if (pDX->m_bSaveAndValidate && (CHG_CHECK & m_usChanged))
        m_usChanged = CHG_CHANGED;
}
```

The `m_usChanged` member variable has a flag bit for each editable data item, and the high order bit is used to note that a change in any data item has occurred. During the loading of the dialogue box, the `DoDataExchange` function is called with the `pDX->m_bSaveAndValidate` flag set to FALSE, and all data exchanges are processed. Note that the `CAngle` class includes a data exchange function, and that a data exchange function for linear dimensions is also provided (the `V3dLinearDDX()` function is included in *vit3dlib\jack_dlg.cpp*). An edit control in the dialogue processes the EN_SETFOCUS, EN_KILLFOCUS, and EN_UPDATE messages. The message processing functions look like this:

```
void CJackDlg::OnSetfocusEdit()
{
    CWnd*   cWnd = GetFocus();
    cWnd->PostMessage(EM_SETSEL,0,-1);
}

void CJackDlg::OnKillfocusEdit()
{
    UpdateData(TRUE);
```

```
    }

    void CJackDlg::OnUpdateEdtCtrX()  {m_usChanged |= CHG_CTR_X;}
```

The `OnSetfocusEdit` handler is selecting all of the text in the edit control when focus shifts to the control (this is a matter of personal behavioural preference). The `OnUpdateEdtCtrX` message handler is called when text displayed in the edit control is changed, and simply sets the bit in the `m_usChanged` member variable corresponding to the changed data item, in this case, the X center. The `OnKillfocusEdit` calls the `UpdateData` function which, in turn, calls the `DoDataExchange` function. Only the flagged data item is read. If the user simply skips through a field, there is no read or write because no changed bit has been set. Immediate processing of the new value provides formatted feedback (particularly important if the user has not specified the units and you are assuming something), and an immediate invalid value message if value checking is done with the data exchange. Note that the `OnSetFocusEdit` and `OnKillFocusEdit` functions are common to all edit controls while the update processing is the only control specific processing.

3.3.4 Grab and Drag

We can think of direct manipulation as a grab (a thing) and drag (the thing) kind of manipulation. The vital aspect of this type of interaction is immediacy. We do not think of the lines on the computer screen having a greater weight or inertia than the mouse, and expect, therefore, that they should be able to move at the speed of the cursor. If you have been playing with *viewit3d* very much, particularly as an OLE server to a container application, you will have noted that interaction is so dismally slow that you have hardly a hope of actually using interactive methods to edit 3D data. Let's see if we can do something to improve this situation.

First, lets diagram what is happening, so that we can find places for improvement. Figure P-20 diagrams the events that occur during the grab and drag processing for direct manipulation. To the left is the implementation of the camera grab and drag loop implemented in *JOEY*, the right is the grab and drag processing that we have implemented in *viewit3d*. They look basically the same. The data manipulation is a little different because the manipulation may effect more than one view (the camera is changing the current view only while there may be several views of the data that need to be updated during a data change). In spite of the similarity, data manipulation seems a bit slower during stand-alone operation, and becomes completely useless in the context of an activated in-place server. What is the problem here?

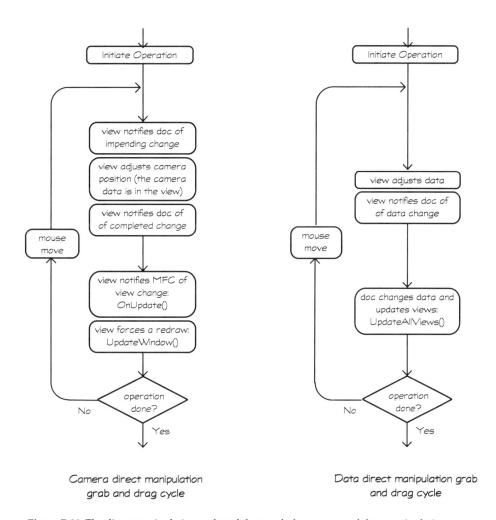

Figure P-20: The direct manipulation grab and drag cycle for camera and data manipulation.

Part of the answer is smart notification of the document about the context of the change followed by smart processing of the change on the part of the document. *JOEY* provides hints to the document when notifying it of changes in the camera. *JOEY* gives the document a hint whether the change happened at the start of interaction, during interaction, at the completion of interaction, or completely unrelated to interaction. In this example we will add similar hints when manipulating data, and improved handling of the change notification by

the document. It is not necessary for the document to flag the data as changed
or to inform the OLE client container that the data has changed until the
interaction is complete. If the document is given a hint about the interaction
context of the change, it can make the appropriate notifications.

♦ In the document header, *objdoc.h*, define flags to hint changes as being either
   from non-interactive operations, or happening at the beginning, end, or
   during the interaction. Add a hint argument to functions that set document
   data to describe the interaction context in which the data is changed:

```
// objdoc.h : interface of the CObjDoc class
//
/////////////////////////////////////////////////////////////
#define NOT_INTERACTIVE    0x0000  // not during interaction
#define START_INTERACT     0x0001  // the start of interaction
#define IN_INTERACT        0x0002  // during the interaction
#define END_INTERACT       0x0004  // termination of interaction

   .
   .
class CObjDoc : public CJoeyOleServerDoc
{
   .
   .
   CXfm4x4f const&   ObjectTransform() {return m_xfmObj;}
   void              ObjectTransform(CXfm4x4f const&,
                           USHORT =NOT_INTERACTIVE);
   CV3dJack&         ObjectJack()      {return m_jack;}
   CXfm4x4f const&   LightTransform()  {return m_xfmLight;}
   void              LightTransform(CXfm4x4f const&,
                           USHORT =NOT_INTERACTIVE);
   CV3dLgtJack&      LightJack()    {return m_jackLight;}
   .
   .
};
```

♦ Add processing of the interaction context hint in the functions that are
   setting document data in *objdoc.cpp*. The processing consists of deferring
   notification until the interaction ends if the change is a result of an
   interaction.

```
void CObjDoc::ObjectTransform(CXfm4x4f const& xfm,
   USHORT usWhen)
{
   m_xfmObj = xfm;
   if (!(usWhen & (START_INTERACT | IN_INTERACT))) {
      SetModifiedFlag();
      if (IsEmbedded()) NotifyChanged();
   }
   UpdateAllViews(NULL);
}
```

```
      void CObjDoc::LightTransform(CXfm4x4f const& xfm,
         USHORT usWhen)
      {
         m_xfmLight = xfm;
➔        if (!(usWhen & (START_INTERACT | IN_INTERACT))) {
            SetModifiedFlag();
            if (IsEmbedded()) NotifyChanged();
➔        }
         UpdateAllViews(NULL);
      }
```

♦ Send the interaction hints from the mouse processing messages when
   document data is being changed. In *objview.cpp*, add this messaging to the
   OnLButtonDown, OnMouseMove, and OnLButtonUp message handlers:

```
      void CObjView::OnMouseMove(UINT nFlags, CPoint point)
      {
         CObjDoc*       pDoc = GetDocument();
         ♦
         ♦
         if ((pDoc->ObjectJack()).IsTracking()) {
            CJoeyMouse      mouse(point);
            PrepareMouse(mouse,MOUSE_WORLD);
➔           pDoc->ObjectTransform((pDoc->ObjectJack()).Track(mouse),
➔              IN_INTERACT);
         } else if ((pDoc->LightJack()).IsTracking()) {
            CJoeyMouse      mouse(point);
            PrepareMouse(mouse,MOUSE_WORLD);
➔           pDoc->LightTransform((pDoc->LightJack()).Track(mouse),
➔              IN_INTERACT);
         }
      }

      void CObjView::OnLButtonDown(UINT nFlags, CPoint point)
      {
         ♦
         ♦
         if ((pDoc->ObjectJack()).Hit(pDoc->ObjectTransform(),mouse,
               fDist,nEditID)) {
            pDoc->ObjectTransform((pDoc->ObjectJack()).TrackStart(
➔              pDoc->ObjectTransform(),mouse,fDist,nEditID),
➔              START_INTERACT);
            SetCapture();
         }else if((pDoc->LightJack()).Hit(pDoc->LightTransform(),mouse,
               pDoc->Light(),fDist,nEditID)) {
            pDoc->LightTransform((pDoc->LightJack()).TrackStart(
            pDoc->LightTransform(),mouse,
➔              pDoc->Light(),fDist,nEditID),
➔              START_INTERACT);
            SetCapture();
         }
      }
```

```
void CObjView::OnLButtonUp(UINT nFlags, CPoint point)
{
    ⋅
    ⋅
    if ((pDoc->ObjectJack()).IsTracking()) {
        CJoeyMouse      mouse(point);
        PrepareMouse(mouse,MOUSE_WORLD);
        pDoc->ObjectTransform(
➔          (pDoc->ObjectJack()).TrackEnd(mouse),
➔          END_INTERACT);
        ReleaseCapture();
    } else if ((pDoc->LightJack()).IsTracking()) {
        CJoeyMouse      mouse(point);
        PrepareMouse(mouse,MOUSE_WORLD);
        pDoc->LightTransform(
➔          (pDoc->LightJack()).TrackEnd(mouse),
➔          END_INTERACT);
        ReleaseCapture();
    }
}
```

You can now build and test *viewit3d*. You will not observe any difference when running *viewit3d* stand-alone, but will observe marked performance improvement when running as a server to an OLE client container. It seems that the container applications (that we have tested) serialize the object data and re-draw cached views when they are notified of a data change  in the server. One reason for this is that the server could terminate without providing another opportunity to update the data. The server needs to notify the container as changes are made so that the container does terminate without ever knowing that there was a change it should have saved. Your application could notify the client constantly, occasionally, or only before the in-place editing window goes inactive.

In addition to reducing time servicing change notifications during the grab-drag cycle, you may be able to decrease drawing time during the re-draw of the data.

The OnUpdate virtual function in the CJoeyView class responds to the request to update a view. This function is passed hints as to what exactly it is that needs updating. When the camera changes, *JOEY* passes the hint UPDATE_HINT_CAM_CHANGED. By default, CJoeyView::OnUpdate requests a complete redraw of the window by invalidating the window with the erase flag set to FALSE. It may be that your application wants to send hints to control the redraw when data changes. For example, you may only need to redraw a small portion of the database during an edit operation.

To make use of the OnUpdate function, use ClassWizard to add the OnUpdate function to your view class. The template provided by ClassWizard should be edited as follows to be a suitable base for use by your applications:

```
void CObjView::OnUpdate(CView* pSender, LPARAM lHint, CObject* pHint)
{
    if ((0 == lHint) || (UPDATE_HINT_CAM_CHANGED == lHint)) {
        CJoeyView::OnUpdate(pSender,lHint,pHint);
    }else {
        InvalidateRect(NULL,FALSE);    // replace with your hint handling
    }
}
```

3.3.5 Enhanced Feedback

Direct manipulation methods also benefit from carefully thought out feedback. The positioning jacks provide a colour change in the selected handle to help inform the user that the handle was actually selected. *JOEY* changes the cursor during camera interaction (which we find often reminds us we are still in left-button camera mode). Cursors are an excellent place to provide feedback because the change in cursor is immediate. In order to change the jack handle colour, the entire scene is redrawn. Numerical positioning information is also useful. In this example, we provide numerical feedback using the status bar, and the TrackStatus member functions provided by the positioning jacks.

♦ Add numerical feedback by calling the TrackStatus function during the mouse tracking message handler in *objview.cpp*:

```
      void CObjView::OnMouseMove(UINT nFlags, CPoint point)
      {
          ♦
          ♦
          if ((pDoc->ObjectJack()).IsTracking()) {
              CJoeyMouse      mouse(point);
              PrepareMouse(mouse,MOUSE_WORLD);
              pDoc->ObjectTransform((pDoc->ObjectJack()).Track(mouse),
                  IN_INTERACT);
→             (pDoc->ObjectJack()).TrackStatus(pDoc->LinearOut());
          } else if ((pDoc->LightJack()).IsTracking()) {
              CJoeyMouse      mouse(point);
              PrepareMouse(mouse,MOUSE_WORLD);
              pDoc->LightTransform((pDoc->LightJack()).Track(mouse),
                  IN_INTERACT);
→             (pDoc->LightJack()).TrackStatus(pDoc->LinearOut());
          }
      }
      void CObjView::OnLButtonDown(UINT nFlags, CPoint point)
      {
          ♦
```

```
     ◆
     if ((pDoc->ObjectJack()).Hit(pDoc->ObjectTransform(),mouse,
           fDist,nEditID)) {
         pDoc->ObjectTransform((pDoc->ObjectJack()).TrackStart(
             pDoc->ObjectTransform(),mouse,fDist,nEditID),
             START_INTERACT);
         SetCapture();
→        (pDoc->ObjectJack()).TrackStatus(pDoc->LinearOut());
     }else if((pDoc->LightJack()).Hit(pDoc->LightTransform(),mouse,
             pDoc->Light(),fDist,nEditID)) {
         pDoc->LightTransform((pDoc->LightJack()).TrackStart(
         pDoc->LightTransform(),mouse,
             pDoc->Light(),fDist,nEditID),
             START_INTERACT);
         SetCapture();
→        (pDoc->LightJack()).TrackStatus(pDoc->LinearOut());
     }
  }
```

You can now re-build and test *viewit3d*. You will have
positional feedback on the status bar for both stand-alone and
in-place activated operation of *viewit3d*. This feedback is of
limited usefulness in stand-alone operation because it lags
behind the movement of the object or light.

The status bar messaging is being displayed using MFC
facilities to get the frame window for the application that contains the *viewit3d*
document and view, then sending a message to that frame window:

```
((CFrameWnd*)AfxGetMainWnd())->SetMessageText(_T("message"));
```

In stand-alone operation, a request is sent to the message queue and ignored
because the application is so busy servicing the grab and drag cycle of the
interaction. The message does not get processed until interaction stops.
Feedback is not received until the interaction is complete and the feedback is no
longer necessary or useful. In order to get immediate feedback in stand-alone
operation, we need to bypass the message queue or provide other feedback
mechanisms.[29] In *viewit3d*, we grab a pointer to the status bar during view
initialisation (if the document is not embedded) and we communicate directly
with the status bar to keep the feedback current.

◆   In the header for the application main frame window, *mainfrm.h*, add a
    member function to return a pointer to the application status bar:

```
    class CMainFrame : public CMDIFrameWnd
    {
```

---

[29] For some feedback needs, the status bar is completely inadequate; you may need to use feedback
windows that are child windows to the view, or other mechanisms to provide feedback.

```
          •
          •
   public:
→      CStatusBar* GetStatusBar() {return &m_wndStatusBar;}
   // Generated message map functions
   protected:
          •
          •
   };
```

♦ In the view header, *objview.h*, add a member variable to hold a pointer to the status bar:

```
   class CObjView : public CJoeyView
   {
       int           m_nRenderStyle;
→      CStatusBar*    m_statusBar;
          •
          •
   };
```

♦ In the view OnCreate member function in *objview.cpp*, add initialisation for this pointer. It is set to point to the status bar window if the document is not embedded, and to NULL if the document is embedded.

```
   int CObjView::OnCreate(LPCREATESTRUCT lpCreateStruct)
   {
          •
          •
→      if (!pDoc->IsEmbedded()) {
→          CFrameWnd* pFrame = (CFrameWnd*)AfxGetMainWnd();
→          if (pFrame->IsKindOf(RUNTIME_CLASS(CMainFrame)))
→              m_statusBar = ((CMainFrame*)pFrame)->GetStatusBar();
→      } else
→          m_statusBar = NULL;
       return 0;
   }
```

♦ In each of the four lines added to the mouse message handlers early in this section for status feedback, add a second argument that is the pointer to the status bar window. One instance of this is shown below (change in bold):

```
   (pDoc->ObjectJack()).TrackStatus(pDoc->LinearOut(),m_statusBar);
```

You can now re-build and test *viewit3d*. The positional feedback for stand-alone operation will now track with the movement of the object or light. The status message processing in the jacks sets the status bar window text and then updates the window if it is non-NULL. You may think we have devoted undo attention to some of the minor details, but we have found that these small details are often far more time

consuming and frustrating to implement than the major functional elements of an application, yet, they are often the thing that separates an acceptable application from a great application.

3.3.6 Hit Testing

Hit testing is a subject of vital importance that could fill a volume in itself. It is a key element of any interaction and is often handled through the rendering system. *JOEY* makes hit testing the responsibility of the application programmer, but provides a collection of tools to help make it possible to get exactly the information you need during hit testing and data manipulation. To explore the mouse feedback and hit testing facilities of *JOEY*, we pull together the techniques introduced in earlier sections to add some data editing capability to *viewit3d*. The editing we add is picking 3D points and dragging them in 3D.

This exercise is divided into several segments, and you can test between segments. In this example, we add a mode for vertex position editing. This mode allows selection of a vertex, dragging the vertex to a new location, then releasing it. We address preparing mouse data, hit testing, grid alignment, dialogues, and feedback in this example. The first step is adding a vertex move mode to *viewit3d*.

♦ Edit the project resource file, *viewit3d*, using AppStudio to provide access to a "position vertex" mode with cursor feedback for this mode. In the IDR_3D_GEOTYPE menu Position pulldown, add a Vertex menu entry to the bottom of the pulldown with the ID: IDM_POSITION_VERTEX, Caption: *&Vertex*, and Prompt: *Toggle vertex position mode on/off\ndrag vertices*. Copy the newly created menu item to the Position pulldown in the IDR_3D_GEOTYPE_SRVR_EMB and IDR_3D_GEOTYPE_SRVR_IP menus.

♦ Continue editing the project resource file, *viewit3d.rc*, to add a "position vertex" button to the toolbar bitmaps for the project, IDR_3D_GEOTYPE_SRVR_IP and IDR_MAINFRAME, Figure P-21.

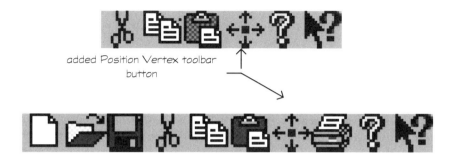

added Position Vertex toolbar
button

Figure P-21: Position vertex button added to the `IDR_3D_GEOTYPE_SRVR_IP` and `IDR_MAINFRAME` toolbar bitmaps.

♦ Continue editing the project resource file, *viewit3d.rc*, to add cursors for the vertex picking and dragging in position vertex mode. The cursors we added looked like those shown in Figure P-22, and were given the IDs `IDC_VERT_PICK` and `IDC_VERT_DRAG`.

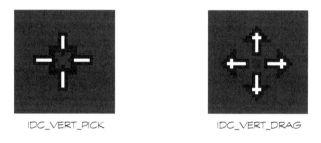

IDC_VERT_PICK   IDC_VERT_DRAG

Figure P-22: Position vertex cursors for vertex picking and vertex drag.

♦ Add member variables in the `CObjView` header file, *objview.h*, to manage the "position vertex" mode, and keep reference data for the move.

```
    class CObjView : public CJoeyView
    {
        int             m_nRenderStyle;
        CStatusBar*     m_statusBar;
→       HCURSOR         m_cursVertPick;     // vertex pick cursor
→       HCURSOR         m_cursVertDrag;     // vertex drag cursor
→       BOOL            m_bVertPosn;        // in vertex position mode
→       BOOL            m_bVertTrack;       // tracking a vertex
→       CPoint3f        m_ptCur;            // current vertex position
→       float           m_fRefDist;         // eye to ref pt
→       float           m_fTargDist;        // eye to target
→       int             m_nIdRef;           // ref vertex ID
```

```
protected: // create from serialization only
    •
    •
};
```

The m_cursVertPick and m_curVertDrag member variables are the handles to the pick and drag cursors. The m_bVertPosn member variable flags whether we are in "position vertex" mode. The m_bVertTrack member variable flags whether we have grabbed a vertex and are currently tracking a move. The remaining additions, m_ptCur, m_fRefDist, m_fTargDist, and m_nIdRef, are reference variables used for positioning the vertex during tracking.

◆ Add initialisation of the new data in the CObjView constructor in *objview.cpp*:

```
    CObjView::CObjView()
    {
→       m_bVertPosn = FALSE;
→       m_bVertTrack = FALSE;
→       m_cursVertPick = LoadCursor(AfxGetInstanceHandle( ),
→           MAKEINTRESOURCE(IDC_VERT_PICK));
→       m_cursVertDrag = LoadCursor(AfxGetInstanceHandle( ),
→           MAKEINTRESOURCE(IDC_VERT_DRAG));
    }
```

◆ Add cleanup in the CObjView destructor in *objview.cpp*:

```
    CObjView::~CObjView()
    {
→       DestroyCursor(m_cursVertPick);
→       DestroyCursor(m_cursVertDrag);
    }
```

◆ Use ClassWizard to add message handling functions in CObjView for the IDM_POSITION_VERTEX menu item. Add message handlers for both the COMMAND and UPDATE_COMMAND_UI messages. Fill in the bodies for these functions as follows:

```
    void CObjView::OnPositionVertex()
    {
→       if (m_bVertPosn) {
→           m_bVertPosn = FALSE;
→           Cursor(NULL);
→       } else {
→           m_bVertPosn = TRUE;
→           Cursor(m_cursVertPick);
→       }

    }
```

```
      void CObjView::OnUpdatePositionVertex(CCmdUI* pCmdUI)
      {
→         pCmdUI->SetCheck(m_bVertPosn);
      }
```

When the m_bVertPosn member is toggled to turn the "position vertex" mode on and off, the cursor is also changed for the window. The CJoeyView::Cursor sets the cursor for the view to the specified cursor, and back to the system cursor if NULL is passed as the cursor handle. The user interface update simply uses the m_bVertPosn flag to set the controls for the mode.

♦ Add the "position vertex" toolbar button to the toolbar initialisation array for CMainFrame in *mainfrm.cpp*:

```
      // toolbar buttons - IDs are command buttons
      static UINT BASED_CODE buttons[] =
      {
          // same order as in the bitmap 'toolbar.bmp'
          ID_FILE_NEW,
          ID_FILE_OPEN,
          ID_FILE_SAVE,
              ID_SEPARATOR,
          ID_EDIT_CUT,
          ID_EDIT_COPY,
          ID_EDIT_PASTE,
→             ID_SEPARATOR,
→         IDM_POSITION_VERTEX,
              ID_SEPARATOR,
          ID_FILE_PRINT,
          ID_APP_ABOUT,
          ID_CONTEXT_HELP,
      };
```

♦ Add the "position vertex" toolbar button to the toolbar initialisation array for CInPlaceFrame in *ipframe.cpp*:

```
      // toolbar buttons - IDs are command buttons
      static UINT BASED_CODE buttons[] =
      {
          // same order as in the bitmap 'itoolbar.bmp'
          ID_EDIT_CUT,
          ID_EDIT_COPY,
          ID_EDIT_PASTE,
→             ID_SEPARATOR,
→         IDM_POSITION_VERTEX,
              ID_SEPARATOR,
          ID_APP_ABOUT,
          ID_CONTEXT_HELP,
      };
```

You can re-build and run *viewit3d*. You now have the new
"position vertex" toolbar button for both stand-alone and
server operation. When the "position vertex" mode is active,
the cursor will be a small crosshair for more precise picking.

We now get into the interesting part of the problem; picking
the vertex (commonly referred to as hit testing), and deciding
how it should move when we drag it. *JOEY* provides a CJoeyMouse class to aid
in hit testing and object tracking. The CJoeyView::PrepareMouse function
loads the CJoeyMouse class with information about a cursor position on the
screen. Within the PrepareMouse function, the CJoeyView maps the cursor to
normalised window coordinates then passes the CJoeyMouse to the camera to
complete the loading of information about the current cursor position. Once the
CJoeyMouse has been prepared, its member functions can be used for hit testing
graphic elements. We now start the example and provide details along the way.

♦   Add member functions to the document to allow the view to access the
    vertex list. In the spirit of maintaining the boundary between view and
    document, the document never allows the view direct access to the data,
    but instead forces access through document member functions. For
    CObjDoc, we add functions to get the point count and to get and set points.
    It is important that the document set the data so that the appropriate
    notification can be given to other views, and to the container if the data is
    embedded. The new member functions are added to the CObjDoc header in
    objdoc.h:

```
    class CObjDoc : public CJoeyOleServerDoc
    {
    •
    •

        void              RenderStyle(int, BOOL =FALSE);
➔       int               NumVerts() const {return m_ptCt;}
➔       CPoint3f const&   GetVert(int) const;
➔       void              SetVert(int,CPoint3f&,
➔                             USHORT =NOT_INTERACTIVE);

    // Operations
    public:
    •
    •
    };
```

♦   Add these document data access functions to CObjDoc in *objdoc.cpp*:

```
➔   CPoint3f const& CObjDoc::GetVert(int nPt) const
➔   {
➔       ASSERT((nPt >= 0) && (nPt < m_ptCt));
➔       return m_pts[nPt];
```

```
➔    }

➔    void CObjDoc::SetVert(int nPt, CPoint3f& pt,USHORT usWhen)
➔    {
➔        ASSERT((nPt >= 0) && (nPt < m_ptCt));
➔        m_pts[nPt] = pt;
➔        if (!(usWhen & (START_INTERACT | IN_INTERACT))) {
➔            SetModifiedFlag();
➔            if (IsEmbedded()) NotifyChanged();
➔        }
➔        UpdateAllViews(NULL);
➔    }
```

Note that the `SetVert` function uses the same hint strategy introduced in
the last section to limit update notifications to non-interactive data editing
and to the end of interactive moves.

♦   Add hit testing to the left button down message handler in the view. We go
    through this in detail after you add handling in the function. This function
    was beginning to get a little messy, so almost all of the code in the
    `OnLButtonDown` function is rearranged and will not be flagged with arrows:

```
void CObjView::OnLButtonDown(UINT nFlags, CPoint point)
{
    // JOEY camera processing
    if (IsCamLeft()) {
        CJoeyView::OnMButtonDown(nFlags, point);
        return;
    }

    CJoeyMouse      mouse(point);
    CObjDoc*        pDoc = GetDocument();
    float           fDist;
    int             nEditID;
    PrepareMouse(mouse,MOUSE_WORLD_TOL);
    // test for vertex move
    if (m_bVertPosn) {
        int         ii = pDoc->NumVerts();
        float       fDistTest = (float)HUGE_VAL;
        m_nIdRef = -1;
        CJoeyMouse mouseObj = mouse;
        mouseObj.BackXfm(pDoc->ObjectTransform());
        mouseObj.BackXfm(pDoc->ObjAxisMap());
        while (--ii >= 0) {
            float       fDist;
            CPoint3f    pt = pDoc->GetVert(ii);
            if ( mouseObj.HitPoint(pt,fDist) &&
                 (fDist < fDistTest)) {
                m_nIdRef = ii;
                fDistTest = fDist;
            }
        }
    }
```

```
        if (m_nIdRef >= 0) {
            // got a hit, start tracking
            m_ptCur = pDoc->GetVert(m_nIdRef);
            m_fRefDist = fDistTest;
            m_fTargDist = mouseObj.TargetDist();
            Cursor(m_cursVertDrag);
            m_bVertTrack = TRUE;
            SetCapture();
        }
        return;
    }
    // test for a hit on the jack handles.  if hit, start the jack
    // manipulation (the jack selects the closest hit).
    if ((pDoc->ObjectJack()).Hit(pDoc->ObjectTransform(),mouse,
            fDist,nEditID)) {
        pDoc->ObjectTransform((pDoc->ObjectJack()).TrackStart(
            pDoc->ObjectTransform(),mouse,fDist,nEditID),
            START_INTERACT);
        SetCapture();
        (pDoc->ObjectJack()).TrackStatus(pDoc->LinearOut(),
            m_statusBar);
    }else if((pDoc->LightJack()).Hit(pDoc->LightTransform(),mouse,
            pDoc->Light(),fDist,nEditID)) {
        pDoc->LightTransform((pDoc->LightJack()).TrackStart(
            pDoc->LightTransform(),mouse,
            pDoc->Light(),fDist,nEditID),
            START_INTERACT);
        SetCapture();
        (pDoc->LightJack()).TrackStatus(pDoc->LinearOut(),
            m_statusBar);
    }
}
```

The standard *JOEY* boilerplate at the beginning of this function is for left button camera control. After this, the mouse is prepared. There are six levels to the mouse preparation, and you specify to what level you want the mouse prepared. These are the choices:

MOUSE_DC   The device coordinate location of the cursor is loaded. This is normally done in the constructor for the CJoeyMouse.

MOUSE_DC_TOL   The hit rectangle is loaded into CJoeyMouse. The width and height of this rectangle come from CJoeyConfig and can be set using the HitTol function. By default, the width and height of the hit rectangle are equal to the width and height of window re-sizing boarders.

`MOUSE_WIND`	The normalised window coordinate for the cursor is loaded.
`MOUSE_WIND_TOL`	The normalised window coordinate hit tolerance in X and Y are loaded into `CJoeyMouse`.
`MOUSE_WORLD`	The cursor position is processed through the camera for the view using the world axis map. The resulting eye point, target point, and target direction are specified in world coordinates (relative to the world axis system) when loaded into `CJoeyMouse`.
`MOUSE_WORLD_TOL`	The hit tolerances and world cursor position are processed to create the volume representing the hit frustum in world coordinates.[30] Anything that falls inside this volume is within the hit tolerance.

Graphically, this is described in Figure P-23. In the mouse down processing, we use the `CJoeyMouse::HitPoint` function to test vertices to see if they fall within the hit frustum. This requires that the mouse be prepared to the `MOUSE_WORLD_TOL` level of information (processing to this level implies that all the lower levels have also been generated).

There is still a problem we must address. The mouse information has been generated in world coordinates, but our object is described in local object coordinates. If the object is located at the origin, these are the same (the world and object axis systems are coincident). As soon as we begin to move the object, the world mouse information is not useful for hit testing. This is solved by transforming the mouse through the same series of transformations that is used to draw the object. Actually, we a back-transforming the mouse since the object transformations map from object coordinates to world coordinates and we want to map the mouse from world coordinates back to object coordinates.

---

[30] A frustum is a truncated pyramid.

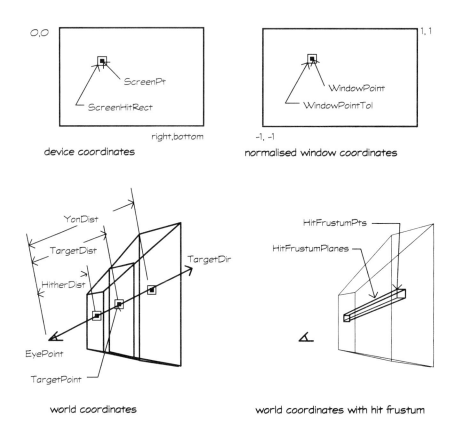

Figure P-23: The properties of the prepared mouse at different levels.

In the document `OnDraw` function, we concatenate the object positioning transformation and the object axis map before drawing the object:

```
    // position in world space
    pRD->XfmPush();
→   pRD->XfmConcat(m_xfmObj);
    m_jack.OnDraw(pRD,m_pMtlJack);
    // draw the object
→   pRD->XfmPushDataDef(m_uvObjAxisMap,
        RENDER_DATADEF_CLOCKWISE | RENDER_DATADEF_CAN_CULL);
```

In the hit testing, we back transform the mouse through the same transformations before hit testing:

```
    mouseObj.BackXfm(pDoc->ObjectTransform());
    mouseObj.BackXfm(pDoc->ObjAxisMap());
```

In the hit testing loop we start by initialising the hit vertex index, m_nIdRef to an invalid index, and the hit distance (distance from the eye to the hit vertex) to infinity:

```
float      fDistTest = (float)HUGE_VAL;
m_nIdRef = -1;
```

As we loop through the points, the mouse HitPoint function returns TRUE if the point falls within the hit frustum. We compare the distance to the point being tested with the closest hit so far, and if it is closer, we replace the test distance and save the index of the vertex. At the end of the search we have either have not hit a vertex (m_nIdRef is still invalid) or we have the closest hit vertex.

In a complex environment, hit testing can be very computationally time consuming. If there are multiple objects, we may want to hit test and sort the bounding volumes of the objects first so that we can then test only objects whose bounding volumes are hit by the mouse vector, and in an order that lets us stop before testing the entire environment. Discussions of sorting for hit testing are found in many references on ray tracing and are not covered in this text, see (Glassner 1989) for a discussion of ray tracing techniques that you might apply to hit testing.

Once we have decided that a vertex was hit, we start the tracking by saving some reference information, changing to the drag cursor, setting the m_bVertTrack tracking flag, and capturing the cursor.

♦ Add termination of the vertex tracking to the left button up mouse handler. Again, we have restructured this function quite a bit, so we present it in full with no flagged change lines:

```
void CObjView::OnLButtonUp(UINT nFlags, CPoint point)
{
    // JOEY camera processing
    if (IsCamLeft()) {
        CJoeyView::OnMButtonUp(nFlags, point);
        return;
    }

    CObjDoc*       pDoc = GetDocument();
    CJoeyMouse     mouse(point);
    PrepareMouse(mouse,MOUSE_WORLD);
    // finish vertex move
    if (m_bVertTrack) {
        Cursor(m_cursVertPick);
        m_bVertTrack = FALSE;
        ReleaseCapture();
    }
```

```
    // finish object or light move
    if ((pDoc->ObjectJack()).IsTracking()) {
        pDoc->ObjectTransform(
            (pDoc->ObjectJack()).TrackEnd(mouse),
            END_INTERACT);
        ReleaseCapture();
    } else if ((pDoc->LightJack()).IsTracking()) {
        pDoc->LightTransform(
            (pDoc->LightJack()).TrackEnd(mouse),
            END_INTERACT);
        ReleaseCapture();
    }
}
```

What is of interest is the processing if the m_bVertTrack flag is set. We end tracking mode by setting the cursor back to the vertex pick cursor, set the m_bVertTrack flag to FALSE, and release the mouse.

You can again re-build and test *viewit3d*. Now, if you select a vertex in your object, it results in a change of cursor to the vertex tracking cursor. You stay in this mode until you release the mouse button. Since we have not added any processing to drag a vertex, there is no change in the data.

Now, we need to get the vertex to move with the cursor. In 2D, moving a point or any other 2D element is relatively well defined; it moves in X and Y and stays in whatever layer it is currently in. In 3D, things are not that simple. The vertex can be anywhere in space along the vector from the eye through the target point, Figure P-23, and it will appear to be in the location of the cursor when projected onto the screen. For this example, we implement a drag that is parallel to the target plane. This means that if we are using an axis aligned view, such as plan, the vertex is constrained in one of the principle directions (e.g. in a plan view, Z is constant; in a front view Y is constant, etc.). This makes it relatively easy to position points if a four view presentation is used, Figure P-17. The geometry of the position computation can be seen by looking at a section through the cursor vector perpendicular to the target plane, Figure P-24.

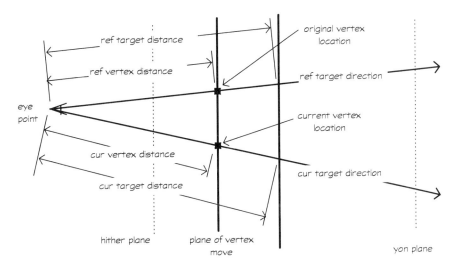

Figure P-24: The geometry of the vertex drag parallel to the target plane.

The target point, eye point, target direction, and target distance are related as:

target point = eye point + (target direction × target distance)

A similar relationship between the eye point, vertex, target direction and vertex distance:

vertex = eye point + (target direction × vertex distance)

The ratio between the target distance and the distance to the picked vertex stays the same if the vertex is moving on a plane parallel to the target plane ("similar triangles" from high school geometry).[31]

---

[31] Many of the relationships and techniques used in programming 3D graphics come from 2D geometry principles generalised to three dimensions. A good geometry text that includes vector notation is invaluable when you are looking for ways to approach problems of controlling interaction. The *Graphics Gems* series from Academic Press is an excellent source for practical solutions to common problems in programming graphic applications.

$$\frac{cur\ vertex\ distance}{ref\ vertex\ distance} = \frac{cur\ target\ distance}{ref\ target\ distance}$$

$$cur\ vertex\ distance = ref\ vertex\ distance \times \frac{cur\ target\ distance}{ref\ target\ distance}$$

We can express the current position of the vertex it terms of eye position, target direction, reference vertex distance, reference and target distance, and current target distance as follows:

$$cur\ vertex = eye\ point + \left(cur\ target\ direction \times ref\ vertex\ distance \times \frac{cur\ target\ distance}{ref\ target\ distance} \right)$$

We work this description of the dragged vertex position into the mouse move and mouse up message processing to complete interactive dragging of the vertex.

◆ Add the processing for the vertex drag to the mouse move message handling function for CObjView in *objview.cpp*. This function has been restructured considerably and changes will not be flagged:

```
void CObjView::OnMouseMove(UINT nFlags, CPoint point)
{
    // allow JOEY to handle camera tracking
    if (IsCamTracking()) {
        CJoeyView::OnMouseMove(nFlags,point);
        return;
    }

    CObjDoc*      pDoc = GetDocument();
    CJoeyMouse    mouse(point);
    PrepareMouse(mouse,MOUSE_WORLD);
    if (m_bVertTrack) {
        int       ii;
        CJoeyMouse mouseObj = mouse;
        mouseObj.BackXfm(pDoc->ObjectTransform());
        mouseObj.BackXfm(pDoc->ObjAxisMap());
        for (ii = PT_x; ii <= PT_z; ii++)
            m_ptCur[ii] = mouseObj.EyePoint()[ii] +
                (mouseObj.TargetDir())[ii] *
                ((mouseObj.TargetDist() * m_fRefDist)/m_fTargDist);
        pDoc->SetVert(m_nIdRef,m_ptCur,IN_INTERACT);
        return;
    }
    if ((pDoc->ObjectJack()).IsTracking()) {
        pDoc->ObjectTransform((pDoc->ObjectJack()).Track(mouse),
            IN_INTERACT);
```

```
        (pDoc->ObjectJack()).TrackStatus(pDoc->LinearOut(),
            m_statusBar);
    } else if ((pDoc->LightJack()).IsTracking()) {
        pDoc->LightTransform((pDoc->LightJack()).Track(mouse),
            IN_INTERACT);
        (pDoc->LightJack()).TrackStatus(pDoc->LinearOut(),
            m_statusBar);
    }
}
```

We do not need the hit frustum for vertex or jack positioning, so the mouse is prepared only to the MOUSE_WORLD level of information. If we are tracking a vertex, it is still necessary to back transform the mouse into object coordinates so that the vertex is moved relative to the object. The mouse is not transformed for the light or object jack move because these are being positioned in world coordinates.

◆   Add the processing for the final vertex location to the mouse button up message handling function for CObjView in *objview.cpp*:

```
    void CObjView::OnLButtonUp(UINT nFlags, CPoint point)
    {
        •
        •
        if (m_bVertTrack) {
➜          int         ii;
➜          CJoeyMouse mouseObj = mouse;
➜          mouseObj.BackXfm(pDoc->ObjectTransform());
➜          mouseObj.BackXfm(pDoc->ObjAxisMap());
➜          for (ii = PT_x; ii <= PT_z; ii++)
➜              m_ptCur[ii] = mouseObj.EyePoint()[ii] +
➜                  (mouseObj.TargetDir())[ii] *
➜                  ((mouseObj.TargetDist() * m_fRefDist)/m_fTargDist);
➜          pDoc->SetVert(m_nIdRef,m_ptCur,END_INTERACT);
            Cursor(m_cursVertPick);
            m_bVertTrack = FALSE;
            ReleaseCapture();
        }
        •
        •
    }
```

The setting of a final position is necessary to make sure that the vertex is actually at the location where the mouse button was released. The SetVert call to the document assures that the update flag will be set and the container application will be notified of the change.

You can now re-build and test *viewit3d*. You have completed the drag vertex interaction for *viewit3d*. Positional feedback and dialogue interaction are still missing. We add feedback, but leave the dialogue as an exercise for the reader. Review the implementation of the jack dialogue and the notes from the dialogue interaction section for hints.

Dragging vertices without updating other information is not a great idea. If you smooth shade or flat shade an object that you have altered, you notice that the shading does not seem quite right. This is because the vertex and face normals are not updated with the changing of the geometry. Also, polygons with more than three vertices may no longer be planar. For some renderers, this is a problem, and results are unpredictable. Ideally, the topology of the object would be adjusted to split faces with more than three vertices into triangles when one of the vertices of such a face is dragged.

Adjusting object topology or re-computing normals and other information can be computationally demanding. You need to consider the impact of these computations in interaction when deciding whether these happen at the start of interaction, at each step during the interaction, at the end of the interaction or upon demand.

We could call the document `InitNormals` function at every step during the interaction, or the document could do this in the `SetVert` function if the change is not during interaction. Our compromise is to add a menu item in the Options pulldown to re-compute normals. This is added along with positional feedback in the next addition to *viewit3d*.

♦ Edit the project resource file, *viewit3d.rc*, using AppStudio to provide access to an update normals function. In the `IDR_3D_GEOTYPE` menu Options pulldown, add a Update Normals menu entry to the bottom of the pulldown with the ID: `IDM_OPTIONS_UPDATE_NORM`, Caption: *Update &Normals*, and Prompt: *Re-compute face and vertex normals\nrecompute normals*. Copy the newly create menu item to the Options pulldown in the `IDR_3D_GEOTYPE_SRVR_EMB` and `IDR_3D_GEOTYPE_SRVR_IP` menus.

♦ Use ClassWizard to add message handling for the COMMAND message of `IDM_OPTIONS_UPDATE_NORM`. Fill in the body of the ClassWizard added message handling function as:

```
    void CObjView::OnOptionsUpdateNorm()
    {
→       CObjDoc*   pDoc = GetDocument();
→       pDoc->InitNormals();
→       pDoc->UpdateAllViews(NULL);
    }
```

♦ Add a status bar feedback function to the header of `CObjView` in *objview.h*:

```
class CObjView : public CJoeyView
{
    •
    •
    int      RenderStyle()  {return m_nRenderStyle;}
    void     RenderStyle(int);
→   void     VertStatus(CPoint3f const&);
    •
    •

};
```

♦ Add the `VertStatus` function in *objview.cpp*. Notice that we use the same strategy as previously described for jack feedback to insure that the feedback is displayed as the vertex tracks:

```
→   void CObjView::VertStatus(CPoint3f const& pt)
→   {
→       CObjDoc*    pDoc = GetDocument();
→       LINEAR_OUT  fncLn = pDoc->LinearOut();
→       TCHAR       outBuff[256];
→       _stprintf(outBuff,_TEXT("vertex at: %s, %s, %s"),
→           fncLn(pt[PT_x]),fncLn(pt[PT_y]),fncLn(pt[PT_z]));
→       if (NULL != m_statusBar) {
→           m_statusBar->SetWindowText(outBuff);
→           m_statusBar->UpdateWindow();
→       } else {
→           ((CFrameWnd*)AfxGetMainWnd())->
→               SetMessageText(outBuff);
→       }
→   }
```

♦ Add position feedback in the message handling functions for mouse left button down, mouse left button up, and mouse track in *objview.cpp*:

```
    void CObjView::OnLButtonDown(UINT nFlags, CPoint point)
    {
        •
        •
        if (m_bVertPosn) {
            •
            •
            if (m_nIdRef >= 0) {
                // got a hit, start tracking
                m_ptCur = pDoc->GetVert(m_nIdRef);
→               VertStatus(m_ptCur);
                •
                •
            }
            return;
        }
```

```
            •
            •
            •
    }

    void CObjView::OnLButtonUp(UINT nFlags, CPoint point)
    {
            •
            •
        if (m_bVertTrack) {
                •
                •
➔           VertStatus(m_ptCur);
            pDoc->SetVert(m_nIdRef,m_ptCur,END_INTERACT);
                •
                •
        }
            •
            •
    }

    void CObjView::OnMouseMove(UINT nFlags, CPoint point)
    {
            •
            •
        if (m_bVertTrack) {
                •
                •
➔           VertStatus(m_ptCur);
            pDoc->SetVert(m_nIdRef,m_ptCur,IN_INTERACT);
            return;
        }
            •
            •
    }
```

You can now re-build and run *viewit3d*. You have positional feedback for your newly added vertex drag function, and the option to update the face and vertex normals after the vertex drag operation. You have done more work with the transformations and learned how they apply to mouse mapping. You have also used `CJoeyMouse` for hit testing vertices. Refer to the on-line documentation and **Implementation** for details on hit testing for other geometric elements.

3.3.7 Grids and Grid Hit Testing

We improved interaction by providing better feedback and the option for dialogue input, but we still have not made it easy to get the desired results through direct manipulation. The positioning for objects and vertices presented in the last several sections allows translation parallel to the screen, which is really only controllable in axis-aligned orthographic views. We still need to make the results of direct manipulation more controlled and predictable.

Grids provide a spatial reference for quick approximate positioning, but do not provide accuracy unless we can lock to the grid. The grids in *JOEY* provide facilities for gridline hit testing and testing against the grid plane. We can use these facilities to make direct manipulation more controllable. To better understand how grid facilities can help, we adjust the light and object positioning jacks so that they can use the world coordinate gridplanes for alignment. The positioning jacks need only be given access to the world axis grid in order to make use of it.

♦ Include the pointer to the current view in the calls to grid tracking functions in the mouse event handlers for the object and positioning jacks. The jacks use the view for access to the world coordinate grid and the current camera. The minor changes in the OnMouseMove, OnLButtonDown, and OnLButtonUp functions in *objview.cpp* are shown in bold underline:

```
void CObjView::OnMouseMove(UINT nFlags, CPoint point)
{
    •
    •
    if ((pDoc->ObjectJack()).IsTracking()) {
        pDoc->ObjectTransform((pDoc->ObjectJack()).Track(mouse,this),
            IN_INTERACT);
        (pDoc->ObjectJack()).TrackStatus(pDoc->LinearOut(),
            m_statusBar);
    } else if ((pDoc->LightJack()).IsTracking()) {
        pDoc->LightTransform((pDoc->LightJack()).Track(mouse,this),
            IN_INTERACT);
        (pDoc->LightJack()).TrackStatus(pDoc->LinearOut(),m_statusBar);
    }
}

void CObjView::OnLButtonDown(UINT nFlags, CPoint point)
{
    •
    •
    if ((pDoc->ObjectJack()).Hit(pDoc->ObjectTransform(),mouse,
            fDist,nEditID)) {
        pDoc->ObjectTransform((pDoc->ObjectJack()).TrackStart(
            pDoc->ObjectTransform(),mouse,fDist,nEditID,this),
            START_INTERACT);
        SetCapture();
        (pDoc->ObjectJack()).TrackStatus(pDoc->LinearOut(),
            m_statusBar);
    } else if ((pDoc->LightJack()).Hit(pDoc->LightTransform(),mouse,
            pDoc->Light(),fDist,nEditID)) {
        pDoc->LightTransform((pDoc->LightJack()).TrackStart(
```

```
                    pDoc->LightTransform(),mouse,
                    pDoc->Light(),fDist,nEditID,this),
                    START_INTERACT);
               SetCapture();
               (pDoc->LightJack()).TrackStatus(pDoc->LinearOut(),m_statusBar);
          }
     }

     void CObjView::OnLButtonUp(UINT nFlags, CPoint point)
     {
          •
          •
          if ((pDoc->ObjectJack()).IsTracking()) {
               pDoc->ObjectTransform(
                    (pDoc->ObjectJack()).TrackEnd(mouse,this),
                    END_INTERACT);
               ReleaseCapture();
          } else if ((pDoc->LightJack()).IsTracking()) {
               pDoc->LightTransform(
                    (pDoc->LightJack()).TrackEnd(mouse,this),
                    END_INTERACT);
               ReleaseCapture();
          }
     }
```

You can now re-build and run *viewit3d*. You have greater control over the movement of the positioning jack by using gridplane lock and gridlock when you are manipulating the object and/or light. By default, an object is loaded with a groundplane grid visible (the XY plane). When no grid locking options are used, the behaviour will be unchanged from the previous example.

Use the grid dialogue to set gridplane lock for the ground plane and motion will be constrained to be parallel with the ground plane. If you set gridline lock, the jack will lock on projected grid locations. To see this, open a second window to the object with a plan camera. As you move the object in a rotated view, the jack will maintain a constant distance from the ground plane and lock onto grid locations when viewed in plan. The other gridplanes can also be used for gridplane and gridline locking.

Using this in your own application is relatively straightforward, but requires maniacal attention to detail if the operation will be correct. We now add grid locking to the "position vertex" mode to show you how to use grids and to introduce you to some of the more subtle aspects of hit testing, tracking, and camera projections.

The first thing we do is to add a local grid to the object to use in positioning object vertices. The reason we use a local grid is that the object exists in its own local space, and we may want to keep alignment with the grid system in which the rest of the object is defined.[32] The default *JOEY* grid is an orthogonal grid. This is not a restriction of the grid implementation, but rather is limited by providing a reasonable user dialogue for controlling the grid. In this example, we make the grid part of the document database instead of using the render environment database facility. This provides an example of manipulation of a *JOEY* resource outside of the render environment.

◆   Add a grid to the CObjDoc object in *objdoc.h*. We hold on to handles for the materials used to draw the grid system for the life of the document, so these are added to the document. A function that allows access to the grid is also provided:

```
class CObjDoc : public CJoeyOleServerDoc
{
    •
    •
    CXfm4x4f      m_xfmObj;              // object transformation
    CUnitV3f      m_uvObjAxisMap[3];     // object axis map
→   CJoeyGrid     m_gridObj;             // object grid
→   CJoeyMaterial const* m_pMtlObjAxis;  // object axis
→   CJoeyMaterial const* m_pMtlObjMajor; // object major gridlines
→   CJoeyMaterial const* m_pMtlObjMinor; // object minor gridlines
    •
    •
    CV3dJack&     ObjectJack()           {return m_jack;}
→   CJoeyGrid*    ObjGrid()              {return &m_gridObj;}
    •
    •
};
```

◆   Add initialisation of the new data in the CObjDoc constructor in *objdoc.cpp*:

```
CObjDoc::CObjDoc()
{
    •
    •
    RE()->MaterialSet("light",mtl);
→   cstr.LoadString(IDS_MTL_WORLD_AXIS);
→   VERIFY(m_pMtlObjAxis = RE()->MaterialGet(cstr));
→   cstr.LoadString(IDS_MTL_GRID_MAJOR);
→   VERIFY(m_pMtlObjMajor = RE()->MaterialGet(cstr));
→   cstr.LoadString(IDS_MTL_GRID_MINOR);
→   VERIFY(m_pMtlObjMinor = RE()->MaterialGet(cstr));
    •
    •
}
```

---

[32] Our first example used the world coordinate grid system for positioning instead of a local coordinate system. This is an interesting exercise if you want to learn a little more about using the transformation stack and the transformed mouse.

JOEY has pre-defined materials for drawing the axis, major gridlines, and minor gridlines. We elected to use these pre-defined materials instead of defining separate object grid materials. The identifiers for these materials are in the string resources included from *joey.rc* into your project resources.

♦ Add cleanup in the CObjDoc destructor in *objdoc.cpp*:

```
CObjDoc::~CObjDoc()
{
    ♦
    ♦
    if (NULL != m_ppPts) delete m_ppPts;
→   if (NULL != m_pMtlObjAxis) m_pMtlObjAxis->Release();
→   if (NULL != m_pMtlObjMajor) m_pMtlObjMajor->Release();
→   if (NULL != m_pMtlObjMinor) m_pMtlObjMinor->Release();
    AfxOleUnlockApp();
}                        ,
```

Whenever we get a material resource from the render environment database, the render environment adds a reference to the material. This reference needs to be released when you are finished with the resource.

♦ In the CObjDoc::DeleteContents function in *objdoc.cpp*, add initialisation for the grid whenever the contents of the database are re-initialised:

```
void CObjDoc::DeleteContents()
{
    ♦
    ♦
    m_jackLight.Resize(RE()->DataSpace() * 0.05f);
    m_gridObj.Attr(JOEY_GRID_DISPLAY_AXIS);
    ♦
    ♦
}
```

We elected to display only the axis of the object grid as the default when an object was loaded. Displaying both the world and object grids results in a very confusing graphic presentation.

♦ Add drawing of the object grid to the document OnDraw function in *objdoc.cpp*:

```
void CObjDoc::OnDraw(PIRenderDevX pRD,
    CJoeyView const *pJView) const
{
    ♦
    ♦
    // draw the object
    pRD->XfmPushDataDef(m_uvObjAxisMap,
        RENDER_DATADEF_CLOCKWISE | RENDER_DATADEF_CAN_CULL);
→   pRD->Draw3dGrid(m_gridObj,0.10f,m_pMtlObjAxis,
```

```
➔                m_pMtlObjMajor,m_pMtlObjMinor);
             if (DRAW_MIN_MAX == nRenderStyle)
                •
                •
       }
```

The grid is drawn after the axis map for the object has been pushed so that the grid is in the same coordinate system as the object. Notice that the materials for the grid are passed to the draw function, so that you could use any materials you want for drawing the grid. The value, `0.10f`, specifies the size of the axis origin icon relative to the width of the window. See the *JOEY* programmer's documentation for details.

♦ Edit the project resource file, *viewit3d.rc*, using AppStudio to provide access to an editing dialogue for the object grid. In the `IDR_3D_GEOTYPE` menu Options pulldown, add an Object Grid menu entry with the ID: `IDM_OPTIONS_OBJ_GRID`, Caption: *Object &Grid*, and Prompt: *Examine or edit the object grid\nobject grid dialogue*. Copy the newly created menu item to the Options pulldown in the `IDR_3D_GEOTYPE_SRVR_EMB` and `IDR_3D_GEOTYPE_SRVR_IP` menus.

♦ Use ClassWizard to add message handling for the COMMAND message of `IDM_OPTIONS_OBJ_GRID`. Fill in the body of the ClassWizard added message handling function as:

```
       void CObjView::OnOptionsObjGrid()
       {
➔          if (((CObjDoc*)GetDocument())->ObjGrid()->Dialogue())
➔              GetDocument()->UpdateAllViews(NULL);
       }
```

The `CJoeyGrid` object provides its own dialogue for editing. This is the same dialogue that the render environment uses for editing grids that are added to the rendering environment database. Materials, cameras, and lights provide editing in the same fashion if you elect not to use the render environment database but instead maintain the database within your own application.

You can re-build and run *viewit3d*. The coordinate axis for the object (which you see when you drag the positioning jack off of the world origin) is immediately noticeable. You can use the grid dialogue to specify which gridplanes to draw and how you would like them drawn. Since the grid is drawn in the same coordinate system as the object, it will move with the object when the object is re-positioned.

The next step is to coordinate the dragging of vertices with the hit testing provided by the grid. This is where we really need to pay attention to details. In the previous section we dragged vertices on a plane parallel to the target plane. We diagrammed the geometry for a perspective camera projection, Figure P-24. The geometry for an orthographic or oblique projection is quite different, but it is serendipitous that the same relationships work for providing the desired movement of the vertex. This is not the case when the plane of dragging is not parallel to the target plane.

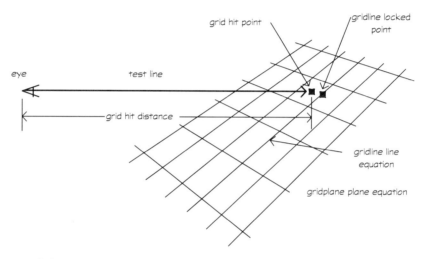

Figure P-25: Information provided by hit testing a `CJoeyGrid` object.

Before we get into the details of the geometry, let us review the information that we can get from a grid when we do hit testing. Figure P-25 depicts a test line intersecting a grid plane. During hit testing, the grid looks at the attributes set for each gridplane to determine the level of hit testing that should be performed (if any). When plane locking is specified, the distance to the gridplane, the intersection point, and the plane equation of the grid plane are returned. If the gridline lock is also specified, the locked point is returned with the line(s) that the point is locked to (provided that the intersection point of the test line and the grid is within hit tolerance of any of the grid lines).

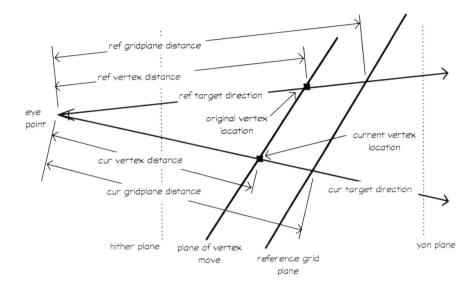

Figure P-26: Vertex dragging in a perspective projection parallel to a reference plane.

Let us look at the geometry of dragging a point along a plane that is not parallel to the target plane for both a perspective projection, Figure P-26, and an orthographic projection, Figure P-27. For a perspective projection, the distances are still related by similar triangles as described in the last section.

The orthographic projection is significantly different. The view rays start from an infinite distance, so they are parallel when the reach the target plane. We generate a pseudo eye point that is closer than an infinite distance, but its location changes for every point on the screen so that all the view rays are parallel. The distance along a view ray from the reference plane to the vertex is:

vertex-to-plane distance = ref plane distance - ref vertex distance

The current vertex position is simply expressed as:

cur vertex = cur plane point - (cur target direction × vertex-to-plane distance)

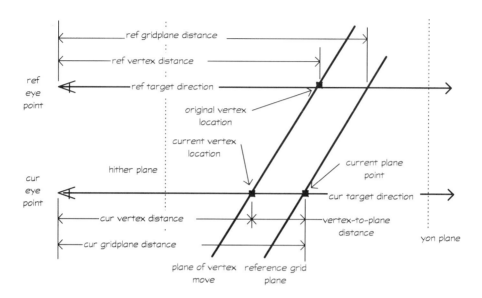

Figure P-27: Vertex dragging in an orthographic projection parallel to a reference plane.

The last part of the vertex positioning is locking onto a projected grid position, Figure P-28. Once we find the vertex location on the drag plane, we use the normal of the plane to project the point onto the gridplane, perform the hit test, and then project it back to the drag plane.

One final detail we need to consider is that when we do the hit testing at mouse button down, the selected point may not be on the cursor vector, it is just somewhere inside the hit frustum. To avoid errors in the reference distances, we need to re-cast the eye vector through the hit point so that all of the reference distances are correct, Figure P-29. You might think that these details are too minute to worry about. If so, try omitting them, and you will find that after several interactions your points have wandered considerably from the plane they we supposed to be constrained to follow. The effects are particularly exaggerated when the reference plane is at a high angle to the target plane.

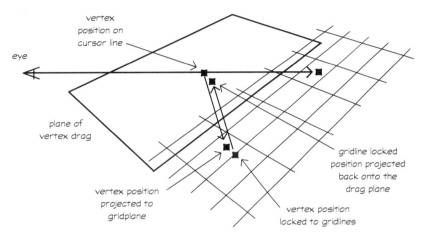

Figure P-28: Projection of a vertext to the grid plane for grid lock testing.

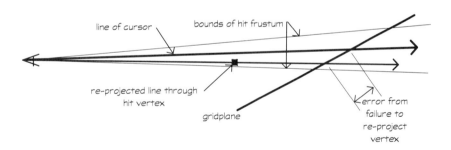

Figure P-29: Error generated by failure to re-project the view vector through a hit vertex.

Since things are getting rather complicated, we elected to break the vertex positioning out of the mouse message handlers and into a separate function. Here are the changes to implement gridlock for vertex dragging:

♦   In the header for `CObjView` in *objview.h*, add member variables to hold reference information for the grid locking, and a position function:

```
class CObjView : public CJoeyView
```

```
    {
        .
        .
        int        m_nIdRef;          // ref vertex ID
➜       BOOL       m_bTestGrid;       // test grid
➜       float      m_fGridDistPsp;    // eye to grid distance
➜       float      m_fGridDistOrth;   // grid to vert
        .
        .
        void       VertStatus(CPoint3f const&);
➜       void       PositionVert(CJoeyMouse const&);
        .
        .
    };
```

◆ Add the PositionVert function *objview.cpp*:

```
void CObjView::PositionVert(CJoeyMouse const& mouse)
{
    CObjDoc*        pDoc = GetDocument();
    int             ii;
    CJoeyGridLock   glock;
    CJoeyMouse mouseObj = mouse;
    // backtransform the mouse
    mouseObj.BackXfm(pDoc->ObjectTransform());
    mouseObj.BackXfm(pDoc->ObjAxisMap());
    if (m_bTestGrid && mouseObj.HitGrid(glock,
            *(pDoc->ObjGrid()),NULL)) {
        CLine3f     lnTest;
        float       fDist;
        // test the camera projection and get the vertex position
        //  on its plane of motion
        if (JOEY_PROJ_PERSPECTIVE & CameraCurrent()->CamType()) {
            for (ii = PT_x; ii <= PT_z; ii++)
                m_ptCur[ii] = mouseObj.EyePoint()[ii] +
                    (mouseObj.TargetDir())[ii] *
                    ((glock.m_fDistPlane * m_fRefDist)/m_fGridDistPsp);
        } else {
            for (ii = PT_x; ii <= PT_z; ii++)
                m_ptCur[ii] = glock.m_ptPlane[ii] -
                    ((mouseObj.TargetDir())[ii] * m_fGridDistOrth);
        }
        // check for a lock on the grid plane - back project the
        // point onto the gridplane
        fDist = m_ptCur.Distance(glock.m_plnLock);
        lnTest.m_pt = m_ptCur;
        lnTest.m_uv.Normal(glock.m_plnLock);
        if (fDist > 0.0f) lnTest.m_uv *= -1.0f;
        pDoc->ObjGrid()->Hit(glock,lnTest,NULL,NULL);
        // project from the hit plane to the plane of motion
        //  if there was not a gridline hit, glock.m_ptLock =
        //  glock.m_ptPlane and the point projects back
        //  where it started
        if (fDist < 0.0f)
```

```
                m_ptCur = glock.m_ptLock + (lnTest.m_uv * fDist);
            else
                m_ptCur = glock.m_ptLock - (lnTest.m_uv * fDist);
        } else {
            for (ii = PT_x; ii <= PT_z; ii++)
                m_ptCur[ii] = mouseObj.EyePoint()[ii] +
                    (mouseObj.TargetDir())[ii] *
                    ((mouseObj.TargetDist() * m_fRefDist)/m_fTargDist);
        }
        // load the vertex and update status
        VertStatus(m_ptCur);
        pDoc->SetVert(m_nIdRef,m_ptCur,IN_INTERACT);
    }
```

We have made liberal use of the geometric functions of the point, line, plane, and unit vector classes in *JOEY* to make the task of programming this example as simple as possible. Refer to the *JOEY* programmer's documentation for details.

◆ Change the mouse handling functions for mouse move, mouse down, and mouse up. Because of the large shifting of code to PositionVert, we show these functions in full:

```
void CObjView::OnMouseMove(UINT nFlags, CPoint point)
{
    // allow JOEY to handle camera tracking
    if (IsCamTracking()) {
        CJoeyView::OnMouseMove(nFlags,point);
        return;
    }

    CObjDoc*      pDoc = GetDocument();
    CJoeyMouse    mouse(point);

    PrepareMouse(mouse,MOUSE_WORLD);
    if (m_bVertTrack) {
        PositionVert(mouse);
        return;
    }
    if ((pDoc->ObjectJack()).IsTracking()) {
        pDoc->ObjectTransform((pDoc->ObjectJack()).Track(mouse,this),
            IN_INTERACT);
        (pDoc->ObjectJack()).TrackStatus(pDoc->LinearOut(),
            m_statusBar);
    } else if ((pDoc->LightJack()).IsTracking()) {
        pDoc->LightTransform((pDoc->LightJack()).Track(mouse,this),
            IN_INTERACT);
        (pDoc->LightJack()).TrackStatus(pDoc->LinearOut(),m_statusBar);
    }
}

void CObjView::OnLButtonDown(UINT nFlags, CPoint point)
```

```
{
    if (IsCamLeft()) {
        CJoeyView::OnMButtonDown(nFlags, point);
        return;
    }

    CJoeyMouse      mouse(point);
    CObjDoc*        pDoc = GetDocument();
    float           fDist;
    int             nEditID;

    // test for vertex move
    PrepareMouse(mouse,MOUSE_WORLD_TOL);
    if (m_bVertPosn) {
        int             ii = pDoc->NumVerts();
        float           fDistTest = (float)HUGE_VAL;
        m_nIdRef = -1;
        CJoeyMouse mouseObj = mouse;
        // back transform the mouse
        mouseObj.BackXfm(pDoc->ObjectTransform());
        mouseObj.BackXfm(pDoc->ObjAxisMap());
        while (--ii >= 0) {
            float       fDist;
            CPoint3f    pt = pDoc->GetVert(ii);
            if ( mouseObj.HitPoint(pt,fDist) &&
                 (fDist < fDistTest)) {
                m_nIdRef = ii;
                fDistTest = fDist;
            }
        }
    }
    if (m_nIdRef >= 0) {
        // got a hit, start tracking
        CJoeyGridLock   glock;
        CLine3f         lnTest;
        m_ptCur = pDoc->GetVert(m_nIdRef);
        VertStatus(m_ptCur);
        m_fRefDist = fDistTest;
        m_fTargDist = mouseObj.TargetDist();
        // re-project the view vector for the grid test to
        //   correct for the hit tolerance
        if (JOEY_PROJ_PERSPECTIVE & CameraCurrent()->CamType()) {
            lnTest.m_pt = mouseObj.EyePoint();
            lnTest.m_uv.UnitDir(mouseObj.EyePoint(),m_ptCur);
        } else {
            lnTest.m_pt = m_ptCur -
                (mouseObj.TargetDir() * fDistTest);
            lnTest.m_uv = mouseObj.TargetDir();
        }
        if (pDoc->ObjGrid()->Hit(glock,lnTest,NULL,NULL)) {
            m_bTestGrid = TRUE;
            m_fGridDistPsp = glock.m_fDistPlane;
            m_fGridDistOrth = glock.m_fDistPlane - fDistTest;
        } else
```

```
            m_bTestGrid = FALSE;
        Cursor(m_cursVertDrag);
        m_bVertTrack = TRUE;
        SetCapture();
    }
    return;
}
// test for a hit on the jack handles.  if hit, start the jack
//   manipulation (the jack selects the closest hit).
if ((pDoc->ObjectJack()).Hit(pDoc->ObjectTransform(),mouse,
        fDist,nEditID)) {
    pDoc->ObjectTransform((pDoc->ObjectJack()).TrackStart(
        pDoc->ObjectTransform(),mouse,fDist,nEditID,this),
        START_INTERACT);
    SetCapture();
    (pDoc->ObjectJack()).TrackStatus(pDoc->LinearOut(),
        m_statusBar);
} else if ((pDoc->LightJack()).Hit(pDoc->LightTransform(),mouse,
        pDoc->Light(),fDist,nEditID)) {
    pDoc->LightTransform((pDoc->LightJack()).TrackStart(
        pDoc->LightTransform(),mouse,
        pDoc->Light(),fDist,nEditID,this),
        START_INTERACT);
    SetCapture();
    (pDoc->LightJack()).TrackStatus(pDoc->LinearOut(),m_statusBar);
}
}

void CObjView::OnLButtonUp(UINT nFlags, CPoint point)
{
    // JOEY camera processing
    if (IsCamLeft()) {
        CJoeyView::OnMButtonUp(nFlags, point);
        return;
    }

    CObjDoc*        pDoc = GetDocument();
    CJoeyMouse      mouse(point);
    PrepareMouse(mouse,MOUSE_WORLD);
    // finish vertex move
    if (m_bVertTrack) {
        PositionVert(mouse);
        Cursor(m_cursVertPick);
        m_bVertTrack = FALSE;
        ReleaseCapture();
    }
    // finish object or light move
    if ((pDoc->ObjectJack()).IsTracking()) {
        pDoc->ObjectTransform(
            (pDoc->ObjectJack()).TrackEnd(mouse,this),
            END_INTERACT);
        ReleaseCapture();
    } else if ((pDoc->LightJack()).IsTracking()) {
```

```
        pDoc->LightTransform(
            (pDoc->LightJack()).TrackEnd(mouse,this),
            END_INTERACT);
        ReleaseCapture();
    }
}
```

With the exception of the mouse down processing, these message handlers just defer to `PositionVert` for tracking a vertex. The hit testing for the grid has been added to the mouse down function. Note that the view vector is re-projected through the hit vertex to get the test line for grid hit testing and that reference variables were saved for both perspective and orthographic projection.

You can now re-build and test *viewit3d*. You may note that the grid lock for vertex move works for any orientation of the object. One thing to point out here is that the final code for this all looks pretty simple, but there is a lot of fussing around to make sure you do not miss anything when you start to work in three dimensions.

3.3.8 Saving State

A significantly annoying behaviour of many applications is the failure of the application to start where you left off in your work. There should be little, if any, difference between the sequence of minimising and restoring and the sequence of exiting and restarting an application.[33] MFC provides an application profile file (*.ini*) that can be used to save and restore application state during the exit and restart sequence. We will explore aspects of state save and restore that are *JOEY* specific, but these are directly applicable to other aspects application state.

As a first step in saving state, we will save and restore the application position on the desktop, the control bar state within the application, and the *JOEY* configuration. If the resolution of the desktop has changed, there are several choices for behaviour - we suggest that the location of the application be the same relative to the desktop and show that implementation. We will not separate the steps for this because the changes for each are localised to the same code. Instead, we highlight the code using ➜ to denote changes made for both screen position and control bar state, ⇨ for screen position specific changes, ◆ for control bar specific changes, and ➔ for *JOEY* configuration specific changes.

---

[33] This is an area that is not really covered by the Microsoft User Interface Design Guide. The behaviour of applications differs greatly in this respect, from programs such as Microsoft Visual C++ that restore your state completely, to those that behave as though each invocation of the application were the first.

We will keep the previous invocation screen size and application rectangle as members in the application class for use in restoring and/or re-sizing child windows. The MFC application profile file facilities are used as much as possible in this implementation

♦ Add members to the `CViewit3dApp` class for previous invocation screen size and application rectangle in *viewit3d.h* as follows:

```
     class CViewit3dApp : public CWinApp
     {
⇨    public:
⇨       UINT      m_uiShowCmd;       // the show command at startup
⇨       SIZE      m_szScreenLast;    // the last screen size
⇨       RECT      m_rectAppLast;     // the last application rect
     public:
        CViewit3dApp();
           •
           •
     };
```

♦ Add string declarations immediately before the `OnCreate` member function in *mainfrm.cpp*. These strings are used to identify the application position information in the application profile file:

```
⇨    static LPCTSTR pszScreenSection = _TEXT("Screen");
⇨    static LPCTSTR pszScreenX =      _TEXT("x");
⇨    static LPCTSTR pszScreenY =      _TEXT("y");
⇨    static LPCTSTR pszFrameSection = _TEXT("Frame");
⇨    static LPCTSTR pszLeft =         _TEXT("left");
⇨    static LPCTSTR pszRight =        _TEXT("right");
⇨    static LPCTSTR pszTop =          _TEXT("top");
⇨    static LPCTSTR pszBottom =       _TEXT("bottom");
⇨    static LPCTSTR pszShow =         _TEXT("show");
     int CMainFrame::OnCreate(LPCREATESTRUCT lpCreateStruct)
     {
```

♦ Save the application screen position and control bar states at the termination of an application by processing the `WM_CLOSE` message sent to the main frame of the application (the main frame owns the control bars). Use MFC ClassWizard to add processing for the `WM_CLOSE` message to the `CMainFrame` class. Edit the `OnClose` message handler in *mainfrm.cpp* to use the `WriteProfileInt` function to write screen position information to the application profile file, and the `SaveBarState` function to save the control bar states:

```
     void CMainFrame::OnClose()
     {
→       CWinApp*            winApp = AfxGetApp();
→       if ( (SW_SHOWDEFAULT != winApp->m_nCmdShow) &&
```

```
→              (SW_HIDE != winApp->m_nCmdShow) ) {
⇨          int            sx, sy;
⇨          WINDOWPLACEMENT    wndpl;
→          // save the application window placement, screen size,
→          //  and toolbar state
⇨          sx = GetSystemMetrics(SM_CXSCREEN);
⇨          sy = GetSystemMetrics(SM_CYSCREEN);
⇨          winApp->WriteProfileInt(pszScreenSection,pszScreenX,sx);
⇨          winApp->WriteProfileInt(pszScreenSection,pszScreenY,sy);
⇨          wndpl.length = sizeof(WINDOWPLACEMENT);
⇨          GetWindowPlacement(&wndpl);
⇨          winApp->WriteProfileInt(pszFrameSection,pszLeft,
⇨              wndpl.rcNormalPosition.left);
⇨          winApp->WriteProfileInt(pszFrameSection,pszRight,
⇨              wndpl.rcNormalPosition.right);
⇨          winApp->WriteProfileInt(pszFrameSection,pszTop,
⇨              wndpl.rcNormalPosition.top);
⇨          winApp->WriteProfileInt(pszFrameSection,pszBottom,
⇨              wndpl.rcNormalPosition.bottom);
⇨          winApp->WriteProfileInt(pszFrameSection,pszShow,
⇨              wndpl.showCmd);
◆          // save the toolbar positions
◆          SaveBarState(winApp->m_pszProfileName);
→          // save the JOEY configuration
→          JoeyConfig->Save();
→      }
       CMDIFrameWnd::OnClose();
   }
```

◆ Restore the application screen position and control bar states when the
  application starts by using the LoadBarState function to load the states
  saved in the previous step. The bars should be restored at the end of the
  main frame OnCreate message handler in *mainfrm.cpp*:

```
int CMainFrame::OnCreate(LPCREATESTRUCT lpCreateStruct)
{
    ◆
    ◆
→   // restore the screen position and control bar state
→   if ( (SW_SHOWDEFAULT != AfxGetApp()->m_nCmdShow) &&
→       (SW_HIDE != AfxGetApp()->m_nCmdShow) ) {
→       CViewit3dApp*      winApp = (CViewit3dApp*)AfxGetApp();
⇨       int            sx, sy, sx_cur, sy_cur;
⇨       WINDOWPLACEMENT    wndpl;
⇨       // save the application window placement, screen size,
⇨       //  and toolbar state
⇨       sx_cur = GetSystemMetrics(SM_CXSCREEN);
⇨       sy_cur = GetSystemMetrics(SM_CYSCREEN);
⇨       sx = winApp->GetProfileInt(pszScreenSection,
⇨           pszScreenX,sx_cur);
⇨       sy = winApp->GetProfileInt(pszScreenSection,
⇨           pszScreenY,sy_cur);
```

```
⇨              winApp->m_szScreenLast.cx = sx;
⇨              winApp->m_szScreenLast.cy = sy;
⇨              wndpl.length = sizeof(WINDOWPLACEMENT);
⇨              GetWindowPlacement(&wndpl);
⇨              // set the last invocation size to the size read in
⇨              winApp->m_rectAppLast.left = winApp->GetProfileInt(
⇨                  pszFrameSection,pszLeft,wndpl.rcNormalPosition.left);
⇨              winApp->m_rectAppLast.right = winApp->GetProfileInt(
⇨                  pszFrameSection,pszRight,wndpl.rcNormalPosition.right);
⇨              winApp->m_rectAppLast.top = winApp->GetProfileInt(
⇨                  pszFrameSection,pszTop,wndpl.rcNormalPosition.top);
⇨              winApp->m_rectAppLast.bottom = winApp->GetProfileInt(
⇨                  pszFrameSection,pszBottom,
⇨                  wndpl.rcNormalPosition.bottom);
⇨              winApp->m_uiShowCmd = winApp->GetProfileInt(
⇨                  pszFrameSection,pszShow,wndpl.showCmd);
⇨              // set size using the ratio of last to cur screen size
⇨              wndpl.rcNormalPosition.left =
⇨                  (winApp->m_rectAppLast.left * sx_cur) / sx;
⇨              wndpl.rcNormalPosition.right =
⇨                  (winApp->m_rectAppLast.right * sx_cur) / sx;
⇨              wndpl.rcNormalPosition.top =
⇨                  (winApp->m_rectAppLast.top * sy_cur) / sy;
⇨              wndpl.rcNormalPosition.bottom =
⇨                  (winApp->m_rectAppLast.bottom * sy_cur) / sy;
⇨              // restore the restored position
⇨              wndpl.showCmd = SW_RESTORE;
⇨              wndpl.length = sizeof(WINDOWPLACEMENT);
⇨              SetWindowPlacement(&wndpl);
◆              // restore the toolbars
◆              LoadBarState(winApp->m_pszProfileName);
→              // restore the JOEY configuration
→              JoeyConfig->Restore();
→          }
        return 0;
    }
```

◆ Initialise the `m_uiShowCmd` member in the application constructor in *viewit3d.cpp*:

```
    CViewit3dApp::CViewit3dApp()
    {
⇨       m_uiShowCmd = SW_SHOWDEFAULT;
    }
```

◆ At the end if the application `InitInstance` member function, show the application in the proper state (maximised or restored position as saved when the application was closed):

```
    BOOL CViewit3dApp::InitInstance()
    {
        ◆
```

```
          ◆
          // The main window has been initialized, so show and update it.
  ⇨       if ( (SW_SHOWDEFAULT != AfxGetApp()->m_nCmdShow) &&
  ⇨           (SW_HIDE != AfxGetApp()->m_nCmdShow) &&
  ⇨           (m_uiShowCmd == SW_SHOWMAXIMIZED) )
  ⇨          m_nCmdShow = m_uiShowCmd;
          pMainFrame->ShowWindow(m_nCmdShow);
          pMainFrame->UpdateWindow();

          return TRUE;
      }
```

This completes the first step in saving and restoring state. The application will now start in the same place with the same control bar configuration as when the application was last closed.

State information can be used to re-load objects, views, and other information. If you do tie your application window to the screen resolution, you might also tie the placement of any child windows to the size of the application windows.[34]

3.4 Performance Sensitive Interaction

Performance is of primary importance in interactive applications. Undoubtedly, you have noticed that the speed of interactive operations is related to the complexity of the data being drawn, the rendering styles used, the size of the window on the screen, the number of windows being updated, current background processing demands, the speed of the machine you are using, etc. A user of your application will notice the same thing, and will declare your application unusable if the re-draw speed (frames per second) falls below some tolerable level. Possible solutions to this problem are to require faster hardware, to limit window size, to limit data complexity, and to limit the rendering styles available to the application user. While these tactics have been used by many applications, we believe that functionally crippling an application to improve interactive response is not a viable approach to solving the problem.

Viewit3d is obviously not running at its peak performance because it has been compiled with debug options and no optimisation. This means that there are a large number of ASSERT checks being made throughout the operation of MFC

---

[34] For testing purposes, we constantly change display resolution. Reviewing the operation of different applications after changing the display resolution will give you a good idea of what does and does not work.

and *JOEY*. Some of these checks (e.g., array bounds on some of the basic geometric elements) can have a significant performance penalty. The performance improvement of an optimised release compile will be noticeable but, probably not be significant.

The real world is of infinite complexity, and our experience shows that users will add their own complexity until the speed of the application makes further complexity unreasonable. While we may think that a processor that is twice as fast or a graphics accelerator that improves graphics performance by a factor or 3 or 4 will significantly affect our users, the truth is that they will probably increase the complexity of their data until they are running at a similar interactive speed. The solution to the performance problem can only come through algorithmic methods of reducing data complexity when required, and adaptively determining the amount of complexity reduction required.

We have already discussed what it means to be interactive with respect to both camera positioning and data manipulation. Performance sensitive interaction involves simply monitoring the speed of the re-draw cycle and adjusting the complexity of the data display to maintain a reasonable update rate. It is important to maintain the correspondence of the mouse position and the graphic feedback (e.g., for an object drag, does the object move smoothly as you drag it across the screen and does it track with the cursor?).

We now revise *viewit3d* to provide performance sensitive adjustment during a camera move. *JOEY* provides some hints during the camera move cycle to let the application know what is required to maintain interactive speed. We have already added several rendering styles to *viewit3d* that show the data at various levels-of-detail. We will put the two together to illustrate the concept of performance sensitive interaction.

♦ Add a member variable to CObjView in which to save the rendering in use before the interaction starts, and an override of the CJoeyView::OnCameraChanged notification function. In the CObjView header, *objview.h*, add:

```
    class CObjView : public CJoeyView
    {
        ♦
        ♦
        float      m_fGridDistOrth;   // grid to vert
➜       int        m_nRenderStyleRef;
        ♦
        ♦
    protected:
```

➔   `virtual void   OnCameraChanged(ULONG);   // a change occurred`
          •
          •
`};`

♦ Add the `OnCameraChanged` function to `CObjView` in *objview.cpp*:

```
void CObjView::OnCameraChanged(ULONG ulChange)
{
    if (CAM_IS_INTERACTIVE & ulChange) {
        if (CAM_DECREASE_COMPLEXITY & ulChange) {
            if (m_nRenderStyle > DRAW_MIN_MAX)
                m_nRenderStyle--;
        }
    } else if (CAM_START_INTERACTIVE & ulChange) {
        m_nRenderStyleRef = m_nRenderStyle;
    } else if (CAM_END_INTERACTIVE & ulChange) {
        m_nRenderStyle = m_nRenderStyleRef;
    }

    CJoeyView::OnCameraChanged(ulChange);
}
```

At the beginning of a camera interaction, *JOEY* calls the `OnCameraChanged` notification function with the `CAM_START_INTERACTIVE` flag set before the first re-draw of the data. We save the current rendering style at the beginning of the interaction. At each step in the interactive cycle, *JOEY* notifies the view about the camera change with the `CAM_IS_INTERACTIVE` flag set before the re-draw. In addition to letting the view know another draw in an interactive camera move is about to happen, it gives the view some hints about performance. The `CAM_DECREASE_COMPLEXITY` hint tells the view that the performance target has not been reached on the last update, giving the view an opportunity to do something about it before the next re-draw. Here, we use the next lowest rendering style if there is one. At the end of the camera move, *JOEY* notifies the view with the `CAM_END_INTERACTIVE` flag set before the final re-draw. This gives the view an opportunity to restore the rendering style that existed before the interaction. We then restore the rendering style to what it was before the interaction started.

♦ Edit the project resource file, *viewit3d.rc*, using AppStudio to add access to the update rate target editing dialogue. In the `IDR_3D_GEOTYPE` menu, add a menu item to the <u>O</u>ptions pulldown with the pre-defined <u>I</u>D: `IDM_OPTIONS_UPDATE_RATE` and the <u>C</u>aption: *&Update Rate* (the prompt string is picked up from the *JOEY* resources). Copy this newly created menu item to the <u>O</u>ptions pulldowns in `IDR_3D_GEOTYPE_SRVR_EMB` and `IDR_3D_GEoTYPE_SRVR_IP`.

You can now re-build and run *viewit3d* to see the affects of performance sensitive control on the level-of-detail of the graphic during a *JOEY* camera interaction. You will notice that the display simplifies until the update rate falls within the target rate, or to the lowest level-of-detail if it is not possible to meet the target update rate. Unfortunately, at the start of every interaction, we go through every level-of-detail until we reach one that satisfies the target. Grids are not considered in simplifying the display.

Now that we have a good understanding of what performance sensitive interaction is, we add some intelligence to the simplification. We decided that, at each interaction, we would start only one level-of-detail higher than where we last stopped (this will work the image up to higher levels of detail if the complexity of the data has changed, or the size of the window has decreased, allowing faster updates). We also decided that, at the second request for simplification, we would stop drawing grids if they were currently being displayed.

♦ Add a member variables to CObjView to keep track of both the state before interaction, and simplification requests. In the CObjView header, *objview.h*, add:

```
class CObjView : public CJoeyView
{
    •
    •
    int         m_nRenderStyleRef;
→   ULONG       m_ulWorldGridRef;
→   ULONG       m_ulObjGridRef;
→   int         m_nDecreaseCt;
    •
    •

};
```

♦ Replace the OnCameraChanged member function of CObjView in *objview.cpp* to reflect the new logic for level-of-detail control:

```
void CObjView::OnCameraChanged(ULONG ulChange)
{
    int         nTmpStyle = m_nRenderStyle;
    CObjDoc*    pDoc = GetDocument();
    if (CAM_IS_INTERACTIVE & ulChange) {
        if (CAM_DECREASE_COMPLEXITY & ulChange) {
            // cut grids as the second step
            if ( (++m_nDecreaseCt == 2) &&
                ((JOEY_GRID_DISPLAY_PLANES & m_ulWorldGridRef) ||
                 (JOEY_GRID_DISPLAY_PLANES & m_ulObjGridRef)) ) {
                if (JOEY_GRID_DISPLAY_PLANES & m_ulWorldGridRef) {
```

```
                     // second request, simplify grids
                     CJoeyGrid      grid;
                     grid = *Grid();
                     grid.Attr(m_ulWorldGridRef &
                        ~JOEY_GRID_DISPLAY_PLANES);
                     Grid(&grid);
                 }
                 if (JOEY_GRID_DISPLAY_PLANES & m_ulObjGridRef) {
                     pDoc->ObjGrid()->Attr(m_ulObjGridRef &
                        ~JOEY_GRID_DISPLAY_PLANES);
                 }
             } else
                 // decrese object complexity otherwise
                 if (m_nRenderStyle > DRAW_MIN_MAX)
                     m_nRenderStyle--;
        }
    } else if (CAM_START_INTERACTIVE & ulChange) {
        // start where we last ended
        if (m_nRenderStyleRef < m_nRenderStyle)
            m_nRenderStyle = m_nRenderStyleRef;
        m_nRenderStyleRef = nTmpStyle;
        m_ulWorldGridRef = Grid()->Attr();
        m_ulObjGridRef = pDoc->ObjGrid()->Attr();
        // if we are starting at a reduced complexity, make
        //  sure the grids are the next thing cut
        if (m_nRenderStyle != m_nRenderStyleRef)
            m_nDecreaseCt = 1;
        else
            m_nDecreaseCt = 0;

    } else if (CAM_END_INTERACTIVE & ulChange) {
        m_nRenderStyle = m_nRenderStyleRef;
        // start one level more complex than the end
        m_nRenderStyleRef = nTmpStyle + 1;
            // reset the grid attributes
        if (m_ulWorldGridRef != Grid()->Attr()) {
            CJoeyGrid      grid;
            grid = *Grid();
            grid.Attr(m_ulWorldGridRef);
            Grid(&grid);
        }
        if (m_ulObjGridRef != pDoc->ObjGrid()->Attr()) {
            pDoc->ObjGrid()->Attr(m_ulObjGridRef);
        }
    }

    CJoeyView::OnCameraChanged(ulChange);
}
```

You can now re-build and run *JOEY* and you will have more intelligent control of level-of-detail. This example provides only a cursory overview of how performance sensitive interaction can be managed. The techniques will be similar for all applications, but the decisions about how data can be simplified (while retaining the important features for performing the operation) will be very application specific. *JOEY* has provided all of the hints for level-of-detail adjustment. The next step is to implement performance sensitivity for your application's interactive operations.

JOEY provides tools to support similar performance sensitive interaction strategies for data manipulation. Again, the way in which data is simplified is specific to both the application and the manipulation being done interactively. There are some subtleties to be aware of when making your data manipulations performance sensitive.

There are two areas that we must focus; monitoring the update cycle time, and providing a meaningful level-of-detail as the view is simplified. *JOEY* provides a cycle timer for monitoring the update cycle rate. The timer should be started at mouse down (in the `OnLButtonDown` message handler), and updated every time a mouse move event is processed (in the `OnMouseMove` message handler). The `CJoeyConfig::TimeUpdateCycle` function provides cycle timing information. It is called before the first draw of the interaction to initialise the timer, and before each successive draw to report whether the last cycle was within the update target range, or whether it was too slow and simplification is required.

In order for the timing to work correctly, each cycle must include similar operations. If initialisation of the interactive operation requires setup, this happens before the timer is started so that the first cycle time is representative, Figure P-30.

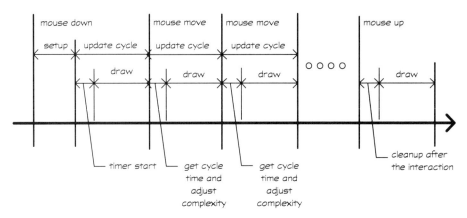

Figure P-30: A schematic abstraction of the event cycle of an interactive manipulation.

Another consideration is the message queue, and how mouse messages are generated. During the interaction, mouse move messages are only generated when the mouse moves. While this seems like an obvious and reasonable way to generate mouse messages, it presents a few problems for performance sensitive interaction. When mouse movement stops, other messages are processed, and the cycle time for that cycle becomes very large, resulting in inappropriate level-of-detail adjustment. The `CJoeyView` class provides a `FlushMouseEvents` function that should be called after re-drawing the vieww occurs. This function flushes all but the last mouse event for the view, and if there is no last event (the mouse has not moved) queues one. This keeps the update cycles flowing smoothly and keeps the interaction synchronised as closely as possible with the mouse movement.

A last consideration in the event processing loop is to make sure that the draw occurs during the timing of the cycle. The update processing of a window normally invalidates the window rectangle and queues a message to re-paint the window. A `ShowWindow` call is necessary to insure that the window is, in fact, re-drawn before the processing of the cycle continues, Figure P-31.

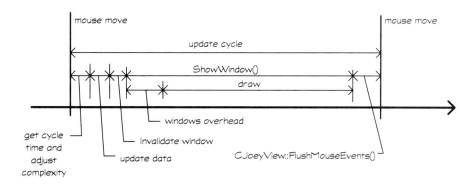

Figure P-31: A detailed look at a single update cycle of an interaction.

Planning the level-of-detail simplification for an interactive operation may not be simple. For example, if we implement performance sensitive interaction for the positioning jacks, it might make sense to simplify the object only as far as wireframe, or perhaps points. The object grid can be eliminated, but the world grid is used for positioning reference and grid hit testing and cannot be removed. During vertex drag, the object grid must be retained, but the world grid can probably be removed. If there is any question what simplification will be appropriate for the action, then the user must be able to control simplification, and turn it off when it prevents performing the desired task.

4. Extending *JOEY*

JOEY cannot be all things to all people, so you will probably want to extend and modify *JOEY* to suit your application specific needs. This chapter provides some hints on extending *JOEY* to meet those needs.

4.1 Dimensioning

With the exception of mathematicians and computer graphics developers, who seem to survive perfectly well in a dimensionless world, most of us rely on some system of measurement to quantify the world around us. Announcing to a waiter that "I would like one, please" might get you one of something, but it is unlikely (unless the menu is numbered) that you would get one of the item you desire. It is hardly any wonder that computer programs get misused when there is no differentiation between input of inches, feet, meters, or miles and the user is supposed to interpret dimensions without units in the resulting output. In short, some indication of units is required when addressing real world problems.

But how can we really deal with units when graphics is dimensionless? This is a good question. The space in which we draw graphic representations and move cameras implicitly takes on the dimensions in which the data is described. When you are writing your application, you know whether parsecs, meters, or angstroms, etc. are your basic unit of measure and you can convert from other units to your basic unit of measure. But how does the user interface know? The user interface is responsible for positioning the camera and providing other dialogue and positional feedback in a meaningful form (consistent with other information presented by the application). But the user interface exists in the dimensionless world of graphics.

When you write an application, or perhaps when the user uses an application, a choice is made about the appropriate unit for representation. Usually, we pick a unit that is representative of the scale of the problem being addressed (e.g., feet or meters for architectural work; angstroms or microns for molecular modeling; parsecs or light years for astronomical modeling, and miles or kilometers for geographic mapping). These units are generally selected so that the numbers used in describing the problem don't get too large or too small. This is a fortunate coincidence for computer modeling since digital representation suffers a loss in resolution when numbers get too large or too small. Since the data is expressed in these units when drawn, the size of the dataspace and parameters describing both the graphics and the camera implicitly use those units.

Before we describe the process for introducing units to the user interface, let us consider the types of values that *JOEY* uses. The user interface locates things in the world coordinate system. Positions are generally given as three orthogonal linear distances from the origin. Orientations are given either by direction vectors or angular orientations. The notion of angular dimensioning is well defined; it represents the division of a circle into increments. In general, the expression of an angle is not a function of the type of problem being solved (though some problems may require greater precision than others). The linear dimensions, on the other hand, are an expression of the scale of the problem and are very application specific. Fortunately, the graphics and user interface do not manipulate area, volume, force, pressure, or any of the other types of dimensioned quantities we encounter in describing the real world. So, we can restrict our concern to linear dimensions only.

In order for *JOEY* to work in the dimensioned space, all that is required is that the user interface know how to convert a linear dimension data value into an output string (preferably including units), and how to convert an input string (again, including units) into a linear dimension data value. In the case of *JOEY*, since graphic keypad input is supported for all numerical data, it also needs to know how to accept keypad entry of linear dimension data values. Three function definitions; `LINEAR_IN`, `LINEAR_OUT`, and `LINEAR_KEYPAD`; are provided for functions that perform these data conversions and data input. Also, the *JOEY* document classes have member functions to set and get pointers to the functions that they will use for handling linear data. The *JOEY* `CJoeyView` views associated with a document use these functions for any linear dimension data input and output.

JOEY includes a default implementation of `LINEAR_IN`, `LINEAR_OUT`, and `LINEAR_KEYPAD` that treats linear dimension values as dimensionless floating point values (perfect for all you mathematicians). The formatting is controlled by the *JOEY* configuration, `CJoeyConfig`. The application can get the pointers to the linear I/O functions from the document for consistent formatting.

Dimensioned linear value implementations of the LINEAR_IN, LINEAR_OUT, and LINEAR_KEYPAD functions are provided in *vit3dlib.dll*. These use meters as the implicit internal dimensioning unit for all values, but provide formatting in both metric and English units in a range suitable for architectural applications. We will not review the code for this, only the connection of these functions to a *JOEY* application, like *viewit3d*.

♦ In the constructor for the CObjDoc document in *objdoc.cpp*, set the linear input, linear output, and linear keypad functions to the dimensioned functions provided in *vit3dlib.dll*:

```
CObjDoc::CObjDoc()
{
        •
        •
        // alternate dimensioning
→       LinearIn(V3dLinearIn);
→       LinearOut(V3dLinearOut);
→       LinearKeypad(V3dLinearKeypad);
        •
        •
}
```

♦ Edit the project resource file, *viewit3d.rc*, using AppStudio to add access to the dimension formatting dialogue. In the IDR_3D_GEOTYPE menu, add a menu item to the <u>O</u>ptions pulldown with the <u>I</u>D: IDM_OPTIONS_DIMENSION, <u>C</u>aption: *&Dimensioning*, and Pro<u>m</u>pt: *Start a dialogue for setting dimensioning style\ndimensiong style*. Copy this newly created menu item to the <u>O</u>ptions pulldown in IDR_3D_GEOTYPE_EMB and IDR_3D_GEOTYPE_SRVR_IP.

♦ Use ClassWizard to add in message handler to CObjView for the COMMAND message to IDM_OPTIONS_DIMENSION. Fill in the body of the message handling function generated by ClassWizard as:

```
void CObjView::OnOptionsDimension()
{
→       V3dLinearDialogue();
}
```

V3dLinearDialogue is a dialogue box function provided with *vit3dlib.dll* that brings up a dimension formatting dialogue that allows you to specify the dimensioning conventions you would like the V3dLinearIn, V3dLinearOut, and V3dLinearKeypad to use.

You can now re-compile and run *viewit3d*. Note that
dimensional units are included in all feedback provided by
JOEY. Note also that since the document linear dimension data
formatting has been used for feedback generated by the
application, that it also includes dimensional units. Another

thing you should note is that it is now assumed that all the data in the *.a3d* file
is expressed in meters.

4.2 Adding Render Devices

Adding a rendering device requires that you supply a component object with an
IRenderDevX interface. A template for this type of component object is found in
the *template* subdirectory (on the *JOEY* disk). To make the template functional,
a unique class ID (CLSID) needs to be created using the *uuidgen* program
(supplied as part of Visual C++). Consult the *readme.txt* file in that directory for
details

This template is provided primarily for educational purposes. It shows the
structure of the component objects that support OpenGL, ADI 3D and the *JOEY*
3D metafiles.

As a template, it does nothing but allow an application to use its interface
without failing. All of the work to fill in the driver for a specific graphic
subsystem (or to write your own) is undone. This template could be used to add
support for another rendering system, or could be the basis for building a
special purpose renderer for your application. An example of a special purpose
renderer would be an XOR renderer that renders line through the
transformation and camera matrices to the screen using Win32 GDI calls in XOR
drawing mode. This would allow wireframe representations to be overlayed
and quickly moved on a rendered background.

Implementing a render device is not a task for the weak at heart, but can be
done to satisfy special needs. Providing a detailed description of how to
implement a render device is beyond the scope of this text.

4.3 Creating a *JOEY* Extension *.dll*

JOEY provides a collection of common graphic services in a "thin" layer of MFC extension classes between MFC and your applications classes, and in a collection of graphic entity and geometry classes that service the thin *JOEY* layer and the application, Figure P-32.

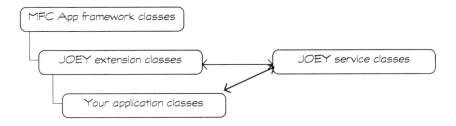

Figure P-32: *JOEY* extension and service classes in the application framework.

The *JOEY* extension classes such as `CJoeyView` and `CJoeyOleServerDoc` fit into the application framework provided by ClassWizard and augment the existing MFC functionality. The *JOEY* service classes such as `CPoint3f` and `Cline3f`, `CJoeyGrid` and `CJoeyCamera` provide completely new services in areas not previously covered by MFC. In many cases, this structure will be sufficient for your needs.

What do you do if you need different functionality for your own family of applications or if the *JOEY* services are not quite right for your application? You provide your own extensions of both the *JOEY* extension classes and the *JOEY* services classes, Figure P-33.

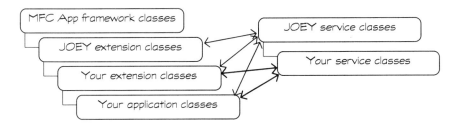

Figure P-33: Adding extension classes and service classes to *JOEY*.

Programming examples of this are beyond the scope of this text but we will provide some hints. Adding your own application extension classes is, conceptually, very simple. You derive your classes from the *JOEY* classes and then use them as the base for your own application classes. If you are extending *JOEY* classes, you are probably using these new classes in a number of places and want to build a *.dll* that contains these extensions. This is not as simple as it seems; in order for you to be able to export the classes in your *.dll*, they must be based on classes that can be exported. Although the MFC and *JOEY* classes are exported from their respective *.dlls*, the compiler doesn't know that and, therefore, provides a plethora of warnings. There are a collection of technical notes and examples from Microsoft that help guide you through the process. We encourage you to review these before you attempt to build your extension *.dll*. You can also review the source code for *vit3dlib.dll* which is a *JOEY* extension *.dll*.

Extending *JOEY* service classes is also conceptually simple but again, reality is much more complicated. The primary complication is that these classes are at the core of the *JOEY* user interface and the *JOEY* 3D metafile. For example, if you provide an extension camera, how does *JOEY* know how to edit it or save it to the 3D metafile. This may not be too tricky if you will be running the viewer on the same machine that created the camera object that is written into the 3D metafile. The difficulties arise when that metafile is used on a machine that doesn't have your camera object available. Providing the architecture to allow extension of the *JOEY* service classes is clearly desirable but beyond the scope of the toolkit supplied with this text. Extension of the *JOEY* service classes and the impact on system architecture are discussed in more detail in the corresponding section of **Theory**.

4.4 3D OLE Extensions

OLE has been used to integrate 3D *JOEY* applications with 2D container applications. *JOEY* does not attempt to go beyond 2D OLE integration. Embedding 3D data into a 3D container is beyond the current definition of OLE.

We could expect, in the future, that the object OnDraw function could draw into a 3D container as it now draws into its own application or to a 2D container. Drawing the 3D object is not the difficult part of this problem.

Throughout the example, we have shown that working in three dimensions is quite different than working in two dimensions. The dialogue that is required between a three dimensional container application and a three dimensional server in order to setup a render device to receive the object that a server would draw is not trivial, and is beyond the scope of this text.

IMPLEMENTATION

Table of Contents: Implementation

Figures

1. A Framework for Interactive 3D Applications

Whenever we use tools developed by someone else, we wonder about the preposterous logic that led to doing things in a way that appears to make absolutely no sense (until you try alternatives for awhile and realise some of the non-obvious considerations). We now provide some insight into the logic used to make specific implementation decisions in *JOEY*. There are a myriad of ways in which *JOEY* could have been implemented; we tried many before settling on the choices in this release. Final implementation decisions were based on usability, interaction in the resulting application and integration in the Windows development environment. Some of these are moving targets while others are a matter of personal preference. Where possible, we structured *JOEY* to give the application developer maximum flexibility, Figure I-34.

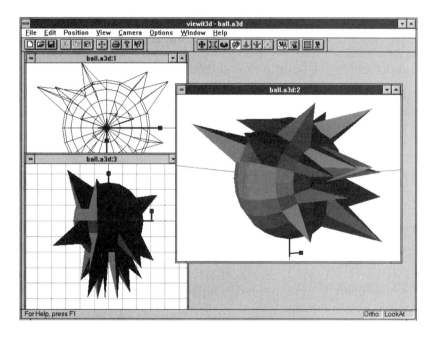

Figure I-34: "Spike-ball" created by editing a sphere in the completed *viewit3d*.

Some of the decisions will seem arbitrary. A difficulty in making *JOEY* decisions is the lack of consideration of 3D data in Windows style guidelines. In making user interface decisions, our first priority was to maintain consistency with Microsoft guidelines and to implement 3D specific features without compromising these guidelines.

Windows applications today are, generally, sophisticated in their user interface and level of integration with other applications. Developing applications with this level of sophistication requires powerful tools to avoid duplication of effort in each application and insure that the application automatically adapts to new guidelines for look and feel.

We selected MFC as the basic toolkit for building Windows integrated applications and added *JOEY* to supply the missing 3D user interface components and to provide easy access to 3D graphics for drawing and rendering. This adds two software components to those typically dealt with by Windows application developers; 3D user interface tools and a 3D graphics subsystem.[35]

We kept the following goals in mind as we implemented *JOEY*:

♦ *JOEY* will maintain the look and feel style guidelines for Windows.

♦ *JOEY* will overlay a user interface for 3D interactive graphics onto MFC that is as "thin" as possible (minimal overhead, no duplication of MFC functionality and exposure of all MFC constructs that developers are familiar with).

♦ *JOEY* will provide easy access to the graphics subsystem by performing common window setup, camera setup and utility tasks facilitating the dialogue between the application, the graphic display and the mouse input.

♦ *JOEY* will facilitate integration of the 3D capabilities into the Windows work environment by supporting OLE server/container services, OLE automation, and printed output.

With these goals in mind, **Implementation** examines the underlying structure of the work done in **Practice**.

---

[35] Various rendering libraries are currently available for Windows and Windows NT. *JOEY* presents a single rendering component object interface. This makes applications "renderer independent" since access to any renderer can be implemented through the component object interface.

1.1 Creating a Framework with MFC AppWizard

The MFC application framework imposes a uniform structure on Windows applications. The framework created by MFC AppWizard implements the base functions of a Windows integrated application. In addition to these base functions, this framework also imposes a uniform architecture on applications that are created using the MFC framework. This discussion focuses on the framework for an OLE Server enabled application.

The MFC architecture for interactive applications splits the functionality of the application into data manipulation and user interface. The role of data manipulation is to maintain the application data, to read/write the application data from/to a storage medium, and to provide functions for manipulating or editing the application data. The user interface provides the interface between the application data manipulation and the user, Figure I-35.

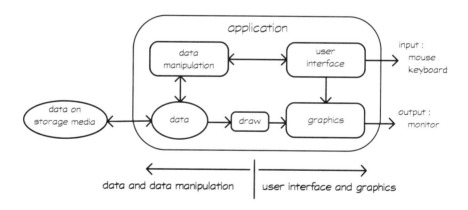

Figure I-35: Conceptual Organisation of the Application.

MFC provides the organisational framework for an application. The interesting parts of the MFC application framework hierarchy (which relate to *JOEY*) are summarised in Figure I-36.[37] The most interesting parts for considering integration of interactive 3D functionality are the branches that end in `CView`, `CDocument`, `COleServerDoc`, `COleServerItem`, and `CDC`.

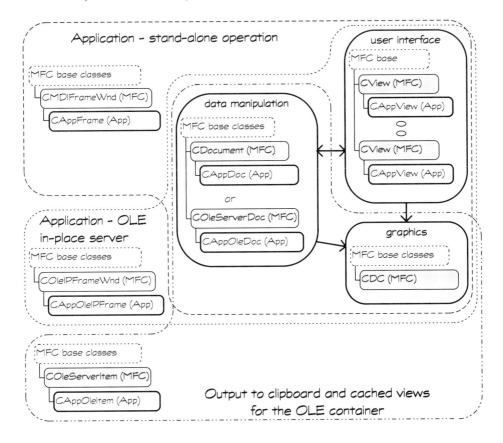

Figure I-36: MFC Application Framework Hierarchy.[36]

---

[36] This figure describes aspects of the framework which are most active in supporting specific functionality. It does not mean that other MFC classes are not involved.

[37] The MFC hierarchy charts and documentation provide a complete picture and discussion of the application framework. The discussion in this text is merely a primer for discussing the implementation of *JOEY* within MFC. It is extremely abstract and leaves out a vast amount of important information. Please consult the MFC documentation for complete details.

It is easy to use the structure provided by MFC to isolate the application specific user interface implementation behind application classes derived from CView, and to isolate application specific data manipulation in application classes derived from CDocument or COleServerDoc. It is also true that the rich event handling and message passing mechanisms provide the opportunity to largely ignore the distinction between data and user interface that has been carefully orchestrated by these classes.

The CView class provides a display window containing a view of the data (CDocument) for manipulation. CView is responsible for orchestrating the interaction between a view and the rest of window system. The application view, derived from CView, orchestrates the connection between user action and the data manipulations that result. The application document, derived from CDocument or COleServerDoc, provides the interface to the data. A view can be connected to only one set of data (one CDocument) while it is possible for data to be connected to several views (in the 3D world, we might want to simultaneously see several different views of the same 3D object).

Drawing the application data to the screen is a weak area of this structure; it sits on the fence between data manipulation and user interface. The CView class includes an OnDraw member function that is called whenever the window system damages a view and needs it to be re-drawn. The CDocument class includes an UpdateAllViews function that notifies each of the views that a change has been made in the document data and the views should be updated. There is a lack of clarity as to whether the data or the user interface is responsible for drawing the data. In the *scribble* tutorial, the drawing functionality is distributed between the CScribView::OnDraw function and members of CScribDoc or related document data classes.

Though we assume familiarity with OLE, let us review a few concepts. An OLE server is an application that creates data that may be used inside another application called a container. The use inside of the container may be through linking (which is a reference to a server's data file that exists outside the container's document data) or through embedding (which is moving the server's data into the container's document data). Through OLE, the container asks the server to create a visual representation of its data for display within the container. Though a container may be able to understand a variety of data types for display, assured understanding is through a metafile.[38]

---

[38] This is somewhat misleading. The server always draws to the container through a metafile that is cached by the container so that it can be displayed without server involvement.

The `COleServerItem` provides the interface between the server data and the container's request for a metafile representation. When data in the server is changed, the server notifies the container. The changes are not reflected in the container until the container requests and displays a new metafile from the server. Through this mechanism, it is possible for the container to display linked or embedded data without any action by the server (if the data has not changed). The implications of this are addressed in Sections 1.2.5, Section 1.2.6 and in greater detail in Section 2.1.

The `COleServerItem::OnDraw` function is called whenever the container needs to have the server provide a drawn representation. Again, there is an ambiguity about whether the document or the interface is responsible for actually drawing the data.

1.2 Adding the *JOEY* 3D Graphic User Interface to the Framework

Introducing 3D Graphics to an application does not change the conceptual organisation of an application, Figure I-35. It extends the user interface to include 3D graphics constructs and extends the graphics to include a 3D graphics subsystem.

JOEY is an MFC extension *.dll*. It provides classes derived from the MFC classes (that are used as the base class for application derived classes). These *JOEY* classes inherit the functionality of the MFC classes and augment them with functionality specific to 3D graphics applications. The *JOEY* classes also provide setup services for the 3D graphics subsystem. Figure I-37 provides an overview of how the *JOEY* classes work within the MFC application framework.

The `CJoeyDoc` and `CJoeyOleServerDoc` classes are extensions to the MFC `CDocument` and `COleServerDoc` classes. They provide notification services to keep the document apprised of changes in the viewing state. These notifications can be used to insure that all document data is current if viewing information is being saved as part of the document.

The `CJoeyView` class is an extension to the MFC `CView` class. It provides viewing (camera) control for the view and the user interface to common graphic elements such as grids, lights and materials. It also orchestrates the services that aid in integrating the graphics application with Windows.

The `CJoeyOleServerItem` is an extension to the `COleServerItem` and provides the services to correctly draw the document into an OLE container application.

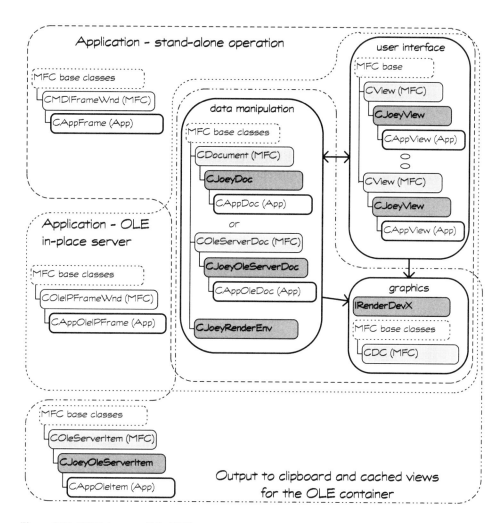

Figure I-37: *JOEY* classes within MFC.

CJoeyRenderEnv has been added to the document data to maintain and manipulate a rendering environment. An instance of this rendering environment is maintained with each document. The rendering environment includes preferred viewing information for use during OLE embedding and facilities for maintaining libraries of materials, lights, cameras, and grids. The rendering environment supplies some useful tools but is not intended to replace or dictate structure of the application database.

The `IRenderDevX` interface provides a 3D drawing/rendering interface for component object access to rendering facilities. It is somewhat limited; it doesn't provide access for "diddling the bits" of the graphics device. On the other hand, it is high level; it describes complex graphic information for rendering to a device with the least possible effort. It also provides the opportunity to get 3D information on the screen with minimal pain and frustration. `IRenderDevX` can be queried for information to allow direct access to the underlying rendering libraries if required (though this is discouraged).[39] `IRenderDevX` is a component object interface to bitmaps, metafiles, windows and *JOEY* 3D metafiles. As a component object interface, `IRenderDevX` can mix and match the low level rendering technology without affecting existing 3D applications. It also enforces a contract for the communication between the view and the document(s) involved in rendering so that there is no risk of the rendering state becoming "broken" through the actions of an object that is drawing itself.

In addition to MFC extension classes, *JOEY* provides a collection of classes that create and manipulate graphic and geometric entities that are commonly used in graphics applications (these are not shown in Figure I-37). These support classes are designed to make life easier by providing the most commonly needed support for 3D manipulation of data.

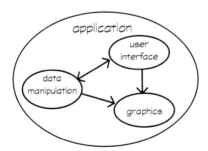

Throughout the implementation of *JOEY*, we constantly question which part of the application structure - data manipulation, user interface or graphics owns the data for an operation and should subsequently own the functionality that manipulates the data. To support this questioning, we use the schematic application organisation shown to the left.

Note that the communication to graphics from data manipulation and user interface is one way.

---

[39] Many of the Windows integration services rely on mapping the `IRenderDevX` output to devices other than a specific renderer. If you bypass `IRenderDevX`, you may lose some of these services.

1.2.1 Including *JOEY* and Graphics

JOEY consists of the *joey.dll* library that is loaded at application run time, and rendering device component objects that are loaded on demand. The *joey.dll* library includes all *JOEY* functionality except the graphic interface to the window, bitmap, metafile, or stream devices. The IRenderDevX component objects provide a mapping between the 3D drawing/rendering interface and the various rendering libraries that exist for use with Windows.[40]

The *joey.h* include file provides all of the declarations and definitions required to use *JOEY*. Each application using *JOEY* has an instance of the CJoeyConfig class allocated for configuration control of *JOEY*. A number of mechanisms could be used to expose the configuration class to the application. By exposing it through the *.dll* export/import mechanism and including it, along with the reference to *joey.h*, within the project *stdafx.h* include file, it becomes accessible to all source files in the application. It also insures that the *JOEY* references are included in the pre-compiled project header.

1.2.2 Adding the Camera Toolbar

JOEY provides camera control for 3D applications. Camera interaction is initiated with the middle or left mouse button. The modes of camera interaction are controlled through a toolbar and/or menu commands. *JOEY* uses a camera toolbar independent of the application toolbar. The use of a separate toolbar makes it possible to encapsulate all of the setup and interaction within the *.dll*. This minimises the demands on the developer for adding the camera toolbar to the application.

JOEY provides the functionality for the camera toolbar, however, the camera toolbar is owned by the application so that creation, docking and tool tips can follow the same conventions as the rest of the application. Immediately after creation, the toolbar is "given" to *JOEY* using CJoeyConfig::SetCameraToolBar. From this point on, *JOEY* assumes responsibility for only the contents of the toolbar. The application is still responsible for docking, visibility, tooltips and other style considerations. This is why the application must provide a menu item for controlling camera toolbar visibility.

---

[40] OpenGL and the ADI 3D are both supported by the release of *JOEY* supplied with this text. The use of component objects in conjunction with the registration of the objects *JOEY* should be using makes it possible to easily add and/or substitute additionally renderers if required.

In **Practice**, we mimic the *JOEY* commands generated by the toolbar using a Camera pulldown menu. The Camera pulldown is provided to demonstrate how to access the toolbar functionality through WM_COMMAND messages. It is possible that your application will want to move the camera and grid dialogue functionality into an Options pulldown or use some other application consistent way of accessing these dialogues. If the user initiates an editing action, the application may want to query for, and cancel, left button mouse control of the camera. This frees the left mouse button for the initiated action.

Resources are a concern when creating MFC extension *.dlls* like *JOEY*. Ideally, the user interface toolkit would be integrated into MFC resources and it would not be necessary to know where to find the user interface resources. Unfortunately, this is not the case. *JOEY* is an extension to MFC. You, the application developer, need to be cognisant of how *JOEY* allocates resources.

MFC uses resource values below 130 for dialogue boxes, icons, cursors, and other resources; and starts the application use of resources at 130, allocating sequential numbers upward as resources are created. *JOEY* starts using these resources at 500 in order to provide substantial room for the application resources. MFC uses command values below 32771 and gives the application commands staring at 32771, allocating sequential numbers upwards as commands are created. *JOEY* starts using commands at 50000 and upwards, again, to provide plenty of room for the application. Most of these resources are exposed in the *JOEY* resource files which should help you avoid conflict between application resources and any of the *JOEY* resources.

1.2.3 Adding Status Bar Camera Feedback

Like the camera toolbar, the application creates panes on the status bar and "gives" them to *JOEY* to use in reporting the camera type and the camera move paradigm. *JOEY* re-assigns the pane IDs. The active *JOEY* view processes the message generated during the MFC idle-time processing of user interface status to update the camera information in the panes. The application may not use the panes once they are given to *JOEY*. We found it necessary for *JOEY* to own the status panes so that size initialisation can be performed by *JOEY*.

1.2.4 Revising the View

The CJoeyView is derived from the MFC Cview class. The CJoeyView class adds camera control and renderer (3D graphic) window setup. It also clarifies some of the ambiguity of the data draw.

Adding the `OnMouseMove`, `OnLButtonDown`, `OnLButtonUp`, and `OnLButtonDblClk` functions is necessary. *JOEY* is intercepting middle mouse button messages for camera control. This template for the `OnMouseMove` function assures that *JOEY* can correctly process camera moves during the interaction. The changes to the `OnLButtonDown`, `OnLButtonUp`, and `OnLButtonDblClk` functions pass left mouse button messages to *JOEY*'s middle mouse button handler when the camera interaction mode has been set for activation by the left mouse button. Applications do not normally process any middle mouse button actions. If your application does process middle mouse button actions, then it is the responsibility of your application to decide if and when the middle mouse messages should be passed on to *JOEY*.

Mouse handling functions are contrary to the normal MFC methodology of having the application view handle the message, passing it on to the base class only if the application has not processed it. This contrary implementation was chosen in order to clearly contain the logic for querying the current camera processing state for the view (and passing the message on to `CJoeyView` if appropriate). If you feel strongly that you would like the first shot at handling the mouse, the handlers can be revised to look more like the typical MFC handlers. If you choose to do this, be sure to pass control to `CJoeyView` for messages you are not handling.

The changes in the `OnDraw` function (for the view) strengthen the division between data manipulation and user interface. The `OnDraw` member function of the application's view calls the `CJoeyView::OnDraw` member function. *JOEY* uses the `IRenderDevX` object to prepare and manage the 3D graphic subsystem. The `CJoeyView::OnDraw` function performs renderer setup and then calls the document `OnDraw` member function. The document `OnDraw` member function is expected to know how to draw the data into a renderer without concern for viewing specifics such as current camera or window sizing for a view.

You may notice that the application view `OnDraw` function only passes the operation to `CJoeyView`, therefore the application view `OnDraw` function could be completely deleted. We retain the function so that you are not tempted to add it at a later time and inadvertently bypass *JOEY* processing.

1.2.5 Revising the Document

The `CJoeyDoc` class is derived from the MFC `CDocument` class, and the `CJoeyOleServerDoc` class is derived from the MFC `COleServerDoc` class. The *JOEY* document classes add some functionality for communicating information about the 3D data to the views for camera and graphics setup. Additional clarification of responsibility for displaying data is also provided.

The document `OnDraw` function is the key element in resolving the ambiguity of the responsibility for drawing the document data. The `OnDraw` function is always called whenever the document data must be drawn. The render device is always correctly configured with the background cleared and the camera loaded so that the document needs only to draw its data.

Every *JOEY* document owns a rendering environment. The rendering environment is serialized with the application data. *JOEY* takes responsibility for the serializing rendering environment through the addition of the *JOEY* document `Serialize` function. The *JOEY* document data is always after the application document data. It is keyed so that *JOEY* knows whether the data is in the file specified and should be read. This facilitates enhancing existing applications to be *JOEY* applications. This issue is further discussed in Section 2.1.

Figure I-38: The render environment data is appended to the end of the data file by the *JOEY* document `Serialize` function.

1.2.6 Revising the OLE Server Item

The `CJoeyServerItem` class is derived from the MFC `COleServerItem` class. The server item is responsible for a large part of the dialogue between an OLE container application and the OLE server application. Along with other interactions, it tells the container how large the drawing of the server document wants to be (the container uses the size for initial display but may subsequently re-size the graphic) and it responds to the container's request for the server to draw its graphic into a CDC supplied by the container.

The AppWizard created `CObjSrvrItem` class provides an override of the `OnGetExtent` function called by the container to get the ideal size of the server graphic.

The default implementation returns a fixed size. When *JOEY* is used, the document size is a part of the render environment and communication is completely handled by the `CJoeyOleServerItem` implementation of the

OnGetExtent function. Removing this function from the CObjSrvrItem removes any temptation to play with it.

The CJoeyOleServerItem class also completely handles the draw operation by setting up a rendering device for the CDC, supplied by the container[41] and calling the document OnDraw function.

You may wonder why the OnDraw function was not also simply deleted. The reason is that you may wish to change something about how the object is drawn depending on the context of the draw. You can also simply delete this function completely if you want to remove all temptation.

1.2.7 Adding Context Sensitive Help for *JOEY*

JOEY uses the same mechanism as MFC to provide help file templates that can be customised for the application.[42]

Context sensitive help files are keyed to the application resource IDs through the help map files (*.hm*). *JOEY* provides a help map file, **$(JOEY_DIR)***include**joey.hm*, for *JOEY* specific help. There will be problems, both with application operation and context sensitive help, if there are conflicts between application resource IDs and those provided by either MFC or *JOEY*. The use of resources is discussed in more detail at the end of Section 1.2.2.

1.2.8 Build and Test the Framework

When you run the framework, most of the functionality is coming from MFC. The 3D capability added by *JOEY* comes from a very "thin" functional layer which uses MFC services and conventions to the greatest possible extent.

1.3 Adding Application Read and Draw

We maintain the integrity of the split between data manipulation and user interface by completely encapsulating data read and display within the document. For many applications, maintaining this boundary is difficult

---

[41] The OnDraw function is also called within the server to draw the metafile representation copied to the clipboard during an <u>E</u>dit, Copy Sp<u>e</u>cial... command.

[42] Refer to MFC and Help Compiler documentation for details.

because it becomes difficult to identify whether elements of the application should be owned by the document or the view.

1.3.1 Object Data Definition

Data creation is generally far more difficult than data display. Therefore, using a data read and display application as the first sample makes sense. However, ASCII data definitions are in conflict with normal practices in MFC. The idea of creating non-textual data in a text editor (and then parsing it into a different form) is foreign to Windows applications so it may not have been appropriate to use such a data source. However, it is easy to write simple data generators for this format, the data is readable without a special viewer and it can be easily extended without need for translation of early versions.

1.3.2 Adding Read and Draw

It is important to keep the application data with the document. Static arrays were used for convenience, though they are generally bad practice. The data structure used is simply vertex and face lists. Each face has a vertex count and a list of vertex pointers as shown in Figure I-39.

You may be curious about the fDataSpace variable in the Serialize function. For now, you can be satisfied with the explanation that it is used to communicate to *JOEY* the volume of space that the object fits into. This information is used by *JOEY* to determine default camera settings so the full object appears in the height of the window. We will explore camera defaults and dataspaces in a later section.

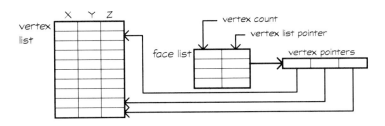

Figure I-39: Document data structure for *.a3d* objects.

The draw function relies on *JOEY* to have the renderer (IRenderDevX) initialised and the camera loaded for the view. The job of the document OnDraw function is to simply draw the data to the IRenderDevX interface. The OnDraw function uses the IRenderDevX::Draw3dPolyline function to draw the object polygons.[43] In this case, the format expected by the draw call (a list of vertex pointers) is nearly identical to the internal database used for the object. Consequently, there is little work to do in the draw routine other than loop through the polygons in the database and send them to the renderer. The important observation is that the OnDraw function just sends the object data to the renderer. It does not worry about window setup, cameras or any other details of the 3D graphic subsystem.

The additions and changes to the CObjDoc document constructor and DeleteContents are primarily database initialisation and deletion operations. Refer to the *scribble* tutorial and MFC documentation for a better idea of how DeleteContents fits in the process of document creation, opening, and closing.

---

[43] This will change to drawing polygons when we explore rendering and materials in later chapters.

2. Integrating the Sample Application into Windows

The process of integrating a graphics application into Windows appears to be easy in the **Practice** section. However, there is more to the problem than meets the eye. Here, we discuss the mechanisms that are at work (in *JOEY*, MFC, and OLE) when applications communicate with each other. In **Theory**, we discuss the considerations for applications which are not as simple as *viewit3d*.

2.1 OLE Server Capabilities - Linking and Embedding

Linking and embedding create a relationship between a server and a client (container) with some very explicit behavioural requirements and some implied expectations of behaviour. We review the example from **Practice** to describe the mechanisms that are at work, and to try to understand both the explicit and implicit demands on the 3D graphic application that is used as an OLE server.

2.1.1 Investigating the workings of OLE

In **Practice**, we added some messaging to *viewit3d* so we could get a better idea of what is happening during OLE interactions.[44] Let us review this in more detail. Please beware; we are not yet OLE experts.

There are three major steps in the process of embedding a server graphic in a container. The first is to serialize the server object into the container's data stream. The second is to provide a graphic representation of the server object that can be drawn into the container's graphic display. The third is to provide in-place activation support for editing the server object.

Processing the request to embed a file starts by using the file extension to look up the appropriate server in the system registration database. The server is started in a hidden window. The server serializes the data from the file into the

---

[44] We found it useful to build a version of *JOEY* that provides messaging on almost every message or overridable function. We learned an amazing amount about the interactions between OLE and MFC this way. You might consider doing something similar if you are having problems with the interaction.

server database. Through OLE, the container provides the server with a stream into the container's data storage.[45] MFC maps the stream into a `CArchive` and asks the document to serialize itself into that `CArchive`, Figure I-40. After the data has been serialized into the container, the server is released and its execution terminates.[46]

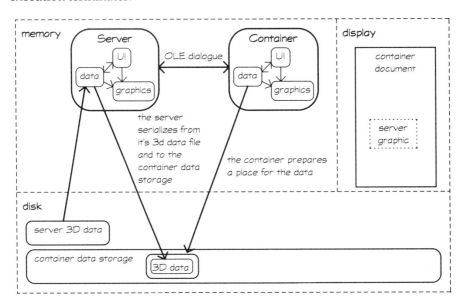

Figure I-40: Server data embedded into a container data storage by the server `Serialize` function.

To make use of the embedded server data, the container re-starts the server application in a hidden window. Metafile views of the object are requested through the `COleServerItem` resulting in representations that will be cached for display, Figure I-41. The server is again released after the graphic representations have been created.[47]

---

[45] Refer to OLE documentation for more information on structured storage and compound files.

[46] If the server is a running MDI application, it appears as though a window is started in the running application rather than starting a new instance of the application. This is especially useful in debugging. If you start the server in the debugger, you can set break points and monitor what is happening during the OLE dialogue.

[47] MS Word asks for two representations while *contain* requests only one. MS Word is requesting one representation for display on the screen and a second representation at the resolution of the current printer.

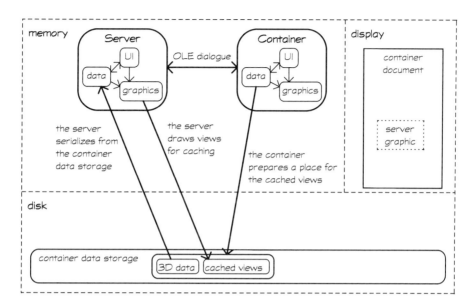

Figure I-41: Cached views created from the embedded data by the server.

Once the server object data has been embedded with cached graphic representations, the server object can be displayed in the container. The cached graphic is the source for the display of the server object, Figure I-42.

In-place activation results in an OLE dialogue between the container and the server to start the server, setup the server menu and toolbar user interface within the container, and correctly position the in-place window over the server graphic in the container. While the server is activated, it serializes to and from a stream in the container's data storage. The stream has been provided by the container, given to the server, and MFC has mapped the stream to a CArchive. The stream may be attached to either a disk file or a memory file. The server also provides new graphic representations for caching, Figure I-43. The server notifies the container that there has been a change and the container requests new representations. Once the server has been activated, it may be closed at de-activation or may not be closed until the container application is closed.[48]

---

[48] Behaviour is container specific. MS Word does not close the server while *contain* does close the server whenever the server is not in-place activated.

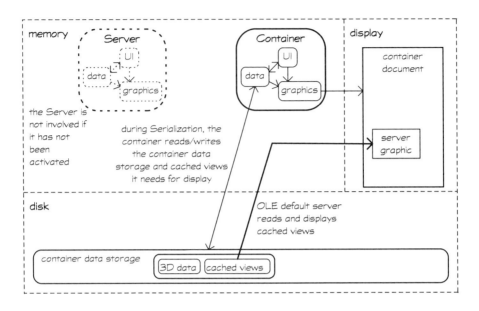

Figure I-42: Cached views provide the graphic for the embedded object in the container document.

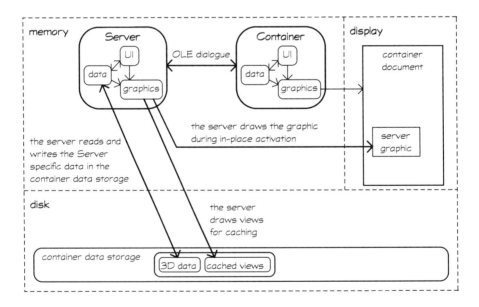

Figure I-43: The server is responsible for the server graphic during in-place automation.

Linking is similar to embedding, except that a file moniker is written into the container data stream instead of the 3D data. The moniker is a pointer or reference to the 3D data files.[49]

In linking, the serialization into the container data storage, Figure I-40, does not occur. The writing of cached views to the container occur as shown in Figure I-41 except that the server reads the data from its 3D data file, Figure I-44 (cached views are created from the server's data file).

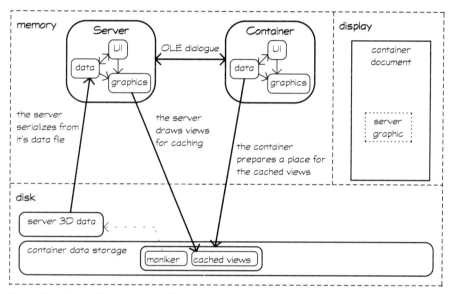

Figure I-44: Server data is separate from the container in linking.

Once a view has been cached, the container can continue to draw that graphic without any action on the part of the server, as shown in Figure I-42.

Activating the linked object results in the server being loaded independently of the container for editing the 3D data file. If the activated server changes the object, the server notifies the container. The container immediately updates both the cached graphic and the displayed graphic when it receives this notification from the server.

---

[49] It is more complicated because the moniker is designed to keep things related even if the container and the server data files are moved. See the OLE documentation for details.

2.1.2 Completing the Implementation as an OLE Server

The primary task was to complete serialization to an archive so that data could be embedded in a container. However, there is a part of that serialization being passed to the *JOEY* document, CJoeyOleServerDoc.

The *.a3d* file is an ASCII geometry file that contains 3D geometry only. Whenever an *.a3d* file is read into *viewit3d*, it appears in the default camera orientation for *viewit3d* because there is no camera data with the geometry. This behaviour would be alarming in the container; you expect the object to stay where you put it during camera adjustment (not to always return to a default position).

In order to get predictable OLE behaviour, *JOEY* saves the OLE view as part of the document data through CJoeyDoc and CJoeyOleServerDoc Serialize function. While this provides a solution for simple applications, the problem of attaching a camera to the data becomes more complex as the server application becomes more complex. See **Theory** Section 2.1 for more discussion on this subject.

When the *.a3d* file is linked into the container, there is only one camera associated with the data. If you link the same file into the document twice, any change in view affects both linkages identically.

Another troubling behaviour occurs when the server graphic is re-sized. If the aspect ratio of the graphic is changed, the graphic is distorted to fit the new window. When the server is activated, the camera is adjusted for the new aspect ratio. There appears to be no mechanism that lets the container know the object must be re-drawn instead of scaled when the aspect ratio of the server window in the container changes. Instead, *JOEY* detects the problem when the server is activated and corrects the distortion in both the in-place activated server window and in the views cached with the server.

2.2 Clipboard, Files and 3D Viewers

Three Dimensional graphic data is implicitly pictures.[50] Special clipboard and file formats are supported for transferring the graphic data from a 3D

---

[50] Though your application may use text to describe data, we will not be covering the use of the clipboard for text. Refer to Win32 API and MFC documentation for details of text transfers using the clipboard.

application to a 2D container application.[51] Transferring data as 2D pictures is well understood. Transferring 3D data is done by embedding either OLE server application data or *JOEY* 3D data. The application creating *JOEY* 3D data does not need to be OLE enabled. The OLE server for *JOEY* 3D data is the *JOEY* Viewer.

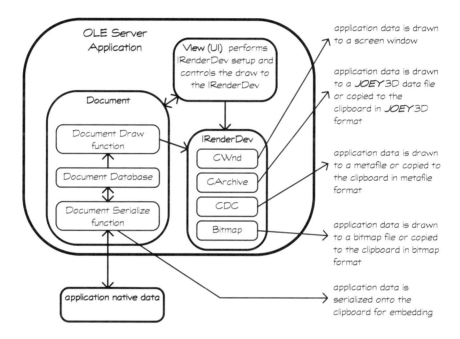

Figure I-45: Implementation of Copy Special and Save Special in an OLE server application.

Special formats are implemented through the `IRenderDevX` interface to a rendering device, Figure I-45. Conceptually, this is similar to drawing (using Win32 GDI functions) to a device context which may be attached to a window, metafile or bitmap. Practically, the result is that only a single draw function for the document data is required (in the case of *viewit3d*, this is the `CObjDoc::OnDraw` function). The `CJoeyView` class that the application view

---

[51] 3D container application interfaces and operation have not yet been defined. These are discussed in OLE extensions sections of the text.

class is derived from takes care of configuring the correct `IRenderDevX` for data output in special formats.

2.2.1 Enabling Special Clipboard Copy Formats

JOEY provides default handling for the Copy S̲pecial.. menu command. The default handling allows selection of one of the special formats to be copied to the clipboard. This handler copies only the selected format to the clipboard. The time involved to copy any format may be substantial so it would take objectionally long to copy them all. Delayed rendering could be used but it may take intolerably long to copy the database and later render it.

In the event that you would like to handle Copy S̲pecial... differently, the functions for copying data to the clipboard are:

application native	`CJoeyOleServerDoc::CopyObjectToClipboard`[52]
JOEY 3D	`CJoeyView::Copy3DMetaToCliboard`
metafile	`CJoeyView::CopyMetaToClipboard`
bitmap	`CJoeyView:CopyBitmapToClipboard`

2.2.2 Enabling Special File Save Formats

JOEY provides default handling for the Save S̲pecial menu command. The default handling allows selection of one of the special formats for output to a file. Once a format has been selected, a F̲ile, O̲pen dialogue box allows selection of the file to save information. We have elected to use Save S̲pecial... instead of tacking it on to Save A̲s...We chose this because this is a one-way save or export of the data in the application. We did not want to have any confusion with the F̲ile, S̲ave and F̲ile, O̲pen menu operation. As with Copy S̲pecial..., the `CJoeyView` orchestrates Save S̲pecial... In the event that you would like to handle Save S̲pecial differently, the functions for saving the data to special file formats are:

JOEY 3D	`CJoeyView::Save3DMetaToFile`
metafile	`CJoeyView::SaveMetaToFile`
bitmap	`CJoeyView:SaveBitmapToFile`

---

[52] Can only be used with OLE server enabled applications.

2.2.3 Playing with the Clipboard and Files

Let's take a look behind the scenes at special format clipboard copy and file save. This should help if you want to customise the operation of these features, add similar features of your own or write documentation for the users of your application.

2.2.3.1 Native Application Data

The standard MFC document `Serialize` function and surrounding functionality handles native application file read and write and is common to all applications. MFC also provides all of the functionality required for using the clipboard for transferring native application data. By understanding what MFC is doing, we can use an identical strategy for other special formats (like *JOEY* 3D metafiles).

The clipboard transfer of a native application database is only meaningful if your application is OLE server enabled. Otherwise, there is no server that can service the data if it is pasted into a container. This means that the native application database will only be copied to the clipboard from a `CJoeyOleServerDoc` derived document (which is, in turn, derived from `COleServerDoc`).

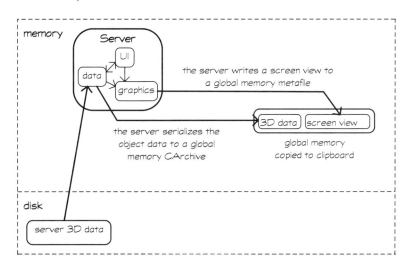

Figure I-46: Copying the native server application data to the clipboard.

Embedding from the clipboard is very similar to embedding from a file. The primary difference is that the server has serialized data to a CArchive that is global memory placed on the clipboard together with a 2D representation for screen display, Figure I-46.

Additional information is also copied describing the data format so that the correct server can be associated with the data. The container's **Paste Special** operation takes this data directly from the clipboard and inserts it into the container data stream, Figure I-47. Existing MFC facilities are used to handle the copy of native application data to the clipboard. Once the server object data and graphic representation has been embedded, operation is identical to that described in Section 2.1 for embedding from a file.

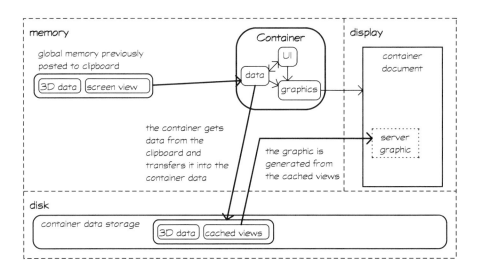

Figure I-47: Pasting (embedding) native server data from the clipboard.

In the MFC documentation, we see that the COleServerItem has a CopyToClipboard function that will put the native object on the clipboard. A COleDataSource is used to put the native application data on the clipboard. Clipboard formats are cached with COleDataSource. The IDataObject interface of the COleDataSource is used with the OleSetClipboard function to get the data onto the clipboard.

To copy data for both embedding and linking, many clipboard formats for data are cached with the `COleDataSource`: "Embed Source", "Object Descriptor", "Link Source", "Link Source Descriptor" and the enhanced metafile format. For each of these formats, data is loaded into a storage medium and cached with the `COleDataSource` object.

2.2.3.2 *JOEY* 3D Data

When *JOEY* 3D data is copied to the clipboard, the operation is very similar to copying the native data. Only data for embedding is copied to the clipboard since there is no *.j3d* file that could be used for linking.[53]

JOEY creates a `COleDataSource` object and builds "Embed Source" and "Object Descriptor" formats in storage mediums which are cached with the `COleDataSource`. The `AddOtherClipboardData` function of the `COleServerItem` is used to add the picture (enhanced metafile) representation to the formats cached with the `COleDataSource` object.

The 3D metafile is a literal record of all of the 3D graphics calls made during a re-draw of the screen. Both the *JOEY* 3D metafile and the screen view are created by calling the same document draw routine. Therefore, the picture copied to the clipboard for use with the 3D metafile is exactly the same as that copied to the clipboard for use with the native data representation. In both cases, they are created by the `AddOtherClipboardData` function of the `COleServerItem`.

The *JOEY* 3D metafile images may seem particularly large. Remember, these are a literal record of the calls made to `IRenderDev` when the image is drawn. Looking at an object (e.g., *ball.a3d* which is made up mostly of quadrilateral polygons), you will notice that each vertex is shared by 4 polygons. Since the draw routine processes the object as polylines, 5 points are sent to `IRenderDevX` for each polygon; each vertex is sent to the graphics an average of 5 times. Each edge is shared by 2 polygons and is therefore drawn twice. The size of the *JOEY* 3D metafile in *viewit3d* is an indication that we are using the graphics very inefficiently. Ideally, objects would be given to the graphics as triangle strips, quadrilateral strips or meshes so that the communication bandwidth is reduced and redundant operations are eliminated. Watching the size of the *JOEY* 3D metafile is one way to evaluate your success at using the graphics more efficiently.

---

[53] The application is using an application native data file to create the *JOEY* 3D data copied to the clipboard. There is no associated *JOEY* 3D file.

2.2.3.3 Metafiles and Bitmaps

The most interesting difference between bitmaps and metafiles is that, with metafiles, it is possible to specify an image size at some specific resolution. The bitmap is the size and resolution of the window on the screen. Using this

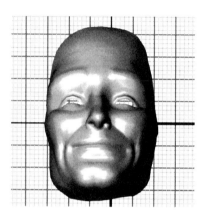

capability of the metafile, it is possible to create very high resolution renderings for printed materials, as shown the small rendering, Figure I-48. This image was created in an enhanced metafile at a colour resolution of 16 bits and a resolution of 1000 dots per inch which is about one half of the resolution of the Optronics 4000 which was used as the camera-ready output for this text.

Figure I-48: High resolution metafile clipboard image (geometry created by Kleiser-Walczak Construction Company).

2.2.4 The *JOEY* Viewer

The *JOEY* Viewer is an OLE server application for which *JOEY* 3D data is the native data type. The *JOEY* 3D data stream has two components: the sequence of IRenderDevX calls made during a draw, and the serialization of the rendering environment. Like GDI metafiles, there is one file record in the file for each IRenderDevX function call during a data draw. When this is read into a database, there is one database record for each IRenderDevX call. Unlike the GDI playback, the *JOEY* 3D data need not be played back verbatim.

The *JOEY* Viewer suppresses the part of the playback that performs window and camera setup and performs its own window and camera setup. Materials and lights are taken from the render environment rather than the IRenderDevX database. This allows the view and appearance of the 3D data to be controlled in the Viewer, Figure I-49.

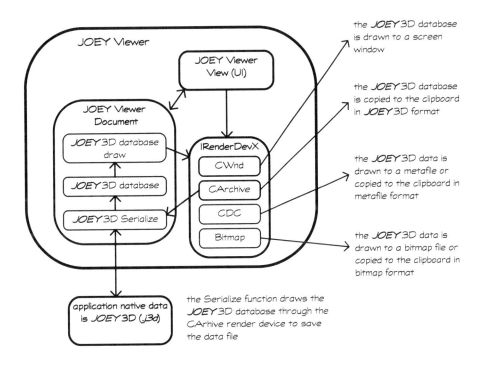

the *JOEY* 3D database is drawn to a screen window

the *JOEY* 3D database is copied to the clipboard in *JOEY* 3D format

the *JOEY* 3D data is drawn to a metafile or copied to the clipboard in metafile format

the *JOEY* 3D data is drawn to a bitmap file or copied to the clipboard in bitmap format

the Serialize function draws the *JOEY* 3D database through the CArhive render device to save the data file

Figure I-49: Implementation of the *JOEY* Viewer.

Serialization from the data file is through a reader that creates the *JOEY* 3D database. Serialization back to the *JOEY* 3D data file happens by drawing the database through the CArchive render device (which is how the file was originally created).

2.3 OLE Automation

JOEY classes have been implemented so that many of the lower level classes can be created using *joey.dll* as the server for the class. Other *JOEY* classes only exist in the context of an application executable. We have attempted to provide a comprehensive OLE automation server interface for *JOEY* classes.

2.3.1 OLE Automation within *JOEY* Classes

Almost all *JOEY* classes can be used as OLE Automation servers. The implementation of the OLE Automation interface is either part of the *JOEY* class or a helper class, Figure I-50.

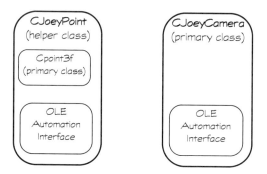

Figure I-50: OLE Automation revealed through a helper class and as part of the primary class.

OLE automation adds a fair amount of overhead[54] in classes that are normally very small and used everywhere, such as points (CPoint2f and CPoint3f), vectors (CUnitV2f and CUnitV3f), colours (CRGBf), etc. For these classes, a helper class is used to support OLE automation. The helper class includes an instance of the class being automated and carries the overhead of OLE automation. The *JOEY* classes that fully support OLE automation are larger and used sparingly (e.g., CJoeyCamera, CJoeyView, CRenderEnv, etc.) and are derived from MFC CCmdTarget. Much of the OLE automation overhead is included as a part of the CCmdTarget class. For these classes, the OLE automation interface is contained within the class and including OLE automation in the class adds negligible additional overhead.

We can see the difference between using an automated class and using a class that has an automation helper class by looking at an example of exposing the IDispatch interface for each. Consider the CJoeyCamera class and the CPoint3f class used as members, m_cam and m_pt, in some application class A.

The CJoeyCamera is exposed through an IDispatch interface using GetCamera and SetCamera functions:

```
LPDISPATCH A::GetCamera()
```

---

[54] As an example, the CPoint3f class has a size of 12 bytes. The CJoeyPoint automation class (for CPoint3f) has a size of 40 bytes. This represents 28 bytes of overhead to support OLE automation.

```
{
    CJoeyCamera*        pCam;

    if (NULL == (pCam = new CJoeyCamera)) {
        AfxThrowMemoryException();
        return NULL;
    }
    *pCam = m_cam;

    return pCam->GetIDispatch(FALSE);
}

void A::SetCamera(LPDISPATCH newValue)
{
    CJoeyCamera*        pCam =
        (CJoeyCamera*)CCmdTarget::FromIDispatch(newValue);
    if ( (NULL != pCam) &&
         pCam->IsKindOf(RUNTIME_CLASS(CJoeyCamera)) ) {
        m_cam = *pCam;
        // TODO - stuff to let A know a m_cam was set
    }
}
```

A copy was made of the m_cam member in the GetCamera function and that no additional reference was added to the created camera when its dispatch interface was returned. An alternate implementation would be to return the m_cam member IDispatch so the m_cam member could be operated on directly. This eliminates the need for the SetCamera function, but can pose problems because A does not know when the m_cam member is affected by an automation client. This implementation of GetCamera is shown below:

```
LPDISPATCH A::GetCamera()
{
    // add a reference count so the camera does not
    //  get deleted when released on the outside
    return m_cam.GetIDispatch(TRUE);
}
```

The CPoint3f is exposed through an IDispatch interface to the CJoeyPoint helper class. The helper class contains an instance of a CPoint3f as follows:

```
LPDISPATCH A::GetPoint()
{
    CJoeyPoint*     pPt;

    if (NULL == (pPt = new CJoeyPoint)) {
        AfxThrowMemoryException();
        return NULL;
    }
    pPt->SetPoint(m_pt);

    return ptTarget->GetIDispatch(FALSE);
}
```

```
void A::SetPoint(LPDISPATCH newValue)
{
   CJoeyPoint*    pPt =
      (CJoeyPoint*)CCmdTarget::FromIDispatch(newValue);
   if ( (NULL != ptTarget) &&
      pPt->IsKindOf(RUNTIME_CLASS(CJoeyPoint)) ) {
      pPt->GetPoint(m_pt);
      // TODO - stuff to let A know m_pt was set
   }
}
```

In this case, a CJoeyPoint is created to support the IDispatch interface and the CPoint3f within it is either loaded from or read into the m_pt member of A. Unlike the CJoeyCamera class, the CPoint3f is not directly available for OLE automation.

2.3.2 OLE Automation in *JOEY* Applications

If your application wants to expose *JOEY* information for automation, the first (and preferred) method is to expose access to the IDispatch interface of the *JOEY* object. The second is to expose methods that map through your application classes to the *JOEY* properties you want to expose. We will discuss both methods using the example from **Practice**.

In the example, we were interested in getting access to camera information for the current view and background colour information for the document. The example provides the IDispatch interface of the *JOEY* document used for creating the application document and lets the automation client walk through the *JOEY* classes to get to the desired information. The application document exposes a method to get the underlying CJoeyOleServerDoc the CJoeyOleServerDoc gets the active CJoeyView which, in turn, gets the camera. The alternative implementation would expose a GetCamera method from the application document directly.

In order to decide whether you want to make things in the application accessible through the *JOEY* document class or completely control OLE automation access to *JOEY* information, you need to determine:

♦   How do you want to divide the workload in accessing data? The example minimises the workload in the server by making the client walk through the *JOEY* structures to get the required information. You could elect to make the server do more work and expose things so that fewer IDispatch transactions are required to get the desired information. The slowness of the camera automation example compared to interactive camera positioning suggest to us that direct access functions for key automation data will be vital in making automation useful.

♦ Do you want your application to provide uniform access (uniform with other applications) to *JOEY* data? Exposing the *JOEY* document through the `GetJoeyDoc` function assures that *JOEY* related aspects of your application are uniformly accessible from an animation client.

♦ How much work do you want to do? It may make sense to expose the *JOEY* interface during the prototyping in order to minimise the work you need to do, and then add to or replace *JOEY* automation if there are specific functional or performance demands that require special attention.

3. Graphic Display and Interaction

Graphic display and interaction are at the heart of any interactive 3D application. If you are an experienced graphics programmer, you will find the approach that we have taken is unique and you may wonder why certain decisions were made. If you don't have previous 3D graphics experience, you probably need more information than **Practice** provided. This chapter attempts to satisfy both needs.

3.1 Graphic Elements

Three dimensional graphics has traditionally been tough to program because the developer was left to do most of the work. Graphics toolkits provide access to 3D constructs, the means to get these to the screen, and methods to diddle bits in the graphics hardware, but, the work of creating the relationship between the graphics, user interface, and application was left entirely to the developer. In creating *JOEY*, the main goal was to make 3D graphics accessible in a way that lets you focus on building a good application rather than learning the intricacies of graphics programming.

JOEY provides very straightforward access to 3D graphics. You need to deal with only a handful of draw calls in order to get your data on the screen while *JOEY* worries about managing things behind the scene. For the 3D graphics elite, those that want to diddle bits and play games with the hardware and rendering algorithms, this may be a frustrating experience. For the developer that is creating a 3D application and wants to concentrate on the functionality of the application rather than the nitty-gritty of the graphics, this should be a real bonus.

In many ways, the *JOEY* philosophy parallels the MFC goals of providing tools to help the developer move quickly to a running windows application. There is a trade-off between the development time required to create a fully functional application, and the flexibility of having access to every detail in the various supporting APIs. *JOEY* constrains your access to the 3D graphics, but, provides avenues for you to circumvent *JOEY* in order to have direct access to the underlying graphics APIs.

3.1.1 Axis Systems

The axis systems used in computer graphics are no more than notational conveniences that allow us to talk about data and camera objects in isolation and to specify inter-element relationships at a later time. Transformations position one axis system with respect to another. In theory, it is possible to map from any axis system into any other using the transformations that position the axis systems relative to each other. In practice, the mappings are often confusing to the developer, and impossible for the user unless efforts are made to hide the complexity in an intuitive interface.

3.1.1.1 Camera Projections and Conventions

Nagging questions in interactive graphic applications include:

◆   who owns the camera(s)?

◆   who brought the camera(s)?

◆   who is holding the camera(s)?

◆   and how many cameras are there?

In designing *JOEY,* we removed the burden of camera control from the application. We also provided a reasonable default operation (with the opportunity for the application to customise to suit particular application needs). We adopted these conventions for *JOEY*:

◆   Each *JOEY* view brings a camera that it owns and controls. The view is like a professional photographer with a lot of camera gear. You (the application) can tell the view which projections and move paradigms it should have available to the user (using `CJoeyView::CameraMask`). The user normally directs the view as to which projection and move paradigm to use and how to locate and setup the camera through the user interface.

◆   You (the application) can ask the view which camera settings are currently being used (using `CJoeyView::CurrentCamera`).

◆   You (the application) can tell the view which projection and move paradigm to use and how to locate and set up the camera (using `CJoeyView::CameraType` and `CJoeyView::CurrentCamera`).

◆   The 3D data (document) can save as many camera settings as the application deems appropriate. The document never owns a camera, it just owns the settings, and can always request that the view use a particular camera with a particular setting.

♦ The *JOEY* 3D data must always have access to the camera settings for a preferred view. This is the OLE camera provided by the `CJoeyRenderEnv`, an instance of which is owned by every *JOEY* document class. The OLE camera is normally updated (automatically) to the last active camera (default *JOEY* operation), or set by the application (using `CJoeyRenderEnv::OleCamera`).

♦ The *JOEY* `OleServerItem` owns one camera that it uses when satisfying OLE draw requests. It requests settings for this camera from the *JOEY* document's rendering environment.

We show this graphically in Figure I-51. The *JOEY* view owns the camera communication with `IRenderDevX`. The view maintains a current setting, and a default setting. The view has a dataspace default position that can be derived for the camera based on the current dataspace. With the exception of initialisation and establishment of camera availability, it is almost always the application user who is in control of the projection, move paradigm, location and settings for the current and default cameras.

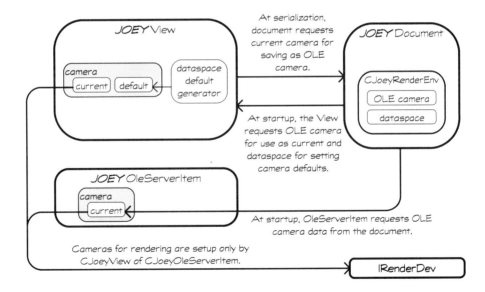

Figure I-51: Default camera operation in *JOEY*

The *JOEY* document maintains the dataspace size, the setting for a default OLE camera, the axis map and size for drawing in a 2D container. The OLE camera information is updated during the document `Serialize` operation by reading the current camera from the currently active view, or the first view associated with the document if none of the views is active. When a *JOEY* view is first created and associated with a document, the *JOEY* default implementation sets the camera for the view to the OLE camera. This is also the case when an application is an OLE server and the *JOEY* Ole server item is responsible for orchestrating the draw.

In order for this to make sense, we examine 2D applications. A 2D graphic is normally thought of as having a top and left boundaries, and some size that determines the right and bottom boundaries. The up orientation is implicit in the creation of the graphic. This defines a preferred view of the graphic. When the graphic is embedded in a container, there is a dialogue in which the container asks the server what the size of the graphic is and requests a drawing of the graphic. The standard operation of a container allows sizing and positioning the graphic. The graphic is treated as a unit in the container. While it can be sized to fit a rectangular hole in a container, there is generally no control that lets you position, scale, and crop the graphic relative to the hole in the container.

Three dimensional data is quite different. It is often difficult to distinguish top from bottom, or front from back. Thus there is no preferred view for the data. We could arbitrarily assign a preferred view, but we consider it to be an absolute necessity to be able to specify a preferred view independent of the 2D rectangle where the view is embedded in the container. This is particularly important when the data is viewed in applications other than the one that creates and edits the data.

Let's look at where the problem arises. Consider 3D data, an OLE Server application that creates and edits the data, an OLE Container that uses the data, and an OLE Viewer that works with application independent 3D data. A good example are the ASCII 3D data files, **.a3d*, with the OLE server sample application, *viewit3d*. MS Word or the MS Visual C++ tutorial *contain* are good examples of container applications. The *JOEY* viewer supplied with this text is a good example of a viewer for application independent 3D data.

When data is embedded, the server performs the serializations that transfer the data from the server data storage (either disk or memory) into the container storage (which may be either disk or memory). When the server draws the data, it is either responding through the MFC `OleServerItem` to a request for a drawing (usually into a metafile), or has been activated, and is drawing to the window directly. Most of the mechanics are hidden in MFC and in the OLE default server.

In the case of the ASCII *.a3d* 3D data files, the data is simply 3D geometry. The *viewit3d* application makes the (rather arbitrary) decision to accept the default orthographic "look at" camera provided by the render environment. In the absence of any view information associated with the 3D data, the embedded view in the container will **always** be a "look at" camera initialised to a front view (you can test this by deleting the call to the *JOEY* document serialize within the `CObjDoc::Serialize` function in the *viewit3d* sample). It is particularly distressing to the user to find that although the view can be changed in the activated application, this change will not be reflected in the embedded graphic in the container document. This is why *JOEY* needs to keep the render environment as a part of the application document database.

The application can bypass *JOEY*, and save and restore camera information in any way it desires. *JOEY* provides this default implementation for ease in prototyping a well integrated 3D interactive application with minimal developer effort.

3.1.1.2 World Axis System and Axis Mapping

Axis mapping has been included in *JOEY* because it is inevitable that the default axis conventions for your data will not match those used by *JOEY*. Many applications use only a single axis system for data because they do not build assemblies of objects. Examples include finite element analysis and mathematical simulations of physical phenomena. In these cases, the axis map would normally be set in the constructor for the application's document class.

In addition to the axis map for the world axis system, new axis maps can be specified for any part of the drawing. This sounds like an unnecessary complication but this facility helps when 3D objects from a wide variety of applications are being collected into assemblies. You will probably use only the axis mapping for the world axis system in your applications and you would probably never expose it directly to the user in a dialogue.

3.1.1.3 Object Axis Systems and Transformations

As noted in the previous section, your application is likely to have only one axis system (which is also the axis system for your data). If you are assembling a collection of objects or repeating an object in multiple positions, the transformation stack becomes very important.

You may ask why we use a transformation stack instead of simply having the application get the current transformation before it changes the transformation and then restoring the current transformation when finished. Saving and storing is the method that we are familiar with when we change cursors or other states in most Windows programming. There are several reasons that we used stacks.

In addition to transforming points from object to world coordinates, the current transformation also defines the transformations for vectors and surface normals to and from world coordinates. These additional transformations are derived as needed and cached with the current point transformation on the stack. Therefore, saving and restoring the current transformation would result in re-computation of the related data. The second and more important reason for using the stack is that there may be many objects that you call upon to draw themselves. Some of these objects may not be completely under your control. To protect yourself from bad behaviour that could damage your rendering state, you need to save the rendering state before you ask an object to draw itself and restore the state when the object is done drawing itself. The stack facilitates the implementation of this in the `IRenderDevX::StateLock` and `IRenderDevX::StateRestore` functions. In the example in **Practice**, we observe that there are two transformations being pushed and two transformations being popped during the document `OnDraw function,` Figure I-53.

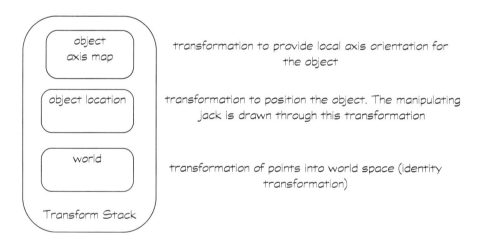

Figure I-53: Transformation stack when object is being drawn in *viewit3d*.

We try adding a second positioning jack for the object within the object axis system. The transformation associated with this jack is concatenated to the "object axis map" transformation and the jack is drawn with the object. To get a better feeling for axis mapping, you can draw the object to world space before the push of the first transformation for the object location. This highlights the differences between changing the object axis map and the world axis map.

One thing you may question about the example is that the *viewit3d* document contains and draws the positioning jack while it clearly a user interface element. This is something that violates the separation of data from user interface. The example was written this way for simplicity. Ideally, the view would own and draw these user interface elements.

Separating the drawing of the interface from the drawing of the document can be accomplished by over-riding the `CJoeyView::OnDrawInterface` function. Drawing is completely orchestrated by either the *JOEY* view or the *JOEY* OLE server item; both prepare the render device and then ask the document to draw itself. In the case of a *JOEY* view, the `OnDrawInterface` function is also called. This provides an opportunity to separate drawing the document from drawing the interface, and to display view specific interface elements.

3.1.2 Rendering

The last thing that the world needs is yet another rendering API. In spite of this, we created another one. We would like to believe that there are some unique features about this API which make it a good idea.

Rendering has been implemented through an `IRenderDevX` component object interface. The key reasons for this implementation are:

♦ To support for a collection of output devices through a common interface.

♦ To provide a "renderer neutral" high level interface so that the application does not need to worry about the specifics of different renderers or low level bit picking.

♦ To provide a "render independent" interface so that applications can take advantage of new rendering technologies simply by using the component object driving that particular technology.

♦ To provide an interface that allows 3D container applications to adequately protect and isolate themselves from the actions of 3D server applications.

Each of these reasons in isolation is significant. Taken together, they build an overwhelming case in favour of a single component object interface used by the application to access rendering services. The practical reasons for choosing this approach are:

♦   it is unclear which rendering technology is best suited for application needs

♦   it is unknown which rendering technologies will be available on the platform that your users are using

Currently, OpenGL is supported as a part of Windows NT. There is no rendering solution included with Windows 95 at the time that this book is going to press. While OpenGL is a good general rendering technology, it is missing the high end realism offered by ray tracing and radiosity, has speed penalties for low end use and is a rather low level rendering interface.[55]

There are some differences between 2D and 3D rendering that must be considered in creating a rendering strategy or Windows integrated applications. Consider the possible output from Windows GDI calls:

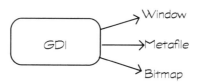

The window is a collection of pixels on the screen that have been set to different colour values. The Bitmap is simply a copy of those pixels (with some additional information for mapping the colours of the pixel onto different devices). The Metafile is the most interesting because it captures the GDI calls so that they can be re-played to a different window. If mapping modes have been correctly set, it is possible to map the metafile into a window of any size and resolution and get the highest quality output.

When we move to 3D, additional possibilities are created. 3D images are normally rendered to a pixel grid. There are really no GDI elements in play other than bitmaps (unless hidden surface removal is not being used in rendering).

---

[55] We do not mean to downplay the significance of OpenGL. The GL libraries have been a model for many other graphics systems. The OpenGL implementation does make this functionality widely available through a common interface. But, OpenGL is clearly not the solution to all rendering problems.

The metafile has been reduced to a bitmap. Because there is more information to support device independence, the metafile bitmaps are easier to use in specifying the desired size and resolution. There is an obvious 3D counterpart to the metafile that is missing.

We have added a 3D metafile with a viewer for using the metafile. Similarly to the GDI metafile, the 3D metafile captures the stream of rendering calls to the rendering interface (in this case, IRenderDevX instead of GDI). Unlike the GDI metafile, the playback is not so direct. A part of the 3D metafile is geometry. Another part is renderer configuration, camera information, etc. In one sense, the 3D metafile contains the data to allow examination and presentation of the 3D geometry. It also contains information about the structure of the geometry making it possible to easily edit the graphic presentation of the data without altering the geometry.

The IRenderDevX interface is a first cut at an application interface to the renderer. The goal in specifying this interface was to allow the most complete specification of rendering data possible so that very realistic images could be created while still allowing for degradation to the best level supported by the renderer. This may be somewhat alarming because there is no assurance that a renderer supporting this interface will create the imagery that you request. All you can expect is for the rendering system to do the best that it knows how to do and to gracefully ignore things it cannot handle.

The philosophy behind the IRenderDevX interface is to provide a high level interface to rendering which minimises the pain and frustration for the application developer. An important aspect of the high level interface is that it provides a structure for the 3D metafile that promotes using the 3D viewer for manipulating the 2D view of the 3D data.

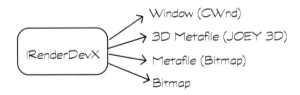

JOEY keeps separate CLSIDs for the implementations of IRenderDevX to be used for CWnd, CDC (Metafile), CArchive (3D Metafile) and Bitmap devices. The CLSIDs of the default implementation that *JOEY* uses for these devices are kept in the system registry under HKEY_CLASSES_ROOT\Joey\IRenderDevX with the sub-keys CWnd, CDC, CArchive and Bitmap. The default implementation of IRenderDevX supplied with *JOEY* maps to OpenGL for the CWnd, CDC, and Bitmap devices. *JOEY* provides the implementation of the 3D Metafile (CArchive) IRenderDevX.[56]

Although implementations of IRenderDevX that *JOEY* will use by default are set in the system registry, it is possible to use other IRenderDevX implementations in an application. It is extremely poor etiquette to change the system registry of IRenderDevX interfaces that *JOEY* uses just to suit your application - DON'T DO IT! When an application starts, it can use the CJoeyConfig::RenderDevClsid function to set application specific renderers for the different devices on an application wide basis or CJoeyView::RenderDev to set IRenderDevX interfaces on a view specific basis.

The IRenderDevX interface is modeled after rendering APIs targeted towards z-buffer or pipeline graphics systems. The implications are that very little data is cached in the renderer, and all the information required for rendering a piece of geometry must be specified before the geometry is drawn through the interface. This has some peculiar ramifications for lights since the lighting must be fully specified before geometry is processed.

A stack model is used for transformations, materials, and lighting. These are considered to be the rendering state. At any time, there is one object-to-world transformation, one material and a lighting state that the geometry is being passed through for rendering. The stack model makes it easily possible to save and restore rendering states during the rendering process. In an object oriented environment, this makes it easier to protect against damaging actions in a poorly implemented object which is changing the state as it draws itself.

We were also concerned about limiting the breadth of the interface. There are very few interface functions but they are generally working with large parcels of information. There are material, light, camera and geometry classes that support conditioning a large body of data so that actions like setting a material can be accomplished with a single render device function.

We have discussed why there is a IRenderDevX interface and what the goals were in defining the interface. Now, we look more closely at the interface and examine how to use it.

JOEY starts a render device object by first looking up the CLSID of the render device for the physical device that the rendering is targeted to, then uses the

---

[56] We are trying to stay current with available rendering technology. Consult the *readme.txt* file on the disk supplied with this text for the latest updates on rendering systems that can be used with *JOEY*.

OLE CoCreateInstance function to have the object started and get a pointer to the IRenderDevX interface.

Once you have a pointer to the interface, it is necessary to attach a physical device to the render device. The only IRenderDevX functionality that can be accessed prior to attaching a render device is retrieving attributes and capabilities of the render device using the IRenderDevX::DeviceCaps and IRenderDevX::RendererCaps. These will return the device capabilities (the physical devices this render device will attach to) and the renderer capabilities (the rendering styles that the device supports).

The *JOEY* view gets a CWnd rendering device during the creation of the *JOEY* view window in the CJoeyView::OnCreate function. It immediately attaches the rendering device to its window using IRenderDevX::Attach, and sets the renderer type to the default renderer type for the view using IRenderDevX::RendererType. This render device is held by the *JOEY* view until the destruction of its window. The window is released during processing of the WM_DESTROY message.

The *JOEY* view keeps the render device properly sized by resetting the window placement during processing of the WM_SIZE message. and maintains the renderer type in response to application calls to CJoeyView::RendererType.

The IRenderDevX interface update cycle is divided into some very distinct phases, Figure I-53. The update cycle is the re-displaying of an image. The first phase of the cycle is render device initialisation. During this phase the frame is normally set to the background colour, the Z-buffer cleared and the camera is set. The second phase of the update cycle is a draw cycle. During the draw cycle the device cannot be cleared and the camera cannot be set. There may be multiple draw cycles with camera and placement resets between them (this allows drawing multiple views into a single window). The last pass of the update cycle is telling the render device that the update is complete so that any cached information is flushed to the physical device that is attached to the render device.

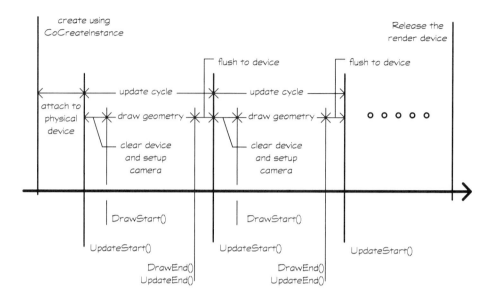

Figure I-53: The life cycle of a render device as used by `CJoeyView`.

The *JOEY* view takes care of the render device update cycle. It prepares the background and camera, and starts the draw cycle. During the first part of the draw cycle, the `CJoeyView::OnDrawInterface` function is called to fill in interface graphics from the view. This is followed by a call to the document `OnDraw` function so that the document data can be drawn. The following code sample includes the `OnDraw` and `OnDrawInterface` functions from `CJoeyView`. This gives you a better idea of how the steps described above are implemented and provides a starting place for creating your own application view handling of `OnDraw` if there are specific needs that are not addressed by the `CJoeyView` implementation of `OnDraw`.

```
void CJoeyView::OnDraw(CDC* pDC)
{
    CJoeyRenderEnv*        pRE = NULL;
    ULONG   ulUpdateKey, ulDrawKey;
    // get a pointer to the render environment
    if (JOEY_OLE_DOC == m_usDocType) pRE = JOEYOLEDOC->RE();
    else pRE = JOEYDOC->RE();
    // make sure there is a renderer device (otherwise we are in setup)
    if ((NULL != m_pRD) && (m_pRD->IsAttached())) {
        if (FAILED(m_pRD->UpdateStart(ulUpdateKey,1,1,0))) return;
        // draw the background
        m_pRD->Clear(*Background());
        // if the render environment is modified, update the camera
        if (m_bCameraModified) {
```

```
                m_pRD->Camera(m_camCurrent,pRE->AxisMap());
                m_bCameraModified = FALSE;
            }

            // start the draw
            if (SUCCEEDED(m_pRD->DrawStart(ulDrawKey))) {
                CJoeyMaterial const*        pMtlDef;
                pMtlDef = pRE->MtlGetLocal(JOEY_RE_MTL_DEFAULT);
                m_pRD->MaterialSet(pMtlDef);
                // draw the interface
                OnDrawInterface(m_pRD);
                // load the default material
                m_pRD->MaterialSet(pMtlDef);
                pMtlDef->Release();
                switch (m_usDocType) {
                    case JOEY_DOC:
                        JOEYDOC->OnDraw(m_pRD,this);
                        break;
                    case JOEY_OLE_DOC:
                        JOEYOLEDOC->OnDraw(m_pRD,this);
                        break;
                }
                // unload the default material
                // end the draw
                m_pRD->DrawEnd(ulDrawKey);
            }
            m_pRD->UpdateEnd(ulUpdateKey);
        }
    }

    void CJoeyView::OnDrawInterface(PIRenderDevX pRD) const
    {
        CJoeyRenderEnv*         pRE = NULL;
        // get a pointer to the render environment
        if (JOEY_OLE_DOC == m_usDocType) pRE = JOEYOLEDOC->RE();
        else pRE = JOEYDOC->RE();
        // draw the grids and axis
        _JoeyDrawGrid(pRD,pRE,m_camCurrent,&m_grid);
        // load the default material - the grid draw does not trash
        //  the current material or transforms, things are in a default
        //  state ready for the application draw.
        return;
    }
```

The *JOEY* view creates other rendering devices for *JOEY* 3D metafiles, 2D metafiles, or bitmaps as needed and releases them immediately after the operation that required their use (Copy Special... or Save Special...) is complete.

The IRenderDevX interface includes support for lines (of infinite extent), half-lines (of infinite extent), grids (of infinite extent), polylines, polygons, triangle strips, quad meshes, and the procedural geometry element CJoeyRenderGeom. CJoeyRenderGeom is a procedural interface to an object that the render device requests to draw itself. During this request, the render device provides the current clipping frustum and other transformed camera information so that the object can perform smart clipping against the view frustum or adaptive level-of-detail based upon the viewing conditions. When the physical render device is a *JOEY* 3D metafile, the CJoeyRenderGeom object is asked to draw itself at it's most complex level of detail. Conspicuously absent from the CJoeyRenderGeom class is support for application sub-classing in a fashion that supports serializing the object into the *JOEY* 3D metafile so that the original object can be used in viewing the *JOEY* 3D metafile if it is available on the system on which the *JOEY* 3D metafile is being viewed.

Objects which encapsulate data for the render device can be easily sub-classed because IRenderDevX queries the class to obtain the information required to draw the entity. This provides a simple mechanism for introducing new classes of objects which can be rendered.

The IRenderDevX functions that you will be using are primarily those for manipulating the transformation stack, manipulation the material stack, manipulating the light stack, and drawing geometric objects. Briefly, these functions are:

Transformation Stack

IRenderDevX::XfmPushDataDef
    Push a definition for subsequent data. The definition consists of the axis map, the face orientation (whether vertices were specified in clockwise or counter-clockwise order when looking from the outside), and whether back facing faces can be culled. A transformation is pushed onto the stack and the axis map transformation is concatenated with it. This becomes the current transformation.

IRenderDevX::XfmPush
    Push a copy of the current transformation onto the stack. This becomes the current transformation.

IRenderDevX::XfmPop
    Pop a transformation that is at the top of the stack.

IRenderDevX::XfmConcat
    Concatenate a transformation to the transformation at the top of the stack.

IRenderDevX::XfmSet
    Set the value of the transformation on the top of the stack. The transformation on the top of the stack is the current transformation. This should be used with extreme caution because you lose the camera

positioning and world axis map transformations when set the current transformation.

Material Stack

`IRenderDevX::MaterialPush`
  Push a copy of the current material on the top of the material stack, and optionally set its properties. This becomes the current material.

`IRenderDevX::MaterialPop`
  Pop the material that is at the top of the material stack.

`IRenderDevX::MaterialSet`
  Set the properties of the current material.

Light Stack

`IRenderDevX::LightPush`
  Push a copy of the current lighting state onto the lighting stack.

`IRenderDevX::LightPop`
  Pop a lighting state from the lighting stack.

`IRenderDevX::LightSet`
  Set the properties of a named light in the current lighting state.

`IRenderDevX::LightRemove`
  Remove a named light from the current lighting state.

Drawing/Rendering Functions

`IRenderDevX::Draw3dPoint`
  Draw an array of points.

`IRenderDevX::Draw3dLine`
  Draw an array of infinite length lines.

`IRenderDevX::Draw3dHalfline`
  Draw an array of infinite length half-lines.

`IRenderDevX::Draw3dGrid`
  Draw a grid object.

`IRenderDevX::Draw3dPolyline`
  Draw a polyline specified by an array of vertices.

`IRenderDevX::Draw3dPolygon`

Draw a polygon specified by an array of vertices.

`IRenderDevX::Draw3dTristrip`

Draw a polygon triangle strip specified by an array of vertices.

`IRenderDevX::Draw3dMesh`

Draw a polygon mesh specified by an array of vertices.

`IRenderDevX::Draw3dGeom`

Draw an object by requesting the object draw itself and providing the viewing frustum, and other viewing information transformed into object coordinates.

If you use a rendering device outside the context of those set up by *JOEY*, you will need to perform your own setup and initialisation.

Initialisation and Configuration Functions

`IRenderDevX::DeviceCaps`

Get a list of the physical devices supported by this render device interface.

`IRenderDevX::RendererCaps`

Get a list of the rendering capabilities of this rendering device. This includes the hidden surface method, illumination method, and illumination model evaluation method. See **Theory** section 3.1.2 for a discussion of rendering methods.

`IRenderDevX::DeviceSpecifics`

Get device specific information about the rendering device. You can use this to get direct access to the OpenGL rendering context, an ADI 3D rendering context and rendition, or other renderer specific information. This allows you to bypass the `IRenderDevX` interface once the rendering device has been setup (not a recommended practice).

`IRenderDevX::Attach`

Attach the render device to a physical device.

`IRenderDevX::IsAttached`

Query the render device to discover whether it is currently attached to a physical device.

`IRenderDevX::RendererType`

Set the renderer type. This includes the hidden surface method, illumination method, and illumination model evaluation method. See **Theory** section 3.1.2 for a discussion of rendering methods.

`IRenderDevX::Placement`
Set the placement of the rendering window on the physical device.

`IRenderDevX::UpdateStart`
Start an update cycle. No drawing operations or manipulation of transform, light, or material stacks is permitted if the render device is not currently in an update cycle.

`IRenderDevX::UpdateEnd`
End an update cycle and flush all data to the physical device to which the render device is attached.

`IRenderDevX::Clear`
Clear the rendering window to a specified colour. Reset the Z-buffer of this is a Z-buffer rendering device. This can only occur after `UpdateStart()` and outside draw block.

`IRenderDevX::Camera`
Set the camera and axis map. This can only occur after `UpdateStart()` and outside a draw block.

`IRenderDevX::DrawStart`
Start a draw block. Drawing and stack manipulation functions can only be called inside a draw block.

`IRenderDevX::DrawEnd`
End a draw block.

`IRenderDevX::FlagStart`
Insert a flag indicating the start of a named block of data. This is only meaningful for output to a *JOEY* 3D metafile and is used to give the viewer hints about the structure of the *JOEY* 3D graphic data.

`IRenderDevX::FlagEnd`
Insert a flag indicating the end of a named block of data. Blocks can be nested, but should not be overlapping.

`IRenderDevX::StateLock`
Lock the state of the transformation, material, and lighting stack. Flags to this function indicate what operations can and cannot be performed between the time the state is locked and the time the state is unlocked with the a call to `StateRestore()`.

`IRenderDevX::StateRestore`
  Restore the transformation, material, and lighting stack to the state they were in when the lock was set.

Refer to the *JOEY* programmer's documentation for more details on each function.

3.1.3 Materials

Materials are challenging because we want the `IRenderDevX` interface to support realistic and physically based renderers (ray tracing and radiosity) in addition to the high speed interactive renderers that must be supported for interactive applications.

In most graphics systems, materials are specified through a large collection of functions with diminutive effects. If you want to switch between two completely different materials, it could require ten or fifteen different function calls. If a material is going to be used for different rendering styles, the programmer is required to include logic to interpret the application material database and call the appropriate material functions to load the material.

JOEY simplifies the specification of materials by encapsulating a material in a `CJoeyMaterial` object. This simplifies the interface to the graphics, reducing the render device interface to `MaterialPush`, `MaterialPop` and `MaterialSet`. The `MaterialPush` and `MaterialPop` functions save and restore the material state for rendering. The `MaterialSet` function sets a new material state. The `CJoeyMaterial` object is responsible for answering queries made within the `IRenderDevX` interface in order to map material properties into those required by the specific renderer being supported. The `CJoeyMaterial` object is responsible for serializing itself and providing a user dialogue for editing the material properties.

The `CJoeyMaterial` is really an interface for querying properties of a surface, serialization, and starting a dialogue for editing the properties. The properties consist of a material name, scalar values and colour values. The value properties provide a functional interface for evaluation at a point on the object surface, `CJoeyColorSpec`, and `CJoeyScalarSpec` for specification of colours and scalars respectively.

JOEY defines the sub-classes of `CJoeyColorSpec` and `CJoeyScalarSpec` to specify constant value, textured value, and composite values. Procedural textures are created by sub-classing the `CJoeyColorSpec` and `CJoeyScalarSpec` classes. One required member function of both

`CJoeyColorSpec` and `CJoeyScalarSpec` is providing a best fit constant value for either a colour or scalar value. In the *JOEY* Toolkit, only constant colours or scalars are supported in editing a `CJoeyMaterial` and in the `IRenderDevX` interface.

The functional specification of colour and scalar properties supports extremely complex definitions of these properties which support the most sophisticated rendering available. Dropping back to best approximation constants will support the vast majority of interactive rendering solutions. Where there is a need to consider units, or the specification of physical properties is sufficiently different from properties used in interactive renderers, separate properties are provided.

We have moved away from specification of line and material point properties in pixel width or diameter to specification in point size (a printer's point is 1/72 of an inch) for device independence (particularly when used for Windows integrated graphics). Printer devices support up to 2,000 dpi resolution. A one pixel wide line is only .0005 inches wide on such a device. In order for printed graphics to be representative of screen graphics, line, point, and text sizes must be specified in absolute size units. We have elected to use standard printing units (points) because the printed medium is most commonly used for recording and distributing graphic information.

The `CJoeyMaterial` interface allows the application to set material properties. We recommend that properties be set only at initalisation or creation, and that further manipulation of properties be left to the user. The editing dialogue should provide the access that users need for specifying materials that they want to see in the image. If it does not, the problem should be corrected by adjusting the editing dialogue.

The material database facilities associated with the render environment maintain a list of named materials and provide serialization, programmatic access and user editing services. Render environments can be linked together to provide material inheritance from other objects. Every document has a unique render environment. In an MDI application, these can be linked to an application render environment and all material queries can be directed there for resolution before the local document render environments are searched. This allows changes to the application render environment material database to be reflected in all objects.

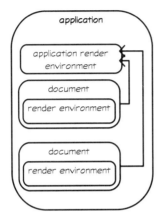

links from document render
environments to the application render
environment allow material sharing,
material inheritance and material
substitution.

Figure I-54: Render environment linking provides inheritance and/or substitution.

Conspicuously missing from the `CJoeyMaterial` class is support for application sub-classing of a material and the use of component object access to the material editing dialogue. With the *JOEY* Toolkit, you can sub-class and replace the material editing dialogue with your own. However, when the render environment is serialized, only the `CJoeyMaterial` will be serialized and the `CJoeyMaterial` dialogue will be associated with the material. If you override the `CJoeyMaterial::Serialize` function, the viewer will not be able to function with the information that your objects have put into the *JOEY* 3D metafile.

Treating materials as component objects is an obvious necessity for the development of applications that integrate well with the rest of the Windows environment.

Functions for manipulating materials are documented in the `CJoeyMaterial` section of the programmer's documentation. There should be no real need to programmatically interact with a `CJoeyMaterial`.

Material Functions

`CJoeyMaterial::Dialogue`
    Provides an editing dialogue for a material.

`CJoeyRenderEnv::MaterialNew`
    Creates a material in the render environment material database.

`CJoeyRenderEnv::MaterialDelete`
Deletes a material from the render environment material database.

`CJoeyRenderEnv::RenameMaterial`
Renames a material in the render environment material database.

`CJoeyRenderEnv::GetMaterial`
Gets a handle to a material in the render envirnoment material database.

`CJoeyRenderEnv::MaterialSet`
Set the properties of a material in the render environment material library.

`CJoeyRenderEnv::MaterialNext`
Get a handle to the next material in the rennder environment database. This is used for iterating through the materials in the database.

`CJoeyRenderEnv::MaterialDialogue`
Provides access to the dialogue for individual materials.

3.1.4 Lights

Lights also pose a problem because the physical properties of a light are significantly different from those used in most interactive renderers. *JOEY* simplifies the specification of light by encapsulating a light in a `CJoeyLight` object. This simplifies the interface to graphics (reducing the render device interface to `LightPush`, `LightPop`, `LightSet`, and `LightRemove` functions. The `LightPush` and `LightPop` functions save and restore the light state. `LightSet` either resets parameters for the light of the same name, or adds a light of this name. `LightRemove` removes the light of this name.

The render device maintains a list of lights that have been set. all lights in this list provide light for every geometric entity drawn until the light state is changed by a `LightSet`, `LightRemove` or `LightPop` function call. This is why lights require both a set and a remove function in the render device interface.

Like `CJoeyMaterial`, `CJoeyLight` is really an interface for querying properties of the light, serialization, and starting a dialogue for editing the properties. The properties consist of a material name, scalar values and colour values. The value properties use a functional interface for evaluating the pseudo-intensity (for interactive renderers) or the energy flux reaching a surface (for physically based renderers).

The implementations of lights in interactive rendering systems usually include a collection of procedural or functionally based lights. The `CJoeyLight` class includes properties common to light in interactive rendering so that the light types internal to a specific interactive renderer can be used where possible.

As with materials, the specification of scalar and colour properties provides for functional evaluation given a specific surface location in space. The functional specification of colour and scalar properties supports complex definitions of light properties which can, in turn, support the most sophisticated rendering available.

The `CJoeyLight` interface allows the application to set light properties. We recommend that properties be set only at initalisation or creation, and that further manipulation of properties be left to the user. The editing dialogue should provide the access that users need for specifying lights that they want to have in the scene. If it does not, the problem should be corrected by adjusting the editing dialogue.

The light database facilities associated with the render environment maintain a list of named lights and provide serialization, programmatic access and user editing services. Render environments can be linked together to provide light inheritance from other scenes. Every document has a unique render environment. In an MDI application, these can be linked to an application render environment and all light queries can be directed there before the local document render environments are searched. This allows changes to the application render environment light database to be reflected in all objects.

Conspicuously missing from the `CJoeyLight` class is support for application sub-classing and the use of component object access to the light editing dialogue. With the *JOEY* Toolkit, you can sub-class and replace the light editing dialogue with your own. However, when the render environment is serialized, only the `CJoeyLight` will be serialized and the `CJoeyLight` dialogue will be associated with the material. If you override the `CJoeyLight::Serialize` function, the viewer will not be able to function with the information that your objects have put into the *JOEY* 3D metafile.

Treating lights as component objects is an obvious necessity for the development of applications that integrate well with the rest of the Windows environment.

Functions for manipulating lights are documented in the `CJoeyLight` section of the programmer's documentation. There should be no real need to programmatically interact with a `CJoeyLight`.

Light Functions

`CJoeyLight::Dialogue`
　　Provides an editing dialogue for a light.

`CJoeyRenderEnv::LightNew`
　　Creates a light in the render environment light database.

`CJoeyRenderEnv::LightDelete`
　　Deletes a light from the render environment light database.

`CJoeyRenderEnv::RenameLight`
　　Renames a light in the render environment light database.

`CJoeyRenderEnv::GetLight`
　　Gets a handle to a light in the render environment light database.

`CJoeyRenderEnv::LightSet`
　　Set the properties of a light in the render environment light library.

`CJoeyRenderEnv::LightNext`
　　Get a handle to the next light in the render environment database. This is used for iterating through the lights in the database.

`CJoeyRenderEnv::LightDialogue`
　　Provides access to the dialogue for individual lights.

3.2 Graphic Representations of Data

There is very little done in *JOEY* that has anything to do with how you present data; data presentation is the responsibility of the application. The *JOEY* Toolkit is conspicuously absent of annotation in the form of both textual elements and markers or icons. These need to be addressed by the graphics development environment in a way that integrates well with other Windows applications. Font sizes and styles must be specified in absolute units such as points. Fonts present a unique problem that is usually renderer specific. The render device must make the appropriate translations to the underlying renderer.

Markers must also be specified in absolute units so that they respond reasonably to different resolution display devices and when images are integrated into 2D container applications.

Encapsulating both text and markers in classes that are passed to the render device, in a similar way that grids are passed to the render device for drawing, is the best way to provide this service. These classes also provide serialization and dialogue editing services so they can easily integrate into the rendering environment database.

3.3 Manipulating Data

Practice introduced a collection of techniques for manipulating data. **Implementation** fills out this discussion by introducing aspects of *JOEY* that were not revealed in the examples in **Practice**.

3.3.1 Direct, Indirect, Immediate, and Delayed Interaction

Throughout the implementation of *JOEY*, we maintained a bias that direct manipulation methods are vital in editing and examining 3D data. We also believe that data and interactions should be exposed to the user in the simplest form possible, exposing more detail, or alternate representation only when the user requests it.

Update rates slower than about five frames per second seem to be difficult to control and objectionable.[57] We don't think of them as being interactive. The elements of interaction that *JOEY* focuses on are:

♦ Immediate feedback: The user needs to know an action was initiated immediately after initialisation regardless of the update rate. During the action, the connection between the cursor movement and the display of graphic feedback must be as closely coupled as possible. When the action terminates, the user must know that it has terminated.

♦ Controlled interaction: An interaction is not useful if it does not achieve the desired result. Constraints are an important part of making interaction controlled.

♦ Maintaining focus: All *JOEY* interaction can occur through the mouse. There is never a need to re-focus attention on another device.

---

[57] This varies greatly across applications and users.

♦ Range of interaction methods: All *JOEY* interactions can be accomplished in a variety of ways.

This list is a bit misleading. The only element of the interaction that *JOEY* actually controls is camera manipulation so these interaction goals may not be met by a *JOEY* application. These goals have, however, been met by *JOEY*, and the tools to promote these goals have been made available to the application developer.

3.3.2 *JOEY* Camera Interaction

Projections and the move paradigms for cameras in *JOEY* were discussed in detail in **Practice**, Section 3.1.1.1, while an overview for screen and dialogue based interaction with the camera was discussed in **Practice**, Section 3.3.2. We have not yet discussed why we chose to implement the camera in this way and what is happening in *JOEY* to coordinate the camera interactions. Camera interaction, as implemented in *JOEY*, does achieve the goals set forth earlier in Section 3.1, and can be used as a model for other interactions.

There is a fundamental difference between *JOEY* views and MFC views for positioning the data relative to the window displayed on the screen. The MFC CScrollView provides the standard positioning scroll bars at the bottom and right edges of the view. The scroll tabs provide both absolute and relative control and good visual feedback about position. Why did we use something different for *JOEY*?

To understand the answer, we need to review some of the differences between viewing 2D and 3D data. The scroll bar concept is based on a flat bounded surface of text and drawings. The size of the surface may grow, but this is usually only in length (by pushing the bottom limit), or in width (by pushing the right side). More of the data can be seen by changing the size of the window, changing the size of the font, scaling, or a combination of all three. Changing the window size is a quick interactive operation. Changing the font or zoom factor is often a trial and error process until a combination can be found that works. Because paper is usually the output medium, there is normally a size (or approximate size of a page) known early in the creation of the document.

Printed materials are usually placed at a constant distance (e.g., arm's length) and at a fixed orientation (few people read upside down!). Try approaching someone with a memo or letter and ask them to look at it. They will generally hold it right side up and at about arm's length. Their response will be similar if the printed material is an image.

Three dimensional objects are manipulated in much less consistent ways. Try approaching someone with an object and ask them to look at it. Most people will view the object from different orientations and distances. These are major considerations when providing good 3D manipulation tools.

Viewing in 2D generally requires only three pieces of information; x position, y position and zoom factor. Viewing in 3D requires six pieces of information to establish location and orientation along with an additional 3 to 6 pieces of information to define the camera used to look at the data. Finally, objects are not fixed in space the way that this text is fixed to a page.

Scrollbars are clearly not the answer for 3D view control, but scroll bars do provide some insight on the required elements of 3D view control. The scroll bar is not moded; you can access it at anytime. It is very simple, the results are predictable, and there are a variety of ways to interact with it, Figure I-55.

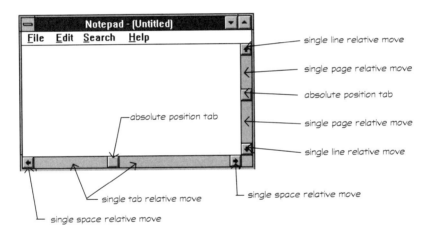

Figure I-55: Absolute and relative modeless scrollbar view control in MS Notepad.[58]

Direct manipulation of an object by pointing and dragging in the window provides the most natural interaction and minimises the use of screen real estate for view control.

Unfortunately, the large number of viewing parameters required to specify a view make it difficult (if not impossible) to provide full control of viewing using a single mouse button without some moded operation.

---

[58] Notepad is a Microsoft accessory shipped with Windows and Windows NT.

The default *JOEY* camera control is the middle mouse button. It was chosen to provide camera positioning without adding a second layer of moded operation.

The axis aligned views are consistent with drawings of objects in machining and illustration, and are common to most users. The constraints imposed by axis alignment remove all of the orientation degrees of freedom and reduce the variables to translation of the centre of view, zoom, and projection parameters. A high degree of control and predictability is provided by these views. Viewing paradigms that allow freedom for both positioning and orientation as well as projection parameters are more interesting. The difficulty is making the interaction controllable and predictable. Translation is always constrained to move the picked translation centre parallel to the plane of the screen. Rotation is a more difficult problem. Many objects have a bottom surface or, as a result of gravity, they rest on some surface. This leads to two distinct manipulations, rotate and orbit, that maintain the notion of a ground plane. Orbit allows two degrees of rotational freedom, but maintains the up direction. Rotate allows rotation only around the vertical axis, so that the elevation angle above the ground plane stays constant. Rotational limits are set so that the object cannot be flipped upside down.

The non-interactive modes for centre, zoom out, and zoom in provide the fastest position specification since there are no intermediate updates of the image during the move.

Other features needed to make camera manipulation useful are:

Absolute and Relative control   Absolute control is good for an individual user, but is very hard to follow for an observer. Relative control is generally more understandable during presentation and examination.

Left mouse button control   Many people do not have a three button mouse or are uncomfortable with the middle button. A necessary feature of the left button mouse control is a cursor that reminds the user that camera mode is on. Programmatic access to enable or disable left button mouse control of the camera is also vital.

Cursor feedback of mode during positioning

It is not uncommon to forget which move mode is active. Unique cursors for each move type provide immediate feedback before you have moved the view.

Camera reset

It is easy to get disoriented when manipulating 3D objects. It is also easy to send them off screen with relative move modes. The camera reset provides immediate return of the object to a recognised reference view.

One feature that was not exercised in *viewit3d* is terminating the camera left button control mode when there is a strong indication that the user is preparing to do something other than position the camera. This can be easily added to the position vertex mode set in the message handler for the IDM_POSITION_VERTEX message. In the IDM_POSITION_VERTEX handler of CObjView in *objview.cpp*, check to see if the left button camera move mode is active. If it is, send an IDM_CAM_LEFT_MOUSE message to the view.

```
       void CObjView::OnPositionVertex()
       {
           if (m_bVertPosn) {
               m_bVertPosn = FALSE;
               Cursor(NULL);
           } else {
→              if (IsCamLeft())
→                  SendMessage(WM_COMMAND,IDM_CAM_LEFT_MOUSE);
               m_bVertPosn = TRUE;
               Cursor(m_cursVertPick);
           }
       }
```

When automatically terminating left mouse button camera move, you need to decide which action (on the part of the user) signifies that the user intends to do something else, and whether the active view is the only one that should be affected. In the above example, only the active view is affected.

Functions that are specifically related to camera interaction are:

```
CJoeyDoc::OnCameraPending
CJoeyOleServerDoc::OnCameraPending
```
    Notification that the camera for a view is about to change. The notification

includes the pointer to the view causing the change and the context in which the change occurred. This notification is sent immediately before the camera for a view of the document changes. Override this function if your document needs to save camera information before the change.

`CJoeyDoc::OnCameraChanged`
`CJoeyOleServerDoc::OnCameraChanged`
Notification that the camera for a view has changed. The notification includes the pointer to the view causing the change and the context in which the change occurred. This notification is sent immediately after the camera for a view of the document has been changed and before the view is updated. The view that sends this notification will be updated by *JOEY*. Override this function if other views need to be updated in response to the change (as in a four-view when view positions are coupled).[59]

`CJoeyView::OnCameraPending`
Notification to the view that the camera is about to change. The notification includes the context in which the camera changed. This notification is sent immediately before the camera is changed. Override this function if you need to save camera information before the change. The default implementation on `OnCameraPending` notifies the document that the camera is about to change by calling the document `OnCameraPending` notification.

`CJoeyView::OnCameraChanged`
Notification to the view that the camera has changed. This notification includes the context in which the camera was changed. This notification is sent immediately after the camera has changed and before the view is updated. Override this function if you want to control the update of the view. The default implementation updates the OLE camera in the render environment, notifies the document of the change, and then updates the view. Use extreme care if you override this function because you can really mess up *JOEY* if you don't know what you are doing.

`CJoeyView::Dialogue`
Starts and editing dialogue for a single camera.

`CJoeyView::IsCamLeft`

---

[59] See Figures P-17 and P-18.

Query the *JOEY* view for the state of the left mouse tracking button on the camera toolbar. If this function returns a TRUE, all left button mouse up, down, or double-click functions should be sent to the corresponding `CJoeyView` middle mouse button handlers.

`CJoeyView::IsCamTracking`
Query the *JOEY* view about mouse tracking. If this function returns TRUE, *JOEY* is tracking the mouse for a camera move and all of the mouse move messages should be sent to the *JOEY* mouse move message handler.

3.3.3 Dialogue Interaction

Practice discusses the dialogue implementation for the positioning jacks and most of the important points in the implementation of the *JOEY* dialogues. *JOEY* editing dialogues can be used by the application whenever required. We recommend using the *JOEY* dialogues and classes without application specific sub-classing because of the implication of embedding you sub-classes in documents which the *JOEY* Viewer will try to read.

JOEY dialogues that your application can use are accessed through the following functions:

`CJoeyConfig::UpdateDialogue`
Dialogue for establishing update rate targets for performance sensitive interaction.

`CJoeyRenderEnv::LightDialogue`
Dialogue for editing the light database of the render environment. This dialogue provides minor editing services, but primarily allows selection of a light and starting its editing dialogue using `CJoeyLight::Dialogue`.

`CJoeyRenderEnv::MaterialDialogue`
Dialogue for editing the material database of the render environment. This dialogue provides minor editing services, but primarily allows selection of a material and starting its editing dialogue using `CJoeyMaterial::Dialogue`.

`CJoeyRenderEnv::GridDialogue`
Dialogue for editing the grid database of the render environment. This dialogue provides minor editing services, but primarily allows selection of a grid and starting its editing dialogue using `CJoeyGrid::Dialogue`.

`CJoeyRenderEnv::CameraDialogue`
> Dialogue for editing the camera database of the render environment. This dialogue provides minor editing services, but primarily allows selection of a camera and starting its editing dialogue using `JoeyCamera::Dialogue`.

`CJoeyCamera::Dialogue`
> Dialogue used for editing a camera. It is the dialogue used by `CJoeyRenderEnv::CameraDialogue` once a camera has been selected for editing.

`CJoeyGrid::Dialogue`
> Dialogue for editing an orthographic grid. It is the dialogue used by `CJoeyRenderEnv::GridDialogue` and the one used in response to the grid dialogue button on the camera toolbar.

`CJoeyLight::Dialogue`
> Dialogue for editing a light. It is used to edit the selected light by `CJoeyRenderEnv::LightDialogue`.

`CJoeyMaterial::Dialogue`
> Dialogue for editing a material. It is used to edit a selected material by `CJoeyRenderEnv::MaterialDialogue`.

Copy Special... dialogue
> This special dialogue is started by sending an `IDM_EDIT_COPY_SPECIAL` command message to a *JOEY* view.

Save Special... dialogue
> This special dialogue is started by sending an `IDM_FILE_SAVE_SPECIAL` command message to a *JOEY* view.

3.3.4 Grab and Drag

The operations that occur during a grab and drag interaction were shown in **Practice**, Figure P-20. The example demonstrated how to cut out unnecessary and time consuming computation that occurs during an update cycle due to unnecessary change notifications. We now take this discussion of reducing update cycle time a step further.

Developers often focus on optimising small, low level parts of an application to improve performance. Our experience has shown that it is seldom possible to identify a specific routine or area of a program that is a computational bottleneck. It is often more fruitful to algorithmically improve how a problem is addressed from a higher level. *JOEY* provides several tools to aid the developer in doing this.

The example in Practice uses hints generated during the interaction to prevent unnecessary drawing updates in the container. There are other areas to focus attention:

♦   Reducing the amount of information drawn at each update.

♦   Reducing the amount of data that is sent to the rendering device.

When the camera is changed, all of the data in the frame must be re-drawn (since its position on the screen has changed). When we manipulate a single data element, the changes may be localised to that element.[60] Can we limit the drawing to just that element? If so, how do we implement it?

One way to do this is to create a background that contains everything except the object being changed. The render device "clear" at the beginning of a frame update would load the pre-computed environment and then the object being moved would be drawn into the z-buffer. Unfortunately, the IRenderDevX interface does not provide the tools to copy the z-buffer to a temporary location and load it as a background, so this is not an option in *JOEY*.

Another commonly used method is to draw the object which is being manipulated in XOR mode over a static image. The original position can be retained in the image for reference. This could be implemented by using an XOR render device for drawing the data which is being manipulated. An XOR render device would reduce everything to lines only, clip and transform to screen coordinates and use GDI calls to draw in XOR mode. This is a good solution to the problem of reducing drawing time. *JOEY* does not currently include an XOR rendering device.[61]

It is also possible to project the bounding volume of the changed item onto the screen and reduce the size of the rendering window and the camera target plane to update only the affected area. Unfortunately, all of the information in the

---

[60] If we consider geometric position only, changes are probably local. When we consider objects that interact with each other, the appearance of other objects (such as lights), is not as simple to decide whether local changes will be sufficient.

[61] But this could be an excellent opportunity for a graduate graphics class!

affected area must be re-drawn. This probably means that you need to send the entire database to the render device.

If your database is large, culling out unseen portions of the database is a good way to reduce the information sent to the graphics system. The `CJoeyRenderGeom` object provides an opportunity to test visibility and size of the rendered object on the screen so that you can skip objects that are not visible and use reduced level-of-detail on objects whose screen projection is very small. When the `CJoeyRenderGeom` is queried by the render device to get the primitives for rendering, it is given a transformed camera so that the eye point, target plane, viewing frustum and other camera parameters are available in object coordinates.

Using `CJoeyRenderGeom` derived objects for communicating data to the renderer provides an opportunity to greatly reduce the data sent for rendering.

A last optimisation is moving from sending data in small data primitives such as polygons to larger aggregate primitives such as triangle strips or meshes. This prevents redundant transfer of data, transformation, colour computation, and setup for scan conversion.

3.3.5 Enhanced Feedback

JOEY provides tools to enhance feedback by simplifying cursor control and providing consistent formatting with other data.

The tools provided by *JOEY* which help with feedback are:

`CJoeyView::Cursor`
> Get/Set the cursor that is used for application action in a view. Use this function to keep the cursor for the view synchronised with the activity that is being performed in the view and to show initiation and completion of an action.

`CJoeyDoc::LinearIn`
`CJoeyOleServerDoc::LinearIn`
> Get/Set the function used for converting input strings to linear data values.

`CJoeyDoc::LinearOut`
`CJoeyOleServerDoc::LinearOut`
> Get/Set the function used for formatting linear data values to output

strings.

```
CJoeyDoc:LinearKeypad
CJoeyOleServerDoc::LinearKeypad
```
Get/Set the function used for linear data keypad entry.

```
CAngle operator TCHAR*
```
Formats an angle string with dimensional units as described in the *JOEY* configuration.

```
CJoeyConfig::AngleType
```
Get/Set the default style for formatting angular dimensions.

```
CJoeyConfig::AnglePlaces
```
Get/Set the default number of places beyond the decimal point used in formatting angular dimensions.

```
CJoeyConfig:FloatPlaces
```
Get/Set the default number of places beyond the decimal point used in linear dimension formatting.

3.3.6 Hit Testing

JOEY provides a collection of services to aid in hit testing. Most of these services centre on `CJoeyMouse`. The current view and camera work together to map the screen location of the cursor into mouse information describing the cursor position in device coordinates, normalised screen coordinates, world coordinates, and a hit frustum in world coordinates, Figure P-23.

In the corresponding section of **Practice**, we used the services provided by the mouse for hit testing points. `CJoeyMouse` will also hit test lines, half-lines, grids, min-max volumes, polylines, and polygons.

A brief summary of functions that control the preparation of `CJoeyMouse` is provided below:

```
CJoeyView::PrepareMouse
CJoeyView::DCtoNormalized
```
Maps the `CJoeyView` window into normalised 2D coordinates from (-1,-1) at the lower left to (1,1) at the upper right of the window. This function is useful for the implementation of screen potentiometres for relative manipulations. The mapping can be linear (`DC_TO_LINEAR`), quadratic

(DC_TO_QUADRATIC) or cubic (DC_TO_CUBIC) for linear, quadratic, or cubic variation across the face of the window. Quadratic and cubic mapping provide greater sensitivity at centre screen while preserving the same values at the edge of the window as linear mapping, Figure I-56.

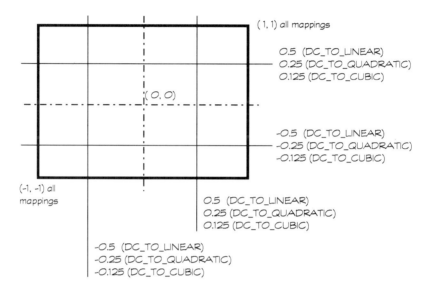

Figure I-56: Linear, quadratic, and cubic mapping of the *JOEY* view window.

CJoeyMouse::BackXfm

Back transforms the mouse position through an axis map, transformation or transformation stack. The axis map, transform or transform stack is mapping from the current object coordinates to world coordinates or to an intermediate coordinate system. The back transformation of the mouse transforms from the world or intermediate coordinates into the current object coordinates.

A brief summary of the hit test functions provided by CJoeyMouse is provided below. The hit tolerance is important in hit testing some geometric elements while others perform hit testing using the cursor vector only.

CJoeyMouse::HitPoint

Tests a point against the hit frustum and returns TRUE if the point lies within the hit frustum. It also returns the distance from the eye point to the point tested. The mouse must be prepared to the MOUSE_WORLD_TOL level so that a hit frustum is available.

The HitPoint function computes the distance from the test point to each of the planes of the hit frustum. A positive distance for any of the planes indicates that the point is outside of the hit frustum.

CJoeyMouse::HitLine

Tests a line against the hit frustum and returns TRUE if the line passes through the hit frustum. It also returns the closest point on the line to the cursor vector and the distance from the eye point to the closest point on the test line. The mouse must be prepared to the MOUSE_WORLD_TOL level so that a hit frustum is available.

The HitLine function computes the distance from the point in the definition of the line to the intersection of the line with the plane. Relying on a property of convex polyhedra (which is what a hit frustum is) if the greatest distance at which the line enters a plane from the frustum is closer than the least distance at which the line leaves a plane of the frustum, then the line passes through the frustum, Figure I-57.

CJoeyMouse::HitHalfline

Tests a half line against the hit function and returns a TRUE if the line passes through or originates in the hit frustum. It also returns the closest point on the half line to the cursor vector and the distance from the eye point to the closest point on the test half line. The mouse must be prepared to the MOUSE_WORLD_TOL level so that a hit frustum is available.

The HitHalfLine function uses the same test as the HitLine function and also tests to make sure that the intersection occurs in the correct half of the line.

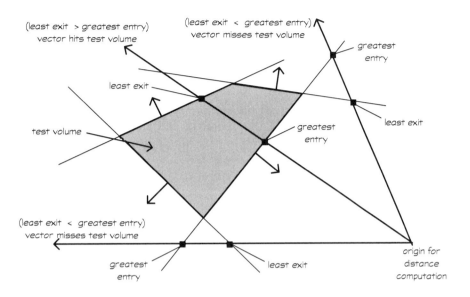

(least exit > greatest entry) vector hits test volume

(least exit < greatest entry) vector misses test volume

greatest entry

least exit

least exit

test volume

greatest entry

(least exit < greatest entry) vector misses test volume

greatest entry

least exit

origin for distance computation

Figure I-57: Intersection test for a vector and a convex polyhedra.

`CJoeyMouse::HitGrid`

Tests the grid against the cursor vector and returns TRUE if there is a lock onto the grid. The attributes of the grid determine the tests that are performed. The results of the test are returned in the `CJoeyGridLock` structure. See Section 3.3.7 for details. The mouse must be prepared to the `MOUSE_WORLD` level so that a cursor vector is available.

The `HitGrid` function defers to the `CJoeyGrid::Hit` function for hit testing the cursor vector against the grid.

`CJoeyMouse::HitMinMax`

Tests a min-max box against the cursor vector and returns TRUE if the min-max box is hit or if the hither point is within the min-max box. The distance to the min-max box is also returned. If the distance is negative, the hither plane point is within the volume. The mouse must be prepared to the `MOUSE_WORLD` level so that a cursor vector is available.

The HitMinMax function creates the 6 planes defining the faces of the min-max box and then uses a test similar to that used in HitLine to test the cursor vector against the bounding volume.

CJoeyMouse::HitPolygon

Tests a polygon against the cursor vector and returns TRUE if the polygon was hit. To improve the speed of the test, the plane equation of the polygon and the closest hit to date can be set as arguments to this function. If the polygon is hit, the distance to the hit and the point of the hit are returned. The mouse must be prepared to the MOUSE_WORLD level so that a cursor vector is available.

The HitPolygon function first intersects the cursor vector with the plane of the polygon to check the distance and confirm that the polygon is a possible hit candidate. The vertices of the polygon are projected onto the plane perpendicular to the cursor vector and the half-line hit test, Figure I-58, is employed to determine whether the intersection point of the cursor vector and the plane of the polygon is within the polygon.

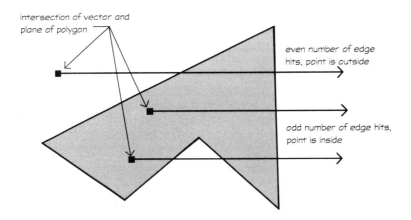

Figure I-58: Polygon-point in-out test using edge intersections on a horizontal half-line.

3.3.7 Grids and Grid Hit Testing

JOEY defines a gridset, CJoeyGrid, as a collection of gridplanes and a gridplane, CJoeyGridPlane, as a collection of gridline sets, CJoeyLine. The only gridline set implemented in the *JOEY* Toolkit is a parallel gridline set. An orthographic gridplane is created by two sets of parallel gridlines at 90° to each other. The orthographic 3D grid used in *viewit3d* is a collection of three gridplanes, one for each of the principle planes, Figure I-59.

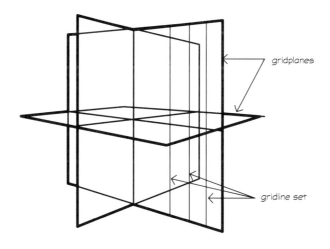

Figure I-59: CJoeyGrid: set of gridplanes containing gridline sets.

Each gridline set is a set of 2D parallel lines. The angular orientation, major spacing, and minor increments define the gridline set, Figure I-60.

Each gridplane is a 2D plane in X and Y (Z=0). Each gridplane has a transformation that positions it relative to the gridset. A gridplane can be bounded by minimum and maximum values in X and Y, Figure I-61. Each gridplane also maintains lock attributes for locking on both gridlines and angle stops.

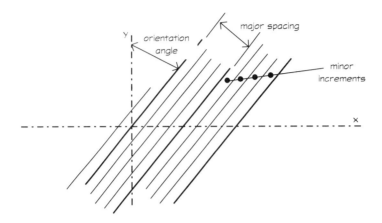

Figure I-60: Definition of a parallel gridline set.

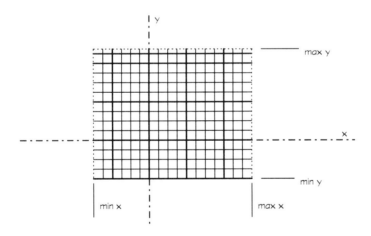

Figure I-61: Definition of the bounds of gridline sets in a grid plane.

You can sub-class `CJoeyGrid` for your application, but the *JOEY* Toolkit does not provide support for using your sub-classed grids in the *JOEY* Viewer. When sub-classing grids, we recommend that you use the grid database, serialization, and hit testing provided by `CJoeyGrid` and modify only the dialogue.

Grid hit testing first checks the gridplanes in a gridset against a test line and finds the closest hit gridplane with hit attributes set. The gridplane is then tested to determine the proximity of the test line intersection point with the gridplane to any of the lock regions. If the point is in a lock region, the lock point is the closest point on the line defining that lock region. If the point falls within two or more lock regions, the lock point is on the closest intersection of lines defining the hit lock regions. If the closest intersection is outside of the lock tolerance, the lock point is on the closest line defining the lock region, Figure I-62.

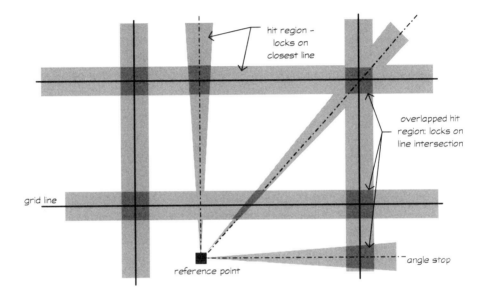

Figure I-62: Hit regions and hit processing for a grid plane.

There are a number of functions for grid definition that are documented in the *JOEY* programmer's documentation for CJoeyGrid, CJoeyGridPlane, and CJoeyGridLine that will not be enumerated here. Important functions for general use of grids in an application are:

CJoeyGrid::Dialogue
    See Section 3.3.3.

`CJoeyGrid::Hit`
> Hit tests a vector against the grid and returns TRUE if the grid was hit and fills in a `CJoeyGridLock` structure defining the grid hit.

`IRenderDevX::Draw3dGrid`
> See Section 3.1.3.

`CJoeyDoc::OnGridChanged`
`CJoeyOleServerDoc::OnGridChanged`
> Notification that the document grid (saved in the render environment) has changed. The grid in the render environment is slaved to the grid for the currently active view of the document. Override this function if grids in other views need to be updated to the grid current view grid.

`CJoeyView:OnGridChanged`
> Notification to the view that the view grid has changed for the view. The default sets the OLE grid in the render environment to the new grid configuration and notifies the document that the grid has changed.

`CJoeyView:Grid`
> Get/Set the grid for a view.

`CJoeyRenderEnv::OleGrid`
> Get/Set the grid that will be used when the document is embedded or linked in a container application.

3.3.8 Saving State

The *JOEY* configuration is saved and restored using the `CJoeyConfig::Save` and `CJoeyConfig::Restore` functions as described in **Practice**. It is up to the application to decide what and how to save and restore other application state information.

3.4 Performance Sensitive Interaction

Practice provided a comprehensive look at the problem of performance sensitivity in the implementation of performance sensitive interaction in your applications. Performance sensitive response is largely the responsibility of the application. In early *JOEY* implementations, we attempted to give *JOEY* more responsibility for providing performance sensitive interaction by automatically simplifying drawing primitives before they reached the render device. Our conclusion was that *JOEY* could not possibly infer what was important about the geometric information and why.

The application, therefore, has the burden of providing the simplified graphics, and *JOEY* can realistically only provide feedback to help in selecting the most appropriate level of detail.

The functions provided by *JOEY* to aid the application in providing performance sensitive interaction:

`CJoeyConfig::UpdateTarget`
   Get/Set update target rates for interactive operations.

`CJoeyConfig::TimeUpdateCycle`
   Time an update cycle, compare this time against the update targets and return a status indicating performance was slower than, faster than, or within the target range.

`CJoeyView::RendererType`
   Get/Set the renderer type. This is used when the render type is part of the control of level-of-detail in performance sensitive rendering.

`CJoeyView::FlushMouseEvents`
   This function flushes the event queue of all mouse functions except the last one in the queue. If there is no last function in the event queue, a duplicate of the last mouse event processed is loaded into the queue. This function is used at the end of an interactive update cycle to assure that there is not extraneous mouse information in the queue, that graphic changes always track the most recent mouse event, and that update cycles don't suffer time lags because there are no mouse messages in the queue.

`CJoeyRenderEnv::RendererType`
   Get/Set the default OLE renderer type for the document to which this render environment is attached.

`CJoeyDoc::OnCameraPending`
`CJoeyOleServerDoc::OnCameraPending`
`CJoeyView::OnCameraPending`
`CJoeyDoc::OnCameraChanged`
`CJoeyOleServerDoc::OnCameraChanged`
`CJoeyView::OnCameraChanged`
   See Section 3.3.2.

4. Extending *JOEY*

It would be a challenge, the magnitude of which is beyond the scope of this text, to include the extensibility we believe is necessary for application development in the *JOEY* Toolkit. The full power of the component object architecture available on Windows can only be realised when the service classes such as the render environment, cameras, grids, light, materials, etc., in addition to the render device, are implemented as component objects. Ideally, these elements of *JOEY* could be replaced fully by application specific component objects, or by favourite component objects of the user.

The degree to which the component object architecture could be exploited by *JOEY* has become apparent to us as a result of the exercises that we went through to build *JOEY* and write a practical guide to getting to the heart of creating interactive 3D applications on windows. The 3D Viewer exposes the extensibility quandary to the greatest extent. Quite simply, if the application developer sub-classes a *JOEY* service class, how does this get serialized into the *JOEY* 3D metafile? and how does the *JOEY* 3D Viewer get one of these special objects to deal with its data in the *JOEY* 3D metafile? The extensions discussed in this section are largely unimplemented, hence the discussion is brief, and is more a critique of shortcomings in the *JOEY* toolkit and thoughts about how they can be corrected.

4.1 Dimensioning

JOEY provides many dialogues for user interaction with *JOEY* objects. Many of these dialogues present linear, and angular dimensions. By default, *JOEY* presents dimensionless values for linear dimensions. *JOEY* includes full dimensioning of angular dimensions for both input and output.

While it is possible for *JOEY* to make some decisions about dimensioning, linear dimensions pose a problem; it is not possible to make any reasonable assumptions about the unit range for an application. As noted in **Practice**, the native unit for an application is application specific and related to the problem that the application is addressing.

Within *JOEY*, any displayed linear information is processed through input and output routines that can be replaced by the application. The replacement of these routines for dimensioning within an application was fully discussed in **Practice**, but what happens in the *JOEY* 3D metafile?

Dimensioning in the *JOEY* 3D metafile and *JOEY* Viewer are not addressed in the *JOEY* Toolkit. Obviously, when a *JOEY* 3D metafile is embedded in a document, the user would like to have linear data presented with an indication of the units used (whenever the Viewer is activated to edit the view). An implementation that could support this would include a dimension component object that provides formatting services and serialization. During the loading of the *JOEY* 3D metafile, the viewer would attempt to get an interface to the dimensioning object. If is was available, any dialogues in the *JOEY* Viewer would reflect the dimensioning of the application that created the *JOEY* 3D metafile data. If the dimensioning object is not available, the default dimensionless presentation would be used.

4.2 Adding Render Devices

A rather sparse render device template has been provided in the *JOEY* Toolkit. It includes little more than the component object framework for a render device. There is another collection of tools used in implementing a render device such as the OpenGL render device. Most of these tools come from the *JOEY* .dll however, there is a body of functionality common to all render devices that is not exposed in the *JOEY* Toolkit.

Since IRenderDevX is not in its final form in the *JOEY* Toolkit, it has not been packaged with libraries used to build the OpenGL, ADI 3D, and *JOEY* 3D Metafile render devices. If you are writing a render device, you probably have enough familiarity with graphics and the specific renderer that you are interfacing with that additional tools would be of limited value. A tip for implementing innfinite length lines, half-lines, and grids: the camera generates a view frustum that can be used for clipping lines, half-lines, and gridplanes. This produces line segments for the underlying renderer.

To make use of the camera frustum, it should be obtained in the IRenderDevX::Camera function (as queries are made for all other camera information so that the camera matrix can be created). The camera frustum must be back transformed through the stack into object coordinates, or lines forward transformed into world coordinates, before clipping can be performed.

4.3 Creating a *JOEY* Extension *.dll*

Practice discusses how to create a *JOEY* extension *.dll.*

It may be important to extend the service classes of cameras, grids, lights, materials, etc. to suit your own application needs. To do this, you can simply sub-class the *JOEY* classes that implement these functions. When you do create a sub-class, it is assumed that you are using the database provided by the *JOEY* class. Most likely, you are revising the dialogue so that presentation of the user interface to the class is more consistent with your application.

This strategy for sub-classing is very limited primarily because these classes are constrained to using the base class database, and because the classes cannot be used in the *JOEY* Viewer. Another limitation is the inability to augment the capability of the class or interface to the class using a favourite component object implementation. **Theory** discusses how these *JOEY* classes could be structured to take advantage of the component object architecture to allow for greater freedom in creating sub-classes of some of the basic *JOEY* service classes.

4.4 3D OLE Extensions

The *JOEY* Toolkit implements no 3D OLE extensions. This should not be taken to suggest that 3D OLE extensions are unimportant. The intricacies of specifying the inter-object relationships required to support embedding 3D object in 3D containers are beyond the scope of this text.

Table of Contents: Theory

Figures

1. A Framework for Interactive 3D Applications

Computer Graphics has been described as "a glorified form of mathematical archeology".[62] The history of interactive computer graphics is very short relative to that of mathematics and it is best left to well known texts on the subject (Foley 1990) (Newman 1979). In this text, we describe how we have used principles described in these archeological graphics explorations to implement *JOEY*. The discussion is brief, conversational, and full of pointers to other references.

Before we focus specifically on 3D graphic theory and techniques, we need to take a small step back and examine why we are using a computer to solve 3D problems. There must be a significant advantage to using the computer if we expect users to choose our applications in lieu of traditional techniques and methods.

A primary goal of an application is to utilise the power of the computer to help a user solve a problem more efficiently and more accurately than would otherwise be possible. This is a rather brash statement, but we believe it expresses the basis for a successful application, particularly in Windows.[63] The current move away from a focus on applications (the tools) to a focus on data (the essence or expression of the problem/solution) supports this statement. We consider the application structure as an expression of the activity of problem solving.

In *Pictorial Conversation: Design Considerations for Interactive Graphical Media,* (Myers 1986) pictorially and entertainingly discusses the interaction between designer and the product of design, or, in the context of the previous paragraph, between the user and the data. We attempt to summarise some of the key concepts that relate to building interactive applications.

First, the designer needs to create a product, or, in the general case, a user needs to solve a problem, Figure T-63.

---

[62] We believe that this description was given by Ken Shoemake during a SIGGRAPH 1985 tutorial entitled Image Rendering Tricks.

[63] An obvious exception is in games where the purpose is entertainment, but even so, the more efficiently and accurately the user can manipulate the elements of the game, the more satisfying the game will probably be.

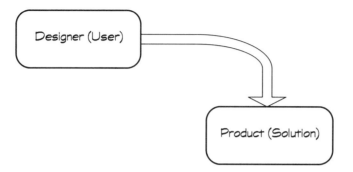

Figure T-63: The basic task is for the designer (user) to create a product (solution).

An intermediate representation, usually drawings and models, is used to explore design possibilities and to substitute for the physical product that will result from the design process.[64] In the general case, the user creates some data that represents the problem. This representation is the data from which the design is built, Figure T-64.

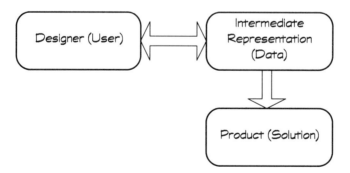

Figure T-64: Designer (users) interaction with an intermediate representation (data) to explore possible solutions.

The intermediate representation is vital because it is the means for recording thoughts and ideas, and for exploring the vast realm of possible solutions to a problem. It also helps the designer to organise ideas and communicate with

---

[64] In architectural design, representation is often talked of as re-presentation of ideas; presenting the idea again to reveal and examine relationships and other considerations that were not apparent when the idea was originally conceived.

others. Most problem solving tasks require an iterative process of representing ideas, interpreting and evaluating the representation, revising the ideas, and representing these new ideas. For an application to be successful, it needs to augment and/or replace traditional media used in this problem solving process.

The insertion of computers into this iterative process creates additional layers of representation and interpretation, Figure T-65.

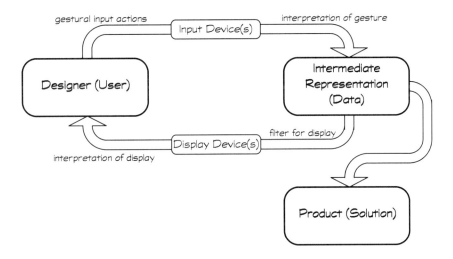

Figure T-65: The dialogue between the designer (user) and the intermediate representation (data) becomes indirect as the application adds layers of interpretation and filtering.

Unfortunately, these additional layers can impede the problem solving process. In the words of (McKim 1972): "*... not all visualisation materials are well-suited to exploring and recording ideas. Materials that involve the visualiser in difficult techniques, for instance, will absorb energy and divert attention away from thinking. Time-consuming techniques also impede rapid ideation, since ideas frequently come more quickly than they can be recorded. Frustration with an unwieldy material can block a train of thought or be reflected directly in diminished quality of thinking.*" Our task is to make sure that the computer is a visualisation medium that is well suited for exploring and presenting ideas. Or, more specifically, that using a computer helps in solving a problem rather than becoming a barrier in solving the problem.

Myers describes traditional media as being a direct experience, while computers provide an indirect experience. With traditional media, the representations are directly manipulated by the user and these representations can be used (as the user requires) in order to capture an idea (e.g., the line a pencil makes on a paper is under direct control and can be used for sketches, layouts, final presentation, annotation or whatever else works to capture the idea). In the case of the computer application, there is a representation internal to the application that must be used by the user. The idea must be turned into gestures that are translated into the representation internal to the application, and then translated again into a display representation that captures the intent of the gesture, Figure T-65. In most cases, this experience is made even more indirect by the physical separation between the input devices and the graphical display.

1.1 Creating a Framework with MFC AppWizard

MFC provides a succinct structure for isolating the manipulation of the intermediate representation (manipulating the database) from the interpretation of the gestures invoking the data manipulation and the display of the results of the manipulation. Specifically, the application takes on a structure that encapsulates, but maintains the separation between the intermediate representation and the input and output functions. The intermediate representation is the handled by the document, and the input and output functions are handled by the view, Figure T-66. MFC then wraps the document and the view in a utility layer that maintains application integration with the look and feel of the Windows operating systems and other Windows applications.[65]

---

[65] The utility layer maintains a look and feel specific to, and changing with, the version of the Windows operating system (i.e. Windows 95, or Windows NT). Also, it provides the appropriate configuration and startup services for stand-alone, OLE in-place activation, or OLE automation activation.

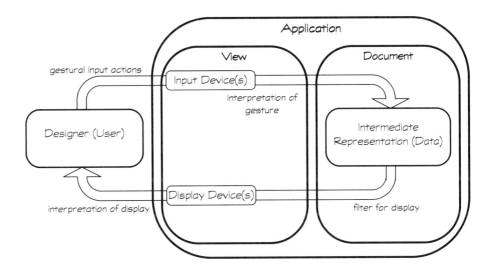

Figure T-66: Encapsulation and separation of the user interface and intermediate representation by the view and document.

The evolution from monolithic application to applications showing a definite split between data manipulation and user interface happened as techniques for structured programming and data encapsulation were evolving (Rupel 1983), (Goldberg et al. 1976), (Hartson 1989). The split provides a way to encapsulate data manipulation so that it can be integrated into a range of different interfaces or applications.

Another force in formalising the split between data manipulation and user interface was the migration of user interfaces from textual terminal interfaces to graphic window interfaces. The lack of a common operating systems and window systems meant that the implementation of the user interface was platform dependent. A more serious problem was that differences in event handling and communication within the window system often required a completely different structure of the user interface for each supported platform. By rigidly enforcing the split between application data functionality and user interface, it is possible to isolate the interface problems.

The practice of writing interactive graphic programs has evolved from an amorphous form where the boundaries between graphics, interface, and application data were not defined, to a form that has a well defined structure using MFC. This structure acknowledges that the look and feel of the operating system is a moving target, and that the results of a data manipulation are independent of how the manipulation is invoked or how the results of the manipulation are displayed.

1.2 Adding the *JOEY* 3D Graphic User Interface to the Framework

JOEY affects all aspects of the final application including the document (data), the view (user interface) and the graphics for creating the image displayed in the view. You may wonder why *JOEY* is so far reaching in how it affects the application. It was our intention to limit the scope of changes to the view. Unfortunately, we found it impossible to get complete functionality without also affecting the document and the interface to the graphics subsystem.

Windows integration and ease of application development were the primary concern in defining the scope of *JOEY*. Windows integration requires some common 3D data elements to support OLE data transfer between applications. It requires 3D graphics support for screen windows (CWnd), metafile (CDC) and bitmap (Bitmap) output. Our belief that 3D data transfer and examination are absolute necessities adds the need for 3D graphic support for a serial output (CArchive or 3D Metafile) device.

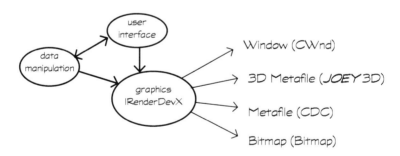

Figure T-67: Integrating 3D graphics with Windows requires 3D metafile support.

JOEY is intended to make writing 3D applications simple. It also insures that these applications can take advantage of new rendering and graphics technologies as they become available. *JOEY* acknowledges that the rendering technologies used to display images are moving targets. The IRenderDevX rendering interface is the 3D analogy to the 2D CDC device context. It hides the user from the mapping of the rendering operations into the specific devices. The IRenderDevX interface goes a step further. The renderer for each device (Window, metafile, bitmap or 3D metafile) is loaded as a component object and can be easily changed.

This structure has two positive side effects. The application is renderer independent (there is no direct interface to a specific graphics subsystem) and new graphics technologies will have an installed application base for which they can serve as accelerators or enhanced renderers.

1.2.1 Including *JOEY* and Graphics

Configuration information or services common to all windows in an application is maintained by CJoeyConfig.

The CJoeyConfig class should be thought of as a part of the application class derived from CWinApp. There is one in existence for each running instance of the application. It provides information common to every document and view within the application.

1.2.2 Adding the Camera Toolbar

Applications can often be divided into functionally distinct modes of operation. This makes it reasonable to have separate toolbars to service these distinct functions.[66] For some applications, it may not make sense to have more than one toolbar. Careful planning of user interaction will determine whether this is the case.

The *JOEY* camera toolbar commands can be easily integrated into a single application toolbar. To do this, copy the bitmaps for *JOEY* camera buttons from the bitmap for the *JOEY* camera toolbar *(include\joey\cam_tbar.bmp)* into your application toolbar bitmap at the desired location. Add the corresponding *JOEY* command to the application toolbar initialisation table in the application frame implementation files (usually *mainfrm.cpp* and *ipframe.cpp*). Camera commands should be correspondingly integrated into your application menu.

The exposure of the camera toolbar, menu commands, view cameras, and view handling of camera control provide opportunities for application specific enhancement or alteration of operation. We discourage changes in the camera interaction controlled by the *JOEY* view because this will introduce paradigms unfamiliar to the *JOEY* based application user.

---

[66] Review Visual C++ and MS Word for examples.

1.2.3 Adding Status Bar Camera Feedback

The importance of feedback has already been established. It will be discussed more formally in Section 3.3. Panes on the status bar are only updated during idle time processing, which does not affect the camera feedback.

1.2.4 Revising the View

Every CJoeyView owns a current camera, a default camera, and a render device that renders to CWnd. In normal operation, the CJoeyView is initialised to use the document camera as both the current camera and default camera, and to use a hidden surface renderer. These are all initialised during the default processing of the WM_CREATE message. Ownership of the render device allows the *JOEY* view to keep the size and aspect ratio of the device synchronised with the window sizing.

In the sample application, we have not added an application message handler for the OnCreate function which processes WM_CREATE. If you do provide application processing of the OnCreate message, it is important for this message handler to call the CJoeyView::OnCreate message handler for correct setup of the CJoeyView. Any additional initialisation performed by your message processor should happen after the CJoeyView handling of the message.

Since the render device is accessed through a component object interface, the reference count for the render device is incremented when the CJoeyView creates the render device. You can replace the render device CJoeyView by using the RenderDev member function, and CJoeyView will release the current IRenderDevX before the replacement. If you supply a pointer to an address to receive the current render device, CJoeyView will add a reference before passing it to you. It is now your responsibility to release it or give it back to CJoeyView at a later date. When you give CJoeyView a new render device, it will add its own reference. You should release your reference once the render device has been given to CJoeyView.

The *JOEY* view orchestrates the copying of special formats to files. During these actions, the view obtains an IRenderDevX for the device representing the special format (*JOEY* 3D metafiles, metafile, bitmap) and initialises it to match the view. It is important that the IRenderDevX initialisation information (in the view) is kept current so that initialisation of rendering devices for special formats matches the currently displayed view. This is also important in assuring correct operation during view re-sizing.

The application should always access the renderer type, camera, axis map, background and placement only through view or document member functions. Direct dialogue with the IRenderDevX interface for this information can damage the connection between the view and the rendering device. The only actions that should be performed by the application in direct dialogue with the render device are drawing actions within the document OnDraw function. If you have other communication with the render device, you are on your own.

The CJoeyView::OnDraw function is a key function in removing the ambiguity of whether the view or the document is responsible for drawing the data. The OnDraw member function performs all of the renderer setup then passes the handle of the rendering device to the view OnDrawInterface and document OnDraw functions for the actual drawing of the document data.

1.2.5 Revising the Document

Every *JOEY* document owns a render environment, CRenderEnv, which is accessible through the RE member function. The render environment contains specific information for viewing the document (a preferred viewing camera, view size, background, grid configuration, etc.). The render environment may also contain graphic database information (materials, cameras, grids, lights, markers, etc.). In many 3D applications, there will be a collection of documents that are connected in 3D assemblies. The render environments of the individual documents can be chained to the assembly document render environment so that data, such as materials, can be inherited from the parent render environment.

The *JOEY* document classes perform important view and render environment setup in the DeleteContents, OnNewDocument, and OnOpenDocument member functions. The code for these functions, along with commentary, is provided in the following code segments. In your application, you may want to override these functions and use their functionality in your processing, or completely replace them with your processing. These code segments are provided to insure that you make sure you don't miss anything. The code segments shown are from CJoeyOleServerDoc Implementation of the CJoeyDoc counterpart is identical.

The DeleteContents handler re-initialises the render environment, which deletes all databases that are part of the render environment and sets the camera, background, axis map, and dataspace to default values:

```
void CJoeyOleServerDoc::DeleteContents()
{
    // call the standard MFC handler
    COleServerDoc::DeleteContents();
    // do some standard setup for a new document (whether it is
    //  a newly created document, or one that is read in -- set
    //  a standard camera with standard update information):
    //      standard render environment setup
```

```
//          view - front orthographic
//          dataspace - 5.0
//          axis map - identity mapping
//          background - white
//       Save current camera as OLE camera by default
//       reset the camera for all views to the OLE camera
//          (this happens as a part of the OnNewDocument
//          or OnOpenDocument so it doesn't need to
//          happen here)
RE()->DeleteContents(FALSE);
m_bSaveCurAsOleCam = TRUE;
}
```

The OnNewDocument member function resets the cameras for all views of the document to the default camera contained in the document render environment:

```
BOOL CJoeyOleServerDoc::OnNewDocument()
{
    //call the standard MFC handler
    if (!COleServerDoc::OnNewDocument())
        return FALSE;

    // set all document views to the ole camera - there is
    // a logic problem here for setting the update flag.
    // The sequence here that does the camera setup DOES
    // NOT affect the document data -- i.e. there are no
    // changes yet. but the aspect ratio correction may
    // throw the changed flag
    POSITION    pos = GetFirstViewPosition();
    CJoeyView* pJVSave = NULL;
    while (pos != NULL) {
        CView* lpView = GetNextView(pos);
        if (lpView->IsKindOf(RUNTIME_CLASS(CJoeyView))) {
            CJoeyView* pJV = (CJoeyView*)lpView;
            float       fAspectCur = pJV->m_camCurrent.Aspect();
            pJV->m_camCurrent = *(RE()->OleCamera());
            if (JOEY_CONSTANT_HEIGHT ==
                    JoeyConfig->CamHoldConstant())
                pJV->m_camCurrent.Width((pJV->m_camCurrent.Width() *
                    pJV->m_camCurrent.Aspect()) / fAspectCur);
            pJV->m_camCurrent.Aspect(fAspectCur);
            pJV->m_camDefault = pJV->m_camCurrent;
            pJV->RendererType(RE()->RendererType());
            pJV->m_grid = *(RE()->OleGrid());
            if ((NULL == pJVSave) ||
                    (pJV == pJV->GetActiveWindow()))
                pJVSave = pJV;
        }
    }
    if (NULL != pJVSave)
        RE()->OleCamera(pJVSave->m_camCurrent);
    // set the modified flag because this camera
```

```
    // reloading may have kicked it
    SetModifiedFlag(FALSE);

    return TRUE;
}
```

The `OnOpenDocument` member function performs essentially the same processing as the `OnNewDocument` member function. It sets the cameras for all views of the document to the render environment camera for the document:

```
BOOL CJoeyOleServerDoc::OnOpenDocument(LPCTSTR lpszPathName)
{
    // call the standard MFC handler
    if (!COleServerDoc::OnOpenDocument(lpszPathName))
        return FALSE;

    // there is a similar problem in to OnNewDocument of
    //  possibly tripping the changed flag. Set it to false
    //  after the view cameras are set
    POSITION   pos = GetFirstViewPosition();
    CJoeyView* pJVSave = NULL;
    while (pos != NULL) {
        CView* lpView = GetNextView(pos);
        if (lpView->IsKindOf(RUNTIME_CLASS(CJoeyView))) {
            CJoeyView* pJV = (CJoeyView*)lpView;
            float      fAspectCur = pJV->m_camCurrent.Aspect();
            pJV->m_camCurrent = *(RE()->OleCamera());
            if (JOEY_CONSTANT_HEIGHT ==
                    JoeyConfig->CamHoldConstant())
                pJV->m_camCurrent.Width((pJV->m_camCurrent.Width() *
                    pJV->m_camCurrent.Aspect()) / fAspectCur);
            pJV->m_camCurrent.Aspect(fAspectCur);
            pJV->m_camDefault = pJV->m_camCurrent;
            pJV->RendererType(RE()->RendererType());
            pJV->m_grid = *(RE()->OleGrid());
            if ((NULL == pJVSave) ||
                    (pJV == pJV->GetActiveWindow()))
                pJVSave = pJV;
        }
    }
    if (NULL != pJVSave)
        RE()->OleCamera(pJVSave->m_camCurrent);
    // set the modified flag because this camera
    // reloading may have kicked it
    SetModifiedFlag(FALSE);

    return TRUE;
}
```

You may wonder why this code is here instead of in **Implementation**. It seemed to flow into this discussion about how an application should be set up to be a predictable application (instead of being part of a discussion about how MFC and *JOEY* work).

The document `OnDraw` function is a key element in the implementation of drawing to windows, drawing to containers, drawing to the clipboard and drawing special file formats. In the future, it could also be used to draw into 3D OLE containers. The document should never attempt any render device setup in the `OnDraw` function (in fact, the setup of the `IRenderDevX` is locked when the document `OnDraw` function is called, precluding any setup operations in the document draw).

No camera actions are allowed inside the `OnDraw` function. The `OnDraw` function should assume that the rendering world is perfectly configured for the draw. Although safeguards are in place in the `IRenderDevX` interface to prevent a poorly implemented `OnDraw` function from affecting other parts of the system, the `OnDraw` function should leave the `IRenderDevX` in the same state it that it was received in (i.e. anything that is pushed should be popped, and nothing that has not been pushed should be popped).

The *JOEY* implementation of the render environment (as part of the document database) and the initialisation of the view windows from the render environment of the document provides a quick solution to a variety of problems that surface during Windows integration, particularly when enabling OLE server capability. We want to stress that our implementation is only one way to handle the problem and may not be appropriate for your application. A typical 3D application will probably have several views of the data. For example, it is common to show three orthographic views and a viewing window that allows any camera or orientation, Figures P-17 and P-18. This means that your application is normally starting four views connected to a single document. Each view has a unique setup.

Although the mechanics (syntax) of communication between an OLE server and container are relatively well defined, the content (semantics) of the communication has been left open. While we normally think of a single view being the content of the embedded graphic, there is nothing in the definition of the OLE mechanism that restricts us to a single view within the embedded graphic. This is discussed further in Section 2.

1.2.6 Revising the OLE Server Item

Dealing with OLE seriously stresses the simple application schematic (as described in **Implementation**). It is one thing to decide whether the document or the view owns and manipulates data inside your application. It becomes another thing completely to make sense of things when a 2D container application is using your application to draw and/or edit a figure in a 2D document.

In this case, we try to put ourselves in the position of the user of the 2D container and try to imagine what this user is trying to accomplish.

Our best guess is that when the user of a container links or embeds server data, they really want a single view. If the user wants multiple views, they will embed or link the data multiple times.

In the linking and embedding model, the container has little information about the server except for the location of the server graphic in the document. A problem arises because we would really like the container to know the camera settings for viewing the 3D server data. Instead, we are forced to keep the camera data with the server data. In addition to camera data, the axis map, ideal size when shown in a container, background colour and other data viewing information is kept in the render environment of the server data. As a result of this structure, *JOEY* is responsible for nearly all of the server-container dialogue for view sizing and drawing.

In Section 2.1, we explore the relationship of OLE to a philosophic scenario of what users want and why they want it. This will help to clarify the comment above.

1.2.7 Adding Context Sensitive Help for *JOEY*

Refer to the MFC documentation for details on how context sensitive help is implemented. The importance of this feature in helping to reduce user confusion and frustration has been well established and requires no further discussion.

1.2.8 Build and Test the Framework

When you observe the operation of the framework, we hope that you will observe that many of the elements of 3D applications are fully operational. They are waiting for the application functionality to be added. In spirit, this is consistent with MFC; you quickly get a reasonable framework in which to build your application. The elements of this framework added by *JOEY* can be easily modified to suit the specific needs of your application.

1.3 Adding Application Read and Draw

Read and draw are completely implemented within the application document. Since there is no data manipulation yet, there is no need to have the view perform any operations that map user actions into data manipulation. The separation of data from user interface is rigidly observed.

1.3.1 Object Data Definition

Structuring 3D data is an interesting problem and a multitude of approaches have been used in 3D applications. The selection of database methodology is probably related to the application needs far more strongly than to the graphic interaction needs. Even though there may be several options that are equally reasonable for application needs, graphic interaction implications may make one clearly preferable to others.

The database used for *viewit3d* is a simple face-vertex model. The topology (or connection) between the graphic elements (i.e., face and vertex) is one way. Specifically, given a face, we know that vertices are used in its definition (the face has pointers to them) while given a vertex, the only way to find out which faces it is used in is to exhaustively search the face list to find pointers to the vertex in the face list.

This structure seems to work well for drawing polygons in *viewit3d*. In the `DrawFlatShaded` and `DrawSmoothShaded` drawing functions for `CObjDoc` which were added in **Practice** Section 3.1.2, the drawing function simply passed the vertex pointer list to the polygon draw function. Before we conclude that it was a good choice for a database, we need to look beyond the simple polygon draw implementation. Here, we consider the *ball.a3d* object, Figure T-68.

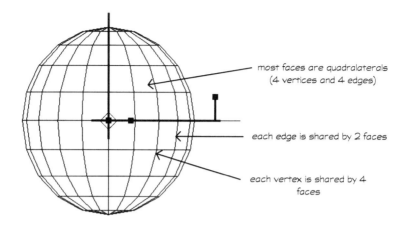

Figure T-68: Face, vertex, and edge relationships in *ball.a3d*.

Draw operations:

as points   The point list is traversed once, points are transformed and drawn only once.

as lines   The face list is traversed once. Each line between polygons is drawn twice (once for each polygon). Each vertex is sent to the rendering system an average of five times (a fifth closing point is required to define the polygon).

as polygons   The face list is traversed once. Each polygon is drawn once. Each vertex is transformed and the lighting is computed four times.

as a mesh   Working back form the face-vertex data to construct a mesh database is extremely difficult. However, once we have the mesh data, each polygon and vertex are only transformed, lit, and drawn once.

Edit operations:

moving a vertex   Picking requires a traversal of the vertex database. If setup for the move requires changes to adjacent polygons (topological changes to the database), another complete traversal of the vertex database is required to find the adjacent polygons.

moving an edge   Picking requires traversing the face list once and testing the edges. All edges are tested twice before the closest edge is found. The closest edge is defined by two points. Finding the adjacent faces may require another search unless data was cached in the first search.

moving a face   Picking requires traversing the face list once. Finding the adjacent faces requires searching through the face list once and comparing each vertex of the selected face with each vertex of the current face in the search.

This data structure often results in redundant work in drawing, and almost any manipulation of a geometric element requires exhaustive searching through the database to find adjacent elements that are affected by the move.

When we implemented the "position vertex" in *viewit3d*, we added a menu button for Update Normals that simply re-computed all of the normals for all other the faces and vertices. A "correct" implementation would have split the four faces adjacent to the moved vertex so that the two polygon halves remained planar, and then re-computed only the normals for the affected faces and vertices immediately after the interaction, Figure T-69. In the face-vertex database, it was far less programming hassle to hope that the graphics would render the resultant non-planar faces (without objectionable artifacts) and to re-compute normals for the entire object upon user request (which is not the right way to handle things).

Other databases that you might consider use a bit more memory to keep topological two way connections between faces, edges, and vertices. While these are a bit more memory intensive, they may provide necessary data for implementing interactive drawing and manipulation. Examples of these databases are face-edge (Mantyla 1982) or winged edge data structures (Baumgart 1975), and radial edge data structures (Weiler 1986). Discussion about implementing these types of databases can be found in (Arvo 1991).

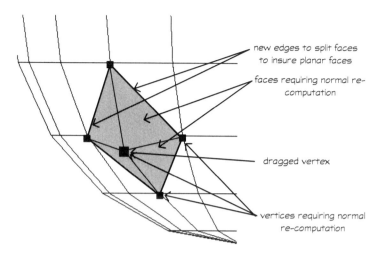

new edges to split faces
to insure planar faces

faces requiring normal re-
computation

dragged vertex

vertices requiring normal
re-computation

Figure T-69: A "correct" implementation of position vertex.

Another drawing and database method that may be useful is the use of implicit surfaces or objects. For example, a sphere can be represented as a centre and a radius. Drawing the sphere can be through pre-computation of the geometry of vertices and faces or by generating them as required. The data for *ball.a3d* was created by a sphere procedure. This procedure could generate data directly in mesh form for optimum rendering speed. If the sphere procedure is encapsulated in a CJoeyRenderGeom object, the level-of-detail that the sphere is drawn at (number of polygons) can be a function of how small or large the sphere appears on the screen or whether is visible at all. *The OpenGL Programming Guide* (Neider 1993) contains an example for a procedural geodesic sphere generator that could be used to play with the concept of variable level-of-detail in a CJoeyRenderGeom object.

1.3.2 Adding Read and Draw

Selecting the file format for 3D data is another interesting problem. The *viewit3d* example used ASCII data that was parsed by keywords. This made it possible to enlarge the definition of data for the examples in the text while assuring that old versions of *viewit3d* would read newer files, simply skipping unrecognised data, and that new versions of *viewit3d* would ready old data files, simply supplying defaults for missing data. The ASCII files are readable in an editor for debugging.

The drawback is that ASCII files are actually much larger that necessary. They are also cumbersome and time consuming to parse and translate from ASCII to binary form, and time consuming to write (because of translation from binary to ASCII). ASCII files are stream oriented an do not fit well into the structured storage model. Although we use ASCII files for the *viewit3d* example, we certainly do not recommend that you use them for your own application.

2. Integrating Graphic Applications into Windows

The most difficult issue, when integrating 3D applications into Windows, is deciding how to make the application intuitive to the user. In **Practice**, we explored the Windows integration facilities offered by *JOEY*. In **Implementation**, we reviewed the mechanisms behind these integration facilities. In this section, we explore intuitive operation further. We discuss the characteristics of an integrated environment and how 3D fits with MFC and OLE.

2.1 OLE Server Capabilities - Linking and Embedding

Embedded documents appear in the container as 2D pictures that can be scaled and positioned by and within the container. The 2D representation has a fixed orientation and fixed bounds. It is normally seen in its entirety and is scaled to fill the window (that the container has allotted to it). The viewing of an embedded 2D object is implicit in the definition of the object.

Three dimensional data does not fit this model well. The major difference is that, unlike 2D data that is typically thought of as text or drawing on a sheet of paper, 3D data exists in a space with infinite bounds and can be meaningfully viewed in a variety of ways. This can be better understood by thinking of text files that are edited in Visual C++. The text file has an implicit origin and layout for viewing. All that is contained in the file is the actual text. During editing, the user interface provides control of the font, colours, window size, and positioning (scrolling) of the text within the window. Three dimensional data, however, does not have well defined conventions for preferred viewing of data. When the data is embedded, there needs to be viewing information included in that embedding so that the data can be meaningfully positioned and presented whenever the server is in-place activated.

In this section, we explore an example where we have users of both an OLE server and an OLE container application. We discuss possible ways that they could interact with the same data sets for entirely different purposes. The objective of this exercise is to understand what intuitive behaviour really is and to then apply this understanding to an analysis of *JOEY* and OLE.

Our scenario has two users; a designer using a 3D design program and a technical writer who writes product documentation. We chose this scenario for several reasons; multiple users are involved, dissimilar tasks are involved and they both need access to the same data for very different reasons. We further complicate the situation by saying that the design is not yet complete; the design continues to change as the documentation is being written. The documentor uses several different views of the model in various sections of the documentation.

In the current model of Windows integration, the documentor could make use of the following techniques for placing views of the design into the document:

Technique	Process
Bitmap	The designer selects views of the design and copies them to the clipboard or to files (as bitmaps) for the documentor to paste or insert into the document.
Metafile	The designer selects views of the design and copies them to the clipboard or to files (as metafiles) for the documentor to paste or insert into the document.
Linked or Embedded 3D Design Data	The designer copies the application database to the clipboard or makes the application file available for linking and embedding in the document.

Using bitmaps requires the designer to be highly involved in the documentation process. Since the bitmap of a 3D database is not easily edited to reflect changes in the design (or the need for a slightly different view), the designer must constantly supply new bitmaps and the documentor must be replacing old bitmap images with new images.

Using metafiles creates a similar situation except that metafiles can be drawn at the resolution of the final output. Therefore, the images in the documentation can be of higher quality than if they were bitmaps.

Embedding provides the documentor with complete design information. The viewing can be manipulated using the design program. The documentor can edit the design so that it looks best in the documentation.[67] This affords maximum flexibility for the documentor since the design data is actually part of

---

[67] Having the technical documentor editing the design may lead to conflicts between a design that works and a design that looks good in the documentation.

the documentation file. It also means that the documentor needs to be proficient in using the design application and that the documentor has a license for the design software on his/her personal computer. The documentor still requires a new database when design changes are made and, after receiving new data, the documentor must re-embed the data in the document and adjust all of the viewing parameters in order to get the desired view.

Linking initially sounds like the best of all worlds. The documentor can link to the design database in several places throughout the document. Whenever the design database changes, the documentor need only update the links and the new design data will be used in the documentation. Unfortunately, things are not so simple.

Before exploring linking and embedding further, let us list some of the behavioural elements that are desirable in the interaction:

Design Database Access	The designer should have full access to the design database. The documentor needs to make images the design database but probably should not have access allowing modification of the data.
Design Database Editing State	If the 3D design application saves and restores state information, it should start in the same state that the designer left it in. The actions of the documentor should not affect the designer's state.
Views of the Design within the Document	Views should be updated to the new geometry of the design without affecting the viewing parameters. The choice of camera location, camera projection, lighting, background, colours and rendering style was probably made to enhance the communication of information about design and they should not change unless the documentor requests a change.
	It should be possible for the documentor to adjust the view (camera position, camera projection, lighting, rendering style, etc.). If the documentor must rely on the designer to provide snapshots of the design, it will impact the designer's productivity and will be a deterrent to the documentor exploring methods of presentation that will provide the best communication.
	When the documentor needs to edit a view, it would be nice if the documentor had the view that was

shown in the document as a starting point. When the documentor double clicks on the graphic in the design (for editing), the editor should start with the graphic of the design that is currently in the document (see the OLE style guidelines for more information).

2.1.1 Investigating the workings of OLE

In previous investigations, we discovered that embedding puts a copy of the current server database into the container object. This means that each instance of the embedded object is unique. It can have settings for cameras, lights, materials, rendering style, etc. that are unique for that graphic. As noted earlier, this does not solve the problem since the 3D design data is still being revised. It also means that there are multiple copies of the database (one for each embedding in addition to the original) and that the document is carrying the overhead of having a complete copy of the design database inside the document for each image of the design.

Linking provides a solution to the problem of keeping the graphics in the document current with the design. Since everyone shares the same database, there is no unique data for any of the uses of the design database, Figure T-70.

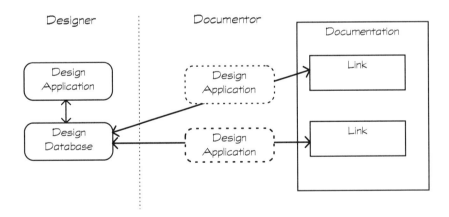

Figure T-70: Linking assures that all users share the same design database.

However, since everyone is using the same data, it shows up in the state in which it was last left. If the documentor changes the camera or rendering parameters, the designer sees those changes when the next design session starts.

When the designer finishes a session, the last viewing parameters become the current view in the document. If the documentor changes the view for one of the links, the other linked views also change.

Clearly, there are elements of both linking and embedding that are important to intuitive behaviour but neither solves the problem alone.

2.1.2 Completing the Implementation as an OLE Server

JOEY adds some state data to the data file in order to solve some of OLE problems. The data has a render environment appended to it so that there is enough data to insure that embedded data looks the same in both the activated and inactive state. The same is true for linked data if there is only one link and one user of the data (though it may require effort to update the container's link if the database is modified).

We discovered, and have shown through this example, that we cannot get intuitive and desired behaviour simply by enabling our 3D application as an OLE server. We need a strategy which insures that use-specific or instance-specific data is embedded in the container, but that the geometry is linked so that it is current and consistent. Also, we do not want to link to the geometry in a way that permits any modifications to the design; it must be a read-only link. This is where the *JOEY* 3D metafile (described in the next section) becomes important.

2.2 Clipboard, Files, and 3D Viewers

The previous section discussed the mechanisms for integrating 2D data using OLE servers and containers. We concluded that simply making a 3D application a server application does not solve the integration problem. In this section, we highlight the *JOEY* 3D metafile as a solution to fill the previously identified gap in techniques for integration of 3D data.

2.2.1 Enabling Special Clipboard Copy Formats

You may wonder why formats that copy the entire applications database to the clipboard are "special" formats. This is a distinction that we were not comfortable in proposing, but found no other clear way to differentiate between selecting and copying all of the object data to the clipboard for pasting into an assembly of objects and copying formats that clearly do not paste back into the application from which they came.

Again, we run up against the distinction between 2D and 3D data. If we pick and copy a vertex, or a collection of faces in *viewit3d*, it would be difficult to make reasonable choices about what that data should be when we paste it back into *viewit3d*. Is it a partial object? Does it get closed and become a solid object? Does it retain some connectivity to the rest of the object? These are all application specific decisions. It is probably true that there is no clipboard representation generated that is compatible with the pre-defined Windows clipboard formats; you probably cannot paste anything meaningful into a 2D document. Conversely, if you copy something from a 2D document, there is probably no way to paste it into the 3D view.

The formats that copy the entire database, either as a 2D image (bitmap or metafile), 3D metafile, or complete application database are special formats for one-way transfer of data out of the 3D application and into a 2D application.

We could have used <u>S</u>elect All followed by <u>C</u>opy to indicate the special formats but this seemed confusing when we thought of how and why we used <u>S</u>elect All in other applications. It may also be extremely time consuming to wait while all of the formats are copied to the clipboard.

We are not recommending presenting the formats designed for export to 2D containers as "special" formats as appropriate for use in your application. Remember, however, that these formats are specifically for export to 2D documents, have size and resolution information that should be set before the copy is performed, and may be very time consuming to copy to the clipboard.

2.2.2 Enabling Special File Save Formats

Every user is familiar with the <u>F</u>ile menu for opening and writing data files. The Save <u>A</u>s menu command is commonly used for saving files in formats native to the application and periodically for saving in data exports formats. Applications generate other files also (e.g., printer files where output goes to a file instead of the physical printer). This is a special type of file for exporting data to a specific type of receiving device. Within this special file, the data no longer reflects the structure of the data within the application (nor can it be read back into the application). We view bitmaps, metafiles and *JOEY* 3D metafiles as being similar in nature to the print file, thus their designation as a "special" file.

Our choice of a **Save Special...** menu item was for consistency with **the Copy Special** menu command. We wanted to leave no doubt that this is a one-way transfer of data. These special file types require size and resolution information before they can be generated. The **Save Special** dialogue provides an opportunity, similar to the print dialogue, to set up specifics for the file that will be created before giving the "OK" for creation of the file. We do not necessarily recommend this for your application.

If you choose a different method for exposing the save of special formats, remember that these are formats specifically for use in 2D documents and use the `OleSize` of the `CJoeyRenderEnv` as the desired size when the graphic is inserted, linked or embedded in a document, and that the Windows metafiles use the resolution (dpi) specified in `CJoeyConfig` as the output resolution of the image. These parameters must be set when these formats are saved to files.

2.2.3 Playing with the Clipboard and Files

Early in the section, we discussed the difficulties with integrating 3D in Windows in an intuitive way. We highlight those again in this section so that you know what to watch for when you play with the methods for transferring 3D data to other applications. We also discuss the *JOEY* 3D metafile and Viewer as one solution to these problems.

2.2.3.1 Native Application Data

Enabling a complex 3D application to be an OLE server is not always a good idea. It may not make sense to run an extremely large and complex CAD package in order to edit a design embedded in a 2D document. If you really want to edit the design, you probably want to use the whole screen. If you are simply viewing data, the CAD application carries tremendous overhead to be used only as a viewer. It is also questionable whether you want to carry a copy of the design database inside your document and, if the document were moved to another machine, whether you would have the necessary access to the CAD application to allow editing of the document.

For simple 3D applications, linking may be an ideal integration method. Linking suffers from the previously mentioned problem of having only a single data source for multiple uses of the data. This is a problem for things like lights and cameras, but it is also the desirable element of linking for geometric data (the view independent data).

For applications that are a part of a suite used by a single user, both mechanisms work well. In a multi-user, distributed environment, neither mechanism works well for 3D data in 2D documents.

2.2.3.2 *JOEY* 3D Data

The *JOEY* 3D metafile and *JOEY* Viewer are based on the notion that 3D geometry exists independently of how it is viewed. The geometry portion of the file is a literal dump of all of the calls to `IRenderDevX` made during an update cycle. The view specific data is in the render environment serialized with the `IRenderDevX` dump, Figure T-71. As noted in this figure, the *JOEY* 3D metafile can exist in three forms.

The first form is simply the dump of an update to `IRenderDevX`. It can be played back literally in order to generate the same picture that was drawn when the file was created. This type of file would be created by a non-*JOEY* application using `IRenderDevX` for rendering support.

The second form includes a render environment. During playback (drawing of the image), elements such as cameras, window placement, etc. are skipped and replaced by loading information from the render environment. For example, camera, background and lighting can be loaded from the render environment and only the draw portion of the *JOEY* 3D metafile could be played back, ignoring lights. This maintains the original geometry but allows complete control of viewing. This is how the *JOEY* Viewer provides view editing.

The third form of the file has a link to a *.j3d* file and a render environment. The viewing information in the render environment overrides any information in the referenced *JOEY* 3D metafile, but preserves the geometry.

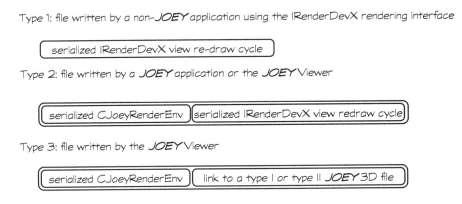

Type 1: file written by a non-*JOEY* application using the IRenderDevX rendering interface

> serialized IRenderDevX view re-draw cycle

Type 2: file written by a *JOEY* application or the *JOEY* Viewer

> serialized CJoeyRenderEnv | serialized IRenderDevX view redraw cycle

Type 3: file written by the *JOEY* Viewer

> serialized CJoeyRenderEnv | link to a type I or type II *JOEY* 3D file

Figure T-71: The three forms of *JOEY* 3D metafiles.

This organisation solves the problem of having a single read-only source for the geometry which is linked to many instances of use, each instance having unique viewing parameters, Figure T-72.

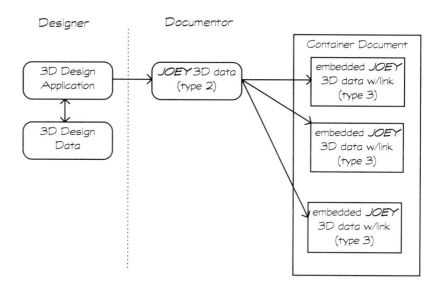

Figure T-72: Multiple embedded *JOEY* 3D metafiles for unique views of a linked 3D geometry.

The designer has control of the 3D design data. A *JOEY* 3D data file can be written into a common location whenever the design changes. The changes are reflected in the document without the loss of the instance-specific viewing information maintained by the serialized `CJoeyRenderEnv` in the embedded Type 3 *JOEY* 3D data files.

2.2.3.3 Metafiles and Bitmaps

Metafiles and bitmaps need to be thought of as snapshots that reflect a specific time and a specific set of viewing parameters. Their utility is somewhat limited where 3D is concerned; they are the basis for transferring imagery into 2D image processing facilities and need to be supported.

2.2.4 The *JOEY* Viewer

The *JOEY* Viewer is a simple OLE server enabled *JOEY* application that plays back a *JOEY* 3D metafile. The render device for the *JOEY* 3D metafile provides serialization of the data for every function in the `IRenderDevX` interface. This serialization often uses the object being rendered (e.g., camera, grid, light, etc.) to serialize itself.

The reader uses the objects to serialize themselves from the *JOEY* 3D metafile. The result of this structure is that the database that the *JOEY* Viewer is using contains objects that include the capability to launch editing dialogues for themselves. This provides the opportunity to use the same tools to edit views in the *JOEY* Viewer as were used to create the data in the application.

JOEY 3D metafiles are generally not useful unless the *JOEY* Viewer is on every machine or can be freely distributed with any document that is using the *JOEY* 3D metafile. Users will undoubtedly become more receptive to using 3D data if tools, like the *JOEY* Viewer are a standard part of the software that they get with the system. For this reason, the *JOEY* Viewer can be freely distributed.

2.3 OLE Automation

Now that you have gone through the tutorial in **Practice** and reviewed the **Implementation** discussion of OLE automation, you probably still have some doubts about the usefulness of OLE automation in the context of *JOEY*. In the *camdriv* and *v3ddriv* examples, you should be asking yourself whether you really want the camera editor to be launching applications (is this what Microsoft had in mind when the did this automation stuff?). No, you don't want editors of small components driving larger applications. Instead, you want to be able to startup the editor or custom control of your choice and have it respond to the editing needs of the main application.

The use of *JOEY* classes as OLE automation servers is part of a larger picture. The larger picture includes custom functionality that can be used across applications and easily replaced when better implementations of these components become available. The camera editor should not be launching the applications, applications should be launching the camera editor!

JOEY classes also need to be able to act as OLE automation clients so that the editors can be implemented as automation servers. In reality, the conversation between the primary applications and the editor "server" is two way, Figure T-73. The application needs to launch the editor server and send it appropriate information. The editor server needs to send edited information back to the application.

Ideally, classes such as CJoeyRenderEnv, CJoeyCamera, CJoeyLight and CJoeyMaterial would have client interfaces to editing servers. Along with providing these interfaces, the editing services now provided by various dialogues such as the camera dialogue, grid dialogue, material dialogue and light dialogue would be implemented as OLE automation servers. This would allow the standard editors shipped with *JOEY* to be replaced with other editing components that have greatly enhanced capability.

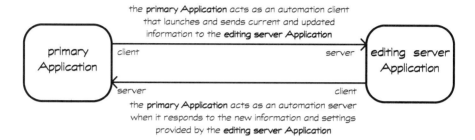

Figure T-73: In the component architecture model, the primary application and the editing server application are both OLE automation clients and OLE automation servers.

The implementation of the complete component architecture was beyond the scope of the *JOEY* toolkit provided with this text, but we believe this introduction will help prepare you to write applications that use the *JOEY* toolkit to promote the idea of component application architecture.

3. Graphic Display and Interaction

Once again, we discuss graphic display and interaction. This time, we try to provide a context for *JOEY* within the history and evolution of techniques in computer graphics and user interface design. If working with this text is your first exposure to 3D graphics, you undoubtedly have a lot of questions about how things are done (and how they were done before). If you have been working in graphics for awhile, you may be wondering how some of the unorthodox approaches in *JOEY* relate to previous work. This section should help to answer both questions.

3.1 Graphic Elements

3D graphics is fraught with matrix mathematics to get 3D into a 2D representation, and with sorting and searching problems to get the objects closest to the viewer drawn over the objects farther from the viewer. Add to this a little bit of optics and physics for determining object colour or shading, some perceptual psychology to determine how to best display the results, and you have the basics of the graphic subsystem. For the graphics programmer and hardware developer, the most difficult part is getting it to all happen fast enough to be useful in an interactive environment. For you, the application developer, the most difficult part is not getting bogged down in the details of the graphics.

Here, we provide more of the "behind the scenes" detail of the services provided by *JOEY* and the graphics subsystem. It is intended to provide insight into the workings you may want to tinker with in more advanced applications, and to point you to references that fully explain details and intricacies in the event you want to really understand what is going on underneath the images on the screen, or implement your own rendering system.

3.1.1 Axis Systems

The introduction of homogeneous coordinate transformations (Plücker 1830) provided the background mathematics for using multiple coordinate systems in computer graphics. The formalisation of the world, camera, and object is probably most clearly presented in some of the Renderman documentation (Upstill 1990). A key concept is that there is really no preferred axis system for describing events or data, but that it makes the most sense to describe an event or data in the axis system in which it can be most easily represented. The mathematics does not favour one axis system over the others, and allows transformation freely between axis systems.

The mathematics of transformations are covered in a multitude of texts (Foley et al. 1990), (Rogers 1990), (Bloomenthal 1994), and others and will not be repeated here. Instead we just gloss over a few concepts that are required for the following discussion. Transformations between axis systems are matrix manipulations at one dimension higher than the space of the data. The extra dimension is added by the homogenous coordinate, which is explicit in the mathematics and the graphics subsystem, but never needs to be seen by the application developer. This means that your 3D point $[XYZ]$ becomes a 4D point $[XYZ1]$. In *JOEY*, points are represented by cPoint3f and transformations by cXfm4x4f. The result is that the transformation between 3D axis systems is a 4x4 matrix.

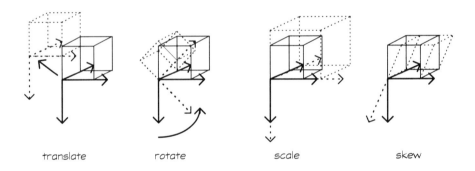

translate   rotate   scale   skew

Figure T-74: Translation, rotation, scale, and skewing transformations.

The mathematics of transformation from coordinate system 1 to coordinate system 2, i.e. from $[X_1 Y_1 Z_1]$ to $[X_2 Y_2 Z_2]$ generally take the form:

$$[X_2 Y_2 Z_2 1] = [X_1 Y_1 Z_1 1] \begin{bmatrix} r_{11} & r_{12} & r_{13} & 0 \\ r_{21} & r_{22} & r_{23} & 0 \\ r_{31} & r_{32} & r_{33} & 0 \\ t_x & t_y & t_z & 1 \end{bmatrix}$$

The homogeneous coordinate, i.e. the 1 in the fourth position of the coordinate specification, is added by graphic subsystem to perform the transformation. The basic transformation operations are translate (shift the origin), rotation (change the direction of the axes around the origin), scale (make things larger or smaller), and skewing or shearing (shifting the axis from being mutually perpendicular), Figure T-74. The translation is represented by the r_x, r_y, and r_z elements of the transformation. The rotation, scale, and skew (or shear) are represented in the upper left 3x3 "r" elements of the transformation. The *JOEY* CXfm4x4f transformation class includes member functions to create identity, rotation, translation, and scale transformations, to multiply transformations, to get the inverse and transpose of a transformation, and to multiply points or vectors by the transformation.

If we call $\left[T_{1\to2}\right]$ the transformation from axis system 1 to axis system 2, then the inverse of this transformation will transform from axis system 2 to axis system 1. Specifically $\left[T_{2\to1}\right] = \left[T_{1\to2}\right]^{-1}$ and the transformation from axis system 2 to axis system 1 is:

$$\left[X_1 Y_1 Z_1 1\right] = \left[X_2 Y_2 Z_2 1\right]\left[T_{2\to1}\right]$$

We can consider adding an axis system 3 with a transformation from axis system 2 of $\left[T_{2\to3}\right]$. We can then describe the transformation from axis system 1 to axis system 3 by first transforming to axis system 2, and then to 3; or, by multiplying the transformations $\left[T_{1\to2}\right]$ and $\left[T_{2\to3}\right]$ to get a transformation, $\left[T_{1\to3}\right]$, between axis system 1 and axis system 3 without intermediate stops:

$$\left[X_3 Y_3 Z_3 1\right] = \left[X_2 Y_2 Z_2 1\right]\left[T_{2\to3}\right]$$

$$\left[X_3 Y_3 Z_3 1\right] = \left(\left[X_1 Y_1 Z_1 1\right]\left[T_{1\to2}\right]\right)\left[T_{2\to3}\right]$$

$$\left[X_3 Y_3 Z_3 1\right] = \left[X_1 Y_1 Z_1 1\right]\left(\left[T_{1\to2}\right]\left[T_{2\to3}\right]\right)$$

$$\left[X_3 Y_3 Z_3 1\right] = \left[X_1 Y_1 Z_1 1\right]\left[T_{1\to3}\right]$$

The multiplication of matrices is key in describing a complex relationship between two axis system. The isolated matrices for scaling, translation, and rotation are easily generated. the relationship between two axis systems is generally described by a sequence of scaling, translation, and rotation operations. The matrices for the individual operations are multiplied to create a single matrix that represents the entire sequence. Multiplication is also important in relating multiple axis systems such as a screw to a carburetor assembly which is mounted to an engine which is in turn mounted to the frame of an automobile. Using multiplication and matrix inverse, it is possible to easily express any of the assembly elements in coordinates relative to the axis system of any of the other assembly elements.

Another useful feature about transformations is they can also be used to transform direction vectors and surface normals. The transformation of a direction vector $\left[\, i_1\, j_1\, k_1\,\right]$ from axis system 1 to $\left[\, i_2\, j_2\, k_2\,\right]$ in axis system 2 is:

$$\left[\, i_2\, j_2\, k_2\, O\,\right]=\left[\, i_1\, j_1\, k_1\, O\,\right]\left[\, T_{1\rightarrow 2}\,\right]$$

For those unfamiliar with vector notation, i, j, and k are unit vectors (vectors of unit length) in the X, Y, and Z directions. $\left[\, i\, j\, k\,\right]$ is a vector that is the resultant of $ii + jj + kk$, Figure T-75.

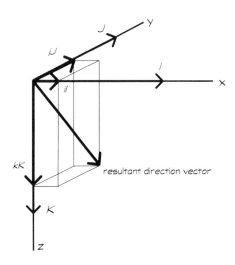

Figure T-75: Vector notation to express direction.

The transformation of a surface normal $\left[\, Ni_1\, Nj_1\, Nk_1\,\right]$ from axis system 1 to $\left[\, Ni_2\, Nj_2\, Nk_2\,\right]$ in axis system 2 is:

$$\left[\, Ni_2\, Nj_2\, Nk_2\, O\,\right]=\left[\, Ni_1\, Nj_1\, Nk_1\, O\,\right]\left(\left[\, T_{1\rightarrow 2}\,\right]^{-1}\right)^{T}$$

This transformation accounts for the possibility of unequal scaling and skew. If the scaling is uniform in X, Y, and Z, and there is no skew (shear), the transpose of the inverse is equal to the original transformation. In that case there is no difference between the transformation of a direction vector and a surface normal.

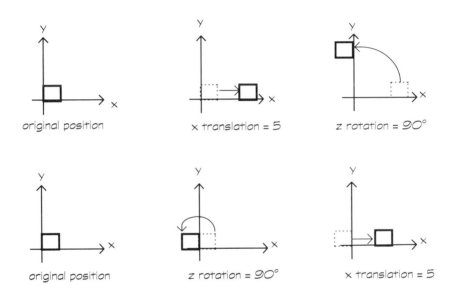

Figure T-76: Example of non-commutative transformation.

A tiring aspect of coordinate transformations is getting the transformations in the correct order to achieve the desired result. They should be multiplied in the order you want the operations to occur. Always keep in mind that transformations are order-dependent and not commutative as shown in Figure T-76.

Another source of confusion is right and left handed coordinate systems. Though the right handed system is the standard mathematical convention, the left handed coordinate system is the standard coordinate system for computer graphics (this does vary between graphics systems).

JOEY uses the left handed coordinate system standard to graphics, but provides an axis map for mapping your native data coordinate system into the *JOEY* coordinate system. The effect of the axis map is to insert a transformation that performs the rotation and/or scaling necessary so that *JOEY* is working in the same axis system as your data is defined in.

3.1.1.1 Camera Projections and Conventions

The computer graphics literature generally describes the generating of a 2D display from 3D data as a process of locating a camera axis system relative to the data axis system, projecting the data into a "camera cube", and then mapping the XY coordinates of the camera cube into a window in the display surface (Foley et al. 1990), (Rogers 1990), Figure T-77. While this provides a mathematical description of the entire process, most of it now happens within either the graphics subsystem and/or the windows subsystem and can be conveniently ignored by the developer.

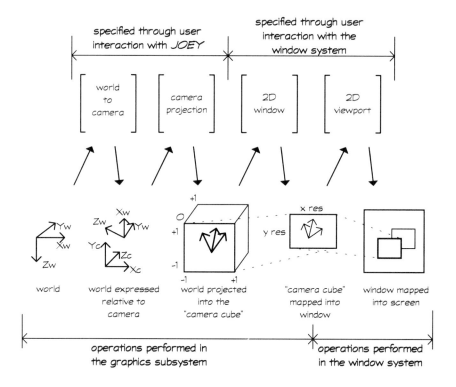

Figure T-77: The process to map world data into a window on the screen.

In *JOEY*, the only aspect of this operation that is revealed to the developer is the model for specifying the camera position and the desired camera projection type. The user is further isolated from the underlying mechanics of camera positioning by an intuitive interactive interface to the positioning model.

The camera positioning model used in *JOEY* describes the position of the camera relative to the world axis system by 3 angles, α, θ, and ϕ, describing the orientation of the camera; and a target point that the camera is aimed at, $\left[T_x\,T_y\,T_z\right]$. In most of the camera interactions, the roll, α, is set to 0.0, and the orientation can be described using only the plan angle, θ, and elevation angle, ϕ.[68] This describes the world to camera rotation transformation as follows:

$$\begin{bmatrix} \cos\alpha\cos\theta - \sin\alpha\sin\theta\sin\phi & \cos\alpha\sin\theta\sin\phi + \sin\alpha\cos\phi & \sin\phi\cos\phi & 0 \\ -\cos\alpha\sin\theta - \sin\alpha\cos\theta\sin\phi & \cos\alpha\cos\theta\sin\phi - \sin\theta\cos\alpha & \cos\theta\cos\phi & 0 \\ \sin\alpha\cos\phi & -\cos\alpha\cos\phi & \sin\phi & 0 \\ 0 & 0 & 0 & 1 \end{bmatrix}$$

A translation is first applied to shift the target point to $0,0,0$ in camera coordinates. This is multiplied by the world to camera rotation to get the final position in the camera coordinate system.

The literature describes camera projections in a variety of ways, differing only in placement of the origin in the camera coordinate system. Some use the camera as the origin, others use the intersection of the view axis (The camera Z axis) and the projection plane as the origin. The choice is arbitrary, with minor differences in the projection matrices.

Camera projections fall into 3 classes, orthographic, perspective, and skewed (as previously described in **Practice**). Orthographic projects all points to the projection plane along lines perpendicular to the projection plane (and parallel to each other). Skewed projection relaxes the requirement that the lines of projection be perpendicular to the projection plane and allows skewed projection lines. Perspective projects all points to the projection plane along lines that intersect at the eye point. The projection plane is defined by a plane perpendicular to the eye vector passing through the target point. The width of the target plane determines the amount of the environment that will be projected onto the plane. Projection mathematics are detailed in other texts, (Foley et al. 1990), (Rogers 1990), and will not be repeated here.

During projection, parts of the environment outside the camera cube are clipped away or discarded. The camera cube is mapped into the window, which is, in turn, mapped onto the screen or other output device. The mapping from the

---

[68] In many disciplines, the plan angle is known as azimuth or bearing, and the elevation angle is known as the altitude.

camera cube to the screen is complicated by computing surface visibility so that objects close to the eye appear in front of objects far from the eye. In addition, surface colour must be determined. Rendering is the term generally used to describe the complete process of projection, shading, and visible surface determination.

3.1.1.2 World Axis System and Axis Mapping

While the notion of axis systems is universal to 3D data, the concept of a standard axis system with a standard orientation is not something we can count on. The axis conventions used may be tied to the operation of a machine tool used to create a part, to some long standing tradition in a discipline or may be completely arbitrary. It is unlikely that your data will follow the conventions of graphics and, if you are integrating data from different systems, they are not likely to be the same.

We use an axis map to solve this problem. The axis map is simply the rotation and scale matrix that transforms data from its native orientation to a similar orientation in the coordinate system used for the camera. This map, combined with a specification of whether polygon vertices are ordered clockwise or counter-clockwise when viewed from the outside are sufficient to relate polygonal data with widely varying axis conventions to both the graphics used for display and to each other.

The axis map is described by giving the plan camera up, side, and view vectors of the mapped axis system in using the *JOEY* conventions for up, side, and view vector direction, Figure T-78.

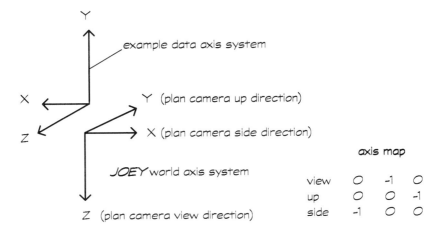

Figure T-78: Defining an axis map.

Reviewing this figure, we see that the view direction, $[0\ 0\ 1]$ in the *JOEY* world axis is $[0\ -1\ 0]$ in the example data axis system. The up and side vectors are similarly mapped. The axis map transformation from the example data axis system $[X_D\ Y_D\ Z_D]$ to the *JOEY* world axis $[X_J\ Y_J\ Z_J]$ is then:

$$[X_J Y_J Z_J] = [X_D Y_D Z_D] \begin{bmatrix} [axis\ map\ side] \\ [axis\ map\ up] \\ [axis\ map\ view] \end{bmatrix}$$

The inverse, to transform from the *JOEY* world axis system to the data axis system is simply the transpose of the transform to the *JOEY* world axis system.

The IRenderDevX interface implements an axis map transformation for every transformation node on the stack. This implementation simply transforms from the axis map of the current node to that of the previous node. If $[M_P]$ is the axis map definition for the previous node and $[M_C]$ is the axis map definition for the current node, the axis map transform from the current node to the previous node is $[M_C][M_P]^{-1}$.

3.1.1.3 Object Axis Systems and Transformation Stacks

The transformation stack has historically been thought of as the series of transformations that an object goes through before it is drawn into the world axis system. An important part of using transformations is getting the order correct. Historically, the stack was treated as a set of individual matrices (not multiplied together). The last transform put onto the stack was the first transform that the object went through so that the transformations were intuitively ordered from most local to most global.

In *JOEY*, the transformation stack always has a single transformation at the top of the stack which represents the whole sequence of transformations below it on the stack. When you push a transform, you get a copy of the last transformation on the stack. Your transformations at this node should happen before this transformation on the stack in order to be local to the data that you will draw. You can achieve this in several ways.

Consider a local positioning of a rotation $[R]$ followed by a translation $[T]$ followed by the positioning already on the stack:

$$\text{my object} \longrightarrow [R] \longrightarrow [T] \longrightarrow [\text{XFM Stack}] \longrightarrow \text{world position of my object}$$

Two ways to write this in pseudo code are:

```
XfmPush()
XfmConcat([T])
XfmConcat([R])
DrawMyObject()
XfmPop()
```

or

```
XfmPush()
[Temp]=[R][T]
XfmConcat([Temp])
DrawMyObject()
XfmPop()
```

Note that concatenating[69] is pre-multiplying what is already on the stack. The local matrices can be multiplied together first and the result concatenated to the stack, or they can be individually concatenated in the reverse order of how they should be applied to the object.

We think of the transformation as the mapping of points from a local axis system to the world axis system. As noted earlier, this transformation also maps vector directions for the local axis system to the world axis system. The inverse of the transformation maps points and vector directions from the world axis system back to the local axis system. Surface normals map from the local axis system to the world axis system using the transpose of the inverse of the point transformation. The *JOEY* transformation class, `CXfm4x4f` and transformation stack class, `CXfmStack4x4f` provide mapping functions to facilitate these operations. For more details, refer to (Foley et al. 1990), (Rogers 1985) and (Glassner 1990).

3.1.2 Rendering

Rendering is a general term used to describe the process of creating a 2D picture from 3D data. While rendering is often discussed as a common problem that should have some common solution, it doesn't. This is because rendering is used to describe anything from wireframe representations to photorealistic representations to physically based simulations. We think it is important for you, the developer of a 3D application, to understand that all renderers are not created equally and to pick the rendering technology appropriate for your application. We will not attempt to provide a comprehensive discussion of rendering, this can be found in standard reference texts (Foley et al. 1990), (Rogers 1985), (Glassner 1989), instead, we highlight points we believe are especially relevant to the renderers you will encounter in practice.

The two most important factors in selecting a rendering technology are speed and realism (or image quality). For interaction with 3D data, speed is generally most important. For presentation, realism is usually most important. Speed and quality are generally mutually exclusive. For many applications, the degree that speed is exchanged for realism is dictated by the needs of the user.

We view rendering as a process solving two fundamental tasks. The first is figuring out where on the screen the 3D geometry should be drawn, and the second is figuring out how the 3D geometry should be drawn there. Projection and visible surface determination are the operations performed in the first task. Local and global illumination are the operations performed in the second task.

---

[69] We are not really sure where the term concatenation (which used to mean pre-multiplied) came from. Used here, it means that the matrix is being placed first in the chain of matrices.

We will spend a bit of time looking at each of these operations in isolation before we talk about combining them into a graphics subsystem.

3.1.2.1 Projection

Projection is the process of mapping the 3D geometry (world space) onto positions on the 2D screen (screen space). There are two techniques for this, the forward mapping of 3D world space into 2D screen space as described in the last section, and the inverse mapping of pixel locations on the screen into the 3D geometry in world space.

The polygon is the lowest common denominator for geometry accepted by renderers. Though some renderers can accept higher level primitives like spheres, quadrics, or surfaces; nearly all renderers break these into polygons for rendering.

In the forward mapping, 3D world space locations are actually mapped into 3D screen space locations. The X and Y positions correspond directly to screen locations, while the Z is the distance from the screen. Matrix techniques are used for forward mapping and are especially suited to geometry that is described polygonally because points, lines, and planes in the 3D world space map to points, lines, and planes in the 3D screen space.

The inverse mapping is referred to as ray tracing. Ray tracing follows vectors (or rays) from the eye through points on the target plane corresponding to pixel locations in the final image. These vectors are followed into world space until an object is encountered. The colour of the object at the point of intersection between the ray and the object is then drawn into that pixel on the screen. Ray tracing is suited to generating realistically shaded images[70], but is not appropriate for wire frame images. Additionally, ray tracing works well with many non-polygonal descriptions of data.

3.1.2.2 Visible Surface Determination

Visible surface determination is the process of determining which object that covers a pixel on the screen is closest to the eye, and drawing that object at that pixel. Essentially all current rendering systems are pixel based, that is, they do the visibility determination at pixel level rather than creating 2D descriptions of

---

[70] When we speak of shading, we are referring to the colouration of surfaces due to surface properties, geometry and lighting.

the visible geometry.[71] This is why Windows metafiles of rendered images are really bitmaps.[72]

Visible surface determination has been a primary area of research since computers were first used to create imagery. One of the best, though dated, discussions of the visible surface problem is "A Characterization of Ten Hidden-Surface Algorithms", (Sutherland 1974), which describes the problem as primarily a sorting problem. The majority current rendering systems use either a z-buffer or ray tracing for visible surface determination.

The z-buffer, developed by (Catmull 1974), and ray tracing, generally attributed to (Whitted 1980)[73] are the two methods used for visible surface determination by most rendering systems. Other methods such as the painters algorithm (Newell 1972) or scanline rendering (Watkins 1970) may be encountered, but their use is rare. The z-buffer is the visible surface technique you most encounter.

The z-buffer sorts in screen space after the forward transformation of the 3D data. The algorithm is quite simple; for each pixel, keep a depth value (distance from hither plane which is the Z coordinate in the screen axis system). The array of pixel depth values is called the z-buffer or depth buffer. At the start of the frame initialise the Z value to the maximum value that will fit in the buffer (z-buffers are commonly 8, 16, or 32 bit values at each pixel). For each polygon, forward transform it to screen space, find the pixel(s) it covers, and if it is closer than the current Z for any of those pixels replace the pixel colour and Z value with those of this polygon.

The popularity of the z-buffer comes from two important properties. First, it can accept and fully process geometry one polygon at a time. Second, it is of a fixed memory size (a function of screen resolution and z-buffer bit depth) regardless of the complexity of the data (number of polygons). These two properties make z-buffer algorithms well suited for pipeline hardware implementations and hardware acceleration. Since geometry can be independently processed one polygon at a time, it is possible to start transformation and colour computations

---

[71] An exception to this is the Weiler-Atherton algorithm (Weiler 1977) that clips and reconstructs visible polygons in screen space. This techniques is not used in any rendering system that the authors are aware of.

[72] The only exception to this is wireframe presentations with no visible surface determination. In this case, it is possible to capture the 2D screen space data as GDI calls, though few rendering systems actually support this.

[73] Ray tracing was first used in computer graphics by (Appel 1968), however, it is the images created by Whitted which are typically associated with ray tracing in computer graphics.

for one polygon while the previous polygon is being loaded (scan converted) into the screen pixel buffer and z-buffer. The predictable fixed memory requirement of the z-buffer makes it possible to dedicated rendering hardware accelerators. Also, the performance of the z-buffer varies linearly (approximately) with the number of polygons processed, i.e. if you have twice as many polygons, it takes about twice as long to render.[74]

The z-buffer does have problems with transparency and with antialiasing. Transparency requires an additional transparency value per pixel, and really only works if the geometry has been presorted and sent to the z-buffer in back-to-front order. Anti-aliasing requires that colours of adjacent polygons be blended in the pixels containing the edge between the polygons, but the z-buffer only keeps one polygon value per pixel. Two major advances, the A-buffer[75] (Carpenter 1984) and the accumulation buffer[76] (Haeberli 1990) addressed these problems, and also added a collection of other capabilities such as motion blur, depth of field, etc. The common aspect of both of these improvements is that each pixel is supersampled, that is, there is more than one sample point per pixel and the final pixel colour is the average of all of the sample points in the pixel.

The A-buffer was a software implementation that resembled the z-buffer, except that for each pixel there was a linked list of polygon fragments that covered the pixel. Once all of the polygons were processed, a post-processing step combined the fragments for each pixel. This made it possible to achieve good handling of transparency and anti-aliasing.

The accumulation buffer simply draws the image multiple times through a standard z-buffer and then accumulates the average pixel values into a final image buffer. Changes in camera position, object position, and object geometry between the images of the single frame produce antialiasing, motion blur, depth of field, and other effects. Refer to (Neider 1993) and (OpenGL 1992) for details.

Ray tracing is a computationally intensive method for visibility determination. The conceptual simplicity of the process coupled with the ease of moving the starting point of the ray has made it a favourite method for certain types of lighting computations. You will probably not encounter it unless you need a high degree of realism (and speed is not an issue) in your application. In

---

[74] There are a collection of other factors such as screen coverage of the polygon, the fixed overhead of clearing the z-buffer, the time to draw from the buffer to the screen, etc. that affect the performance. The linear relationship between time and complexity is reasonably accurate though.

[75] The A-Buffer was originally used in Pixar's Renderman implementation.

[76] The accumulation buffer was first used in Silicon Graphics Workstations and is part of OpenGL.

addition to speed issues, ray tracing requires access to the complete geometric database at all times. This results in memory considerations for complex scenes as the ray tracer usually has a pre-processed copy of the application database lying around during rendering.

In summary, though the z-buffer was originally used because it was well suited for hardware, it has a collection of desirable features that have made it popular for software rendering, and it is what you will most often encounter.

3.1.2.3 Local Illumination

Local illumination is the interaction between light energy and the material a surface is made from. It is local illumination that makes similar geometric objects, such as a tennis ball, a crystal ball, a Christmas ball and a Ping-Pong ball look different when placed side by side.

There are two elements of local illumination that are of practical concern in the renderers that we encounter. The first is the illumination model - or the mathematics that are used to model what happens when light strikes a material. The second is when the illumination model is actually evaluated, and what happens to the pixels in between. We discuss the illumination model in depth as a part of material and lights specifications in future sections. For now, it is sufficient to say that most illumination models abstract the interaction of light with the surface to a non-directional diffuse illumination and a directional specular component. The diffuse component is what we observe with a matte surface (like a tennis ball). It is characterised by smooth change across a continuous surface and an essentially constant colour for a point on the surface regardless of where the surface is viewed from. The specular component provides the highlight or mirror reflections. Specular highlights move across the surface as the viewer moves.

Things are not as obvious when we consider how and when we actually use the illumination model. A colour is computed for every pixel on the screen but this does not mean that the illumination model has been evaluated for every pixel. Illumination computations are expensive so rendering systems take shortcuts wherever possible.

These are the methods which you are most likely to encounter:

Method	How it Works	What it Does
Gouraud Shading (Gouraud 1971)	Uses the illumination model to compute colours at the vertices of a polygon. Linearly interpolates the colour for points on the interior of the polygon	- Good for diffuse surfaces with small colour gradients across the surface - Not rotationally invariant except when used with triangles (if you rotate the object on the pixel grid, the shading changes) - Perspective distortions of shading occur on large polygons - Shading discontinuities are evident in specular or reflective surfaces
Phong Shading (Phong 1975)	Interpolates geometry across the polygon and evaluates the illumination model at each pixel	- Since geometry is interpolated, the surface features important to specular highlights are better approximated. Specular materials render well - Linear interpolation is in screen space and is not rotationally invariant and is also subject to perspective distortion
Ray Tracing (Whitted 1980)	The geometry is explicitly computed and the illumination model is evaluated at each pixel	- Provides the best image but is very time consuming. It is generally overkill unless refraction and reflection are modeled using reflection maps or the ray traced reflections of other objects

3.1.2.4 Global Illumination

Global illumination is the description of the light that reaches a surface. Changes in global illumination are what make the same object look different when lights are turned on and off or when the object is moved to a different environment. Once again, a variety of approximations an simplifications are made to reduce processing time. A breakdown of methods that covers most of those which you will encounter include a constant ambient method, ray tracing, and radiosity. Generally, the constant ambient method is the only one suitable for interactive applications.[77]

Method	How it Works	What it Does
Constant Ambient	Light sources are explicitly considered in the illumination computation A constant global ambient term accounts for background illumination	- Works relatively well for objects in isolation and diffuse environments - Interactions between objects, like reflections or colour bleeding, are not captured
Ray Tracing (Whitted 1980)	Reflections and refractions are followed from reflective and transparent surfaces Colour information is gathered either from the other objects in the environment or from reflection and refraction maps	- Very realistic appearance for reflective environments - Only works when ray tracing is being used for local illumination computation
Radiosity (Goral 1984)	Models energy exchange between diffuse surfaces	- Generates good simulations for lighting studies - Generates realistic images of diffuse environments - Generally used outside of the context of interactive applications - All colours are computed before the image is created and Gouraud shading can generally be used to draw the data to the screen

Ideally, the interface between the application and the graphics supports all of the projections, visible surface methods, local illumination and global illumination methods described. It is not unreasonable for a user to specify a target for the quality of image desired and have the application adjust the rendering used to suit the interaction demands. If the user is idle for a period of

---

[77] This is not strictly true. If the interaction is limited to moving the camera, it is possible to pre-compute the illumination and colour using radiosity methods and display the results using a Gouraud shaded renderer.

time, the application should create increasingly better images while waiting for the user to resume work.

3.1.3 Materials

Materials and lights provide the data for evaluating the colour of surfaces once the geometry has been defined. We have two very separate and district needs for colour in an image to provide visual cues for identification and marking and to provide realistic appearance of the rendered geometry. Our model for materials must satisfy both needs.

Visual cues and identification are vitally important for editing 3D data. In many editing situations, the primary concern is data selection and manipulation. This requires precise identification and alignment of features of the geometry which are often not even part of the geometry that would be drawn for realistic rendering. These features include centrelines and other datum lines, control points for surfaces and spline, gridlines, axis identification, etc. There are commonly drawn in constant colours.[78]

The basic entities used for identification and marking are points, lines and polygons. The constant colour drawing properties associated with these are:

point	colour
	size
line	colour
	width
	style (or stipple)
polygon	edge colour
	edge on/off
	fill colour
	fill on/off
	fill pattern (or
	stipple)

More complex marking entities are usually made up as a collection of points, lines and polygons. Bitmaps are also commonly employed for markers.

When surfaces are rendered or shaded, the specification is significantly more complex. If we want an object to appear realistic, we need a reasonable approximation of both the light reaching the surface and the interaction of light

---

[78] Colours that are not affected by lighting or the position of the geometry.

with the surface. This discussion of materials focuses on light interacting with the surfaces. We can think of the rendering process for a single pixel as one of projecting a cone from the view point through the pixel on the screen into the environment, Figure T-79.

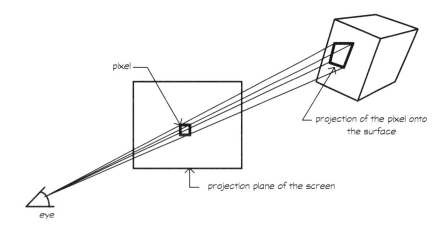

Figure T-79: Projection of a pixel from the projection plane into the environment.

The projected pixel has an area on the object surface and a surface normal. There is also a material associated with that point on the surface of the object. The true colour of the surface is found by gathering the global information about light striking that surface and using a physically based model to compute the interaction of light with the surface to determine the intensity and colour of light reflected from the surface to the viewer. The accuracy of the computed pixel colour is a function of the accuracy of the global lighting information and the model used for computing the interaction between light and the material surface. Instead of digressing into a long discussion (Hall 1989) of these topics, we will focus on the approximations used in the majority of graphics systems and supported by *JOEY*.

3.1.3.1 Colour described as RGB

Colour in computer graphics are characterised by RGB (red, green, blue) values. These are the relative strengths of the signals sent to the colour monitor to control the intensity of the electron guns that illuminate the red green and blue phosphors on the monitor screen. We need a cursory understanding of how colours produced this way relate to colours of lights and objects in the world around us before we can worry about computing the RGB colours of objects.

Visible light is in the wavelength range 380nm (blue-violet) to 770nm (red) and the colours that we see are a function of the distribution of intensity of light through this wavelength range. Colour is quantitatively described using the terms hue, saturation (chroma), and value (brightness or intensity). These terms characterise a natural organising tendency to first group colours such as "red", "blue", and "yellow" (by hue), and then describe brightness and saturation. Saturation can be thought of as the pureness of a colour. Light that has been split by a prism is very saturated, that is, the wavelengths have been separated from each other, so every colour in the spectrum results from a single wavelength. Unsaturated light is "white", or is a mixture of all colours.

Early visual experiments and studies of vision led to the understanding that the retina of the eye contains three different types of colour receptors (cones) that are sensitive to different wavelengths in the visible range. By stimulating these three receptors with three colour primaries correctly spaced in the spectrum, the visual sensation of a vast majority of the colours we see in nature can be reproduced by adjusting the relative brightness of the colour primaries. This is called trichromatic colour reproduction. A property of trichromatic colour reproduction is that the very pure or saturated colours cannot be reproduced. However, with the exception of rainbows and other phenomena that split light into individual wavelengths, these highly saturated colours are seldom found in nature.

Computer monitors rely on trichromatic colour reproduction using red, green, and blue phosphors as the colour primaries. The *JOEY* CRGBf class is used for colour values throughout *JOEY*. In *JOEY*, all RGB values are normalised to be in the range 0 to 1. The colours that can be produced by a monitor can be characterised in a number of ways (Meyer 1983), (Meyer 1986). Two natural ways are the RGB hexcone (Smith 1978) and the RGB cylinder (Joblove 1978), Figure T-80.

The specification of an RGB colour is monitor specific, that is, the colour created by some RGB triplet, say (.2,.3,.5) on our monitor will be different from the colour created by the same values on your monitor. This is due to variations in the colour of the red, green, and blue phosphors, and in the electronics that drive the electron guns illuminating the phosphors. It is possible to measure and characterise a monitor so that colours can be reproduced with great accuracy, but this is beyond the scope of this text.

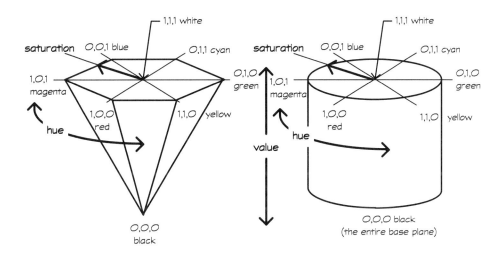

Figure T-80: The colour hexcone and colour cylinder for describing colour.

Colours are perceived based on the wavelength distribution of light that reaches our eye. Normally, this light has been reflected from surfaces. There are then two components that go into producing the colour. The first is the colour of the light that strikes the surface. The second is the reflectivity of the surface. We use RGB values to describe both, but the meanings are very different.

When we use RGB to describe a light, we are describing a distribution of lights at various wavelengths in the spectrum. We commonly think of white (1,1,1) as being an equal distribution of light in all wavelengths, but in fact, it is not. Our perception of white is tuned to daylight, which has an unequal distribution across the spectrum and varies depending on sky conditions, cloud cover, and time of day.[79]

When we use RGB to describe the reflectivity of a surface, white (1,1,1) is an identity reflector. It reflects all of the red, green, and blue light so that the reflected light is the same colour as the illuminating light. The reflected colour is determined by multiplying the colour of the light by the reflectivity of the surface.

---

[79] This leads to a discussion of colour adaptation (that our sense of white adjusts to the surrounding light colour), and other perceptual issues that are outside the scope of this text.

This is a very brief overview of why colour monitors use red, green, and blue phosphours and why colours are specified as RGB triplets for display. A detailed discussion can be found in (Cornsweet 1970), (Hunt 1975) and (Judd 1975). A discussion of colour, specifically focused on computer applications using RGB, can be found in (Meyer 1988), (Hall 1990), and (Borges 1991).

3.1.3.2 Local Illumination Model

The local illumination model is the model of how light and materials interact. It is the model that, given the illumination by incoming light, predicts the reflectivity of a surface in a particular direction, and subsequently, the colour reflected in that direction (usually to the eye). In engineering terminology, the illumination of the surface is the energy that reaches the surface (illuminance), usually measured in footcandles or lumens per square meter. The luminance of the surface (the brightness of the reflected light) is measured in candela per square meter. Associating these quantities with the RGB sent to the monitor is a very difficult and unpredictable task. As a result, we normally rely on a collection of empirical approximations that create images that look pretty good.[80]

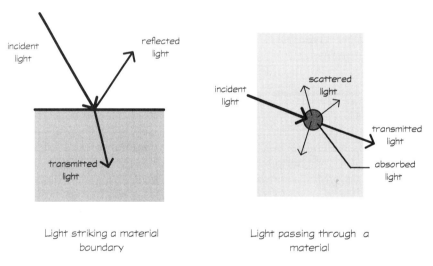

Light striking a material boundary

Light passing through a material

Figure T-81: Light reflected and transmitted at a material boundary, then transmitted, scattered, or absorbed as it passes through a material.

---

[80] Terminology and units in illumination engineering are terribly misused in most discussions of rendering. The IES (Illumination Engineering Society) provides the definitive terminology, refer to (Kaufman 1984) for a complete discussion of illumination and lighting.

The material properties that must be specified to make a surface renderable are a function of the local illumination model that is used. *JOEY* takes a generalised approach to surface modeling which allows the specification of optical and spectral material properties suitable for physically based lighting simulations, as well as defining abstractions that can be used for high speed renderers and constant colour drawing.

The number of parameters that need to be specified for reasonable rendering of a surface are substantial. In some applications, such as animation, the user may want complete control of the material. In most applications, however, the number of parameters that must be specified is daunting to the user and a simplified interface is required. The *JOEY* material editing dialogue relates many of the material parameters to two user choices; whether the material is a conductor of non-conductor; and the shininess of the material. Heuristics are then used to select appropriate coefficients. These are loaded into the material definition. The *JOEY* dialogues are a starting point for more complex application specific material specification.

There is a physical basis from which the empirical models are derived. Physically, there are two things that happen to light when it encounters a boundary between two materials; it is either reflected from the boundary or transmitted through the boundary (Hecht 1987). Once it is transmitted into a material, it is either transmitted, scattered, or absorbed, Figure T-81. For opaque materials, complete absorption occurs before the light is transmitted very far from the surface. The light we see is a combination of light that is reflected from the surface, and light that is transmitted through the surface and then scattered back out, Figure T-82.

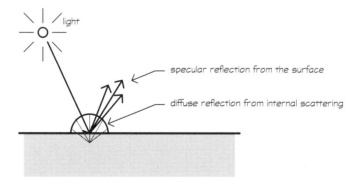

Figure T-82: Diffuse and specular components of light reflection from a surface.

There are two classes of material that exhibit very different behaviour; conductors, and non-conductors (dielectrics). For conductors, almost all of the reflection happens at the boundary. There is negligible transmission and internal reflection. For dielectric materials, there is very little reflection at the surface, and generally, very little absorption within the material. The opaque character comes from light that is scattered and reflected by the pigments suspended in the material. In both cases, a model that includes a non-directional (diffuse) component and a directional (specular) component provide reasonable empirical approximations of behaviour.

Looking at a perfectly smooth surface, the fraction of light energy that is reflected is a function of the angle of incidence, index of refraction, and coefficient of extinction of the material, Figure T-83. Very few surfaces are perfectly smooth, however, and the reflected light is scattered because of the roughness of the surface. This is commonly described by considering the surface to consist of tiny smooth facets (microfacets) and using some probability function, D, to predict the fraction of the microfacets that are correctly oriented for reflecting the light in a particular direction. In the case of conductors, a high percentage of the incoming light is reflected at the boundary (common metals fall in the range of 50% to 90% reflection), while for dielectrics, very little light is reflected at the surface (common dielectrics fall within the range 5% to 10% reflection).

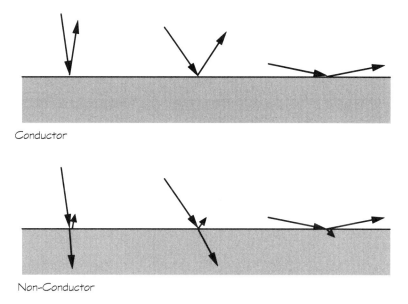

Figure T-83: The ratio of reflected and transmitted energy depends upon the index of refraction, coefficient of extinction, and angle of incidence.

The second major difference between a conductor and a dielectric is that both the diffuse and specular components are the same colour for a conductor, while they are normally different colours for dielectric materials. In a conductor, both diffuse and specular reflection are the result of surface reflection. In the non-conductor, the surface reflection is normally white (about equal across the spectrum), while the diffuse reflection is the colour of the pigment.

The model we have just described is expressed as:

surface colour = light colour x ((Kd x diffuse colour x cos()) + (Ks x specular colour x D))

This is the description of the surface colour resulting from illumination by a single source. When there is more than one source, the surface colour resulting from illumination by each source is computed, and these are summed.

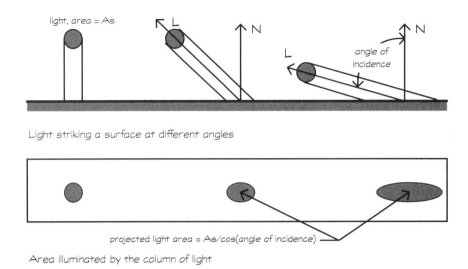

Figure T-84: Illumination intensity as a function of the angle of incidence.

In the diffuse term, the diffuse coefficient, Kd, describes the percentage of reflection that is diffuse. Similarly, in the specular term, the specular coefficient, Ks, describes the percentage of reflection that is specular. A good rule of thumb is that Kd + Ks < 1. The $cos()$ factor is the cosine of the angle of incidence (angle between the surface normal and the light) which can also be expressed as the dot product of the surface normal and the light vector. This factor accounts for the geometry resulting in light being spread over more surface area when the angle of incidence is high, Figure T-84.

D in the specular term is a probability function describing the likelihood that microfacets in the surface are oriented for mirror reflection of the light toward the viewer, Figure T-85. The probability function predicts the percentage of microfacets oriented towards H, and is generally a function of the angle between N and H. H, in turn is a function of the light direction, L, and viewer direction, V. There are many functions that can be used for D. The most common is a cosine power function of the angle between N and H (Blinn 1977).[81] Most renderers use the exponent of the cosine to describe the shininess of the surface. However, *JOEY* uses the angle between N and H at which the specular function drops to a value of .5 so that renderers that use microfacet distribution

---

[81] This is often incorrectly attributed to (Phong 1975), who used the angle between the mirror reflection of L and the view vector, V, in describing D.

functions can be easily mapped (through the `IRenderDevX` interface) to have approximately the same appearance.[82]

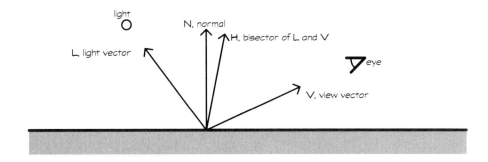

Figure T-85: Geometry of specular reflection.[83]

Another important aspect of materials is transparency. There a two commonly found implementations of transparency. The first simulates the true behaviour of light resulting in refraction (bending) of the light as it passes in to or out of a material, and colour filtering of the light as it passes through the transparent material. The second is, perhaps more appropriately, called pseudo-transparency. It simply allows some fraction of the background to show through the object colour. This is useful in exposing interior details of assembled components without distortion.

As noted previously, z-buffers are sensitive to the order in which objects are drawn for reasonable handling of pseudo-transparency, and for correct operation, objects should be drawn in order from furthest to closest. Real transparency is only available through ray tracing. The details of using transparency are beyond the scope of this text, and transparency is not implemented in the *JOEY* toolkit.

---

[82] The use of the angle, β, at which the distribution function drops to a value of .5 was first suggested by (Blinn 1977). Its use, and a comparison of various microfacet distribution functions is further described in (Hall 1989).

[83] We use the vector convention that all vectors originate from the surface whose colour is being evaluated. The direction of the light from the surface, L, is the inverse of the direction the light is traveling, -L, and the direction of light traveling from the surface to the eye, V, is the inverse of the direction the eye is looking, -V.

3.1.3.3 Texture Mapping

Texture mapping is usually presented as a special and unique feature of the rendering system, but in most cases, it is actually just an extension of material specification. *JOEY* includes texture specification as a part of the material definition.[84] The details of texturing are beyond the scope of this text and we present only a brief conceptual overview of the texturing process.

In the general form, texturing is a process of using a lookup table (Catmull 1975), (Blinn 1976) or a function (Perlin 1985) to generate material parameters or modify surface geometry.[85] The lookup table or parameter generating function is the texture. The mapping is the relationship between the location of points on the surface of the object and the lookup indices for a table, or the input parameters for the parameter generating function (a lookup table is just a special case of a parameter generating function). The highlights of the process of texturing a material are diagrammed in Figure T-86.

The lookup table is most commonly an image. This provides a 2D lookup table of colour values. In order to allow fast hardware rendering implementations, most rendering systems that support textures support only image textures, and limit the material parameters to which the textures can be applied. Support for generalised functional parameter generators is found in very few rendering systems. Instead, functional parameter generators are used to create the image textures are used in rendering.

The common implementation of texturing uses the mapping function to generate texture coordinates for each vertex of a polygon. For a point on the polygon, the texture coordinates are interpolated and then the texture lookup of evaluation is performed. The texture is often preprocessed through area filters so that the area filtering can be done quickly (Williams 1983), (Crow 1984).

---

[84] While texture specification is part of the *JOEY* definition of the material, it is not implemented in the *JOEY* Toolkit supplied with this text.

[85] Texturing is by no means limited to materials. The notion of precomputing scene parameters for reflections, lighting, shadows, etc. all fall under the general heading of texturing.

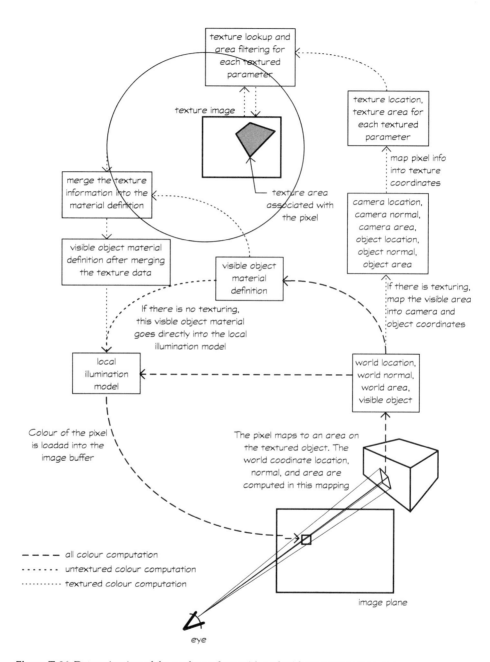

texture lookup and
area filtering for
each textured
parameter

texture image

texture location,
texture area for
each textured
parameter

map pixel info
into texture
coordinates

merge the texture
information into the
material definition

texture area
associated with
the pixel

camera location,
camera normal,
camera area,
object location,
object normal,
object area

visible object material
definition after merging
the texture data

visible object
material
definition

If there is texturing,
map the visible area
into camera and
object coordinates

If there is no texturing,
this visble object material
goes directly into the local
illumination model

local
illumination
model

world location,
world normal,
world area,
visible object

Colour of the pixel
is loadad into the
image buffer

The pixel maps to an area on
the textured object. The
world coodinate location,
normal, and area are
computed in this mapping

image plane

eye

– – – – all colour computation

· · · · · · · untextured colour computation

· · · · · · · · · textured colour computation

Figure T-86: Determination of the surface colour with and without texture mapping.

The *JOEY* material, `CJoeyMaterial`, allows colour and colour coefficients to be stored as composite trees. The composite tree is an idea that originates in 2D image processing and animation (Porter 1984). Each composite step uses a composite rule to combine colours from two sources which could be constant colours, colours generated from an image or texture lookup, functionally generated colours, or colours from previous composite steps. In general, each colour also has an associated transparency. The use of a composite tree allows the specification of multiple bounded textures with different mapping functions. While `CJoeyMaterial` can store a very complex material description, it is the user interface and the renderer that impose limits on what the user can specify as a material, and how the renderer will interpret that specification.

3.1.3.4 Interpolation Artifacts

The question of when the local illumination model is evaluated was introduced in Section 3.1.2.3. As noted, the evaluation of the local illumination model can be computationally demanding, especially when textures and/or multiple lights are involved. Interpolations are a way to reduce computation, but they introduce interpolation artifacts. We discuss this because we feel it is important for you to know when artifacts you see are beyond your control.

When a polygon is drawn into the z-buffer, the vertex positions are transformed from object coordinates into screen coordinates which include XY position on the screen and a depth value. The mathematics of the transformation assure that lines and planes in object coordinates remain lines and planes in screen coordinates. As a polygon is scan converted, there are always 2 active edges that define the span being loaded into the z-buffer, Figure T-87. The endpoints of the span are determined by linear interpolation between the vertices that define the active edges. The Z value for each pixel on the span is determined by linear interpolation between the end points of the span.

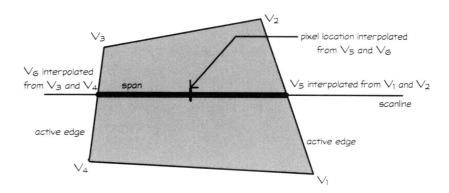

Figure T-87: Span and pixel locations are interpolated in screen coordinates during polygon scan conversion.

Gouraud shading (Gouraud 1971) extends the interpolation to include colour interpolation. The colours are computed at the vertices and interpolated in the same way as other polygon properties. The interpolation requires only a single add for each step (the step to the next span along the active edges, or the step to the next pixel along the span) for each of the interpolated parameters. Thus, interpolating the colour requires only 3 adds for each pixel, which is substantially faster than re-computing the illumination model. It should be noted that the interpolation is relative to screen coordinates and not object coordinates.[86]

A variety of problems have been noted with this approach, including:

♦ Pronounced Mach banding[87] at polygon boundaries due to discontinuities in the first derivative of intensity (Phong 1975). Interpolation keeps the rate of change constant across a polygon, but adjacent polygons will normally have a different rate of change.

♦ Shading is not invariant with scanline orientation, Figure T-88 (Duff 1979). This causes "shimmering" or "crawling" highlights when objects are in motion.

---

[86] Gouraud interpolation of colour is used by OpenGL.

[87] Mach banding is a perceptual phenomena noted by E. Mach in the 1860's. Mach bands are caused when the first derivative (rate of change) of intensity across a scene is discontinous. The perceptual mechanism of the eye enhances the discontinuity by making it appear lighter or darker than the surroundings.

♦ If local illumination models that include specular highlights are used, the highlights are easily misplaced or omitted, Figure T-89 (Phong 1975). This effect is exaggerated with animation, again causing "shimmering" or "crawling" highlights.

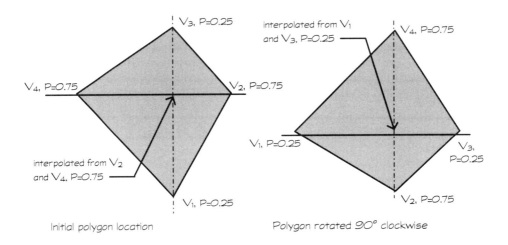

Figure T-88: Variation in interpolated values as a function of screen orientation.

These problems can be easily seen with the hand object, *hand.a3d*, when it is smooth shaded because of polygon size, coarseness of the polygonal approximation, and polygons with more than 3 vertices. Subdividing polygons into triangles eliminates the second problem (invariance with scanline orientation). The other problems can be reduced by using finer polygon approximations, i.e. more polygons to represent surfaces, as this results in the local illumination model being evaluated more often. The problems are eliminated if the polygon size is decreased to roughly pixel size and the local illumination model is evaluated for every pixel. If you experience objectionable problems of the nature described, it really suggests that the renderer you are using is not appropriate for the problem you are trying to solve.

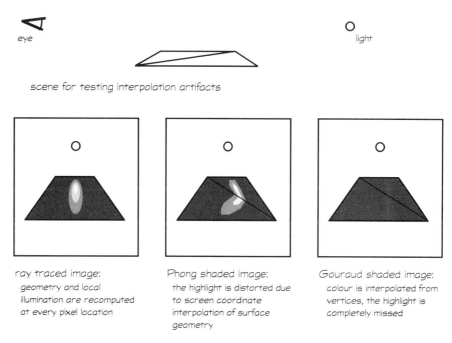

Figure T-89: Interpolation artifacts in the rendering of specular highlights.

Phong presented an alternate to Gouraud interpolation in which the surface normal and pixel location on the polygon are interpolated, then the local illumination model is evaluated at every pixel (Phong 1975). This introduces the problem of highlight misplacement and "shimmering" in perspective projections as a result of the non-linearity of the projection, Figure T-89. Again, this problem can be eliminated if the polygon size is decreased to roughly pixel size so that the geometrically correct information is available when the illumination model is evaluated.[88]

Ray tracing techniques determine the correct geometry and evaluate the illumination model at each pixel. This eliminates interpolation artifacts, though artifacts created by using polygonal approximations of smooth surfaces will remain.

Texturing is subject to interpolation artifacts that are similar to those exhibited in shading. To eliminate them, the mapping function must be evaluated at every pixel rather than interpolating between mapping values at polygon vertices.

---

[88] One thing to note about decreasing polygon size is that this must be done for flat surfaces as well as curved surfaces if interpolation artifacts in shading are to be eliminated.

A common theme in considering whether artifacts of the rendering process are acceptable is the trade between speed and realism. All of the techniques described for reducing or eliminating artifacts significantly affect the speed at which frames can be generated. In interactive applications it is necessary to sacrifice realism and detail in order to maintain interactivity. If high realism is required, then interactive renderers and the associated artifacts must be accepted during scene and animation planning, and the generation of images that make up the presentation sequence should be considered a batch processing activity.

3.1.4 Lights

Lighting is the second half of the illumination problem. The global illumination model is the model that predicts the light that strikes a surface. If you look at the surfaces that surround you, you will notice subtle variations in light, shadows, reflections of light from nearby surfaces, and a collection of other effects. Some careful observation will lead you to the conclusion that the description of the global illumination on a surface is not a trivial function to compute or to represent. Since this is the case, a collection of empirical approximations are typically used to simplify both the user specification of lighting and the computation during rendering.

3.1.4.1 Approximating a Light Source

Light from explicitly defined light sources is always included in the model for illumination. Real light sources have a geometric shape, send different amounts of energy in different directions, and have a colour associated with the light. Light manufacturers can supply catalogues describing light distribution functions for various bulbs and fixtures as well as the colour characteristics of different bulbs. Unfortunately, this information is very difficult to use in the context of computer graphics, so we fall back to some simplifying approximations.

JOEY encapsulates lights in the `CJoeyLight` class. As noted, lights in the "real world" differ from lights used in most renderers. The `CJoeyLight` object tries to reach a compromise so that the description of the light can provide input for very realistic renderers while still providing the information needed for the light approximations used by interactive renderers.

Lights are most commonly approximated as point sources that are either within the scene (local lights) or at an infinite distance from the scene (directional lights). Local lights are described by a location in the scene while directional lights are simply described by the direction the light is traveling. Realistically, there is no limit to the number of lights in a scene. Practically, however, as the number of lights increases, it becomes increasingly difficult to control the final appearance of the image, image computation time increases, and you may run up against limits imposed by the renderer.

An example of a directional light is the sun. If you are modeling something on the scale of a building, a city, or even the earth, the direction of the sunlight is nearly identical for all objects in the model. When the light is within the scene, such as a light in a room, the direction at every point in the room is slightly different. The light types `JOEY_LIGHT_TYPE_DIRECTIONAL` and `JOEY_LIGHT_TYPE_LOCAL` specify that the light is a either a directional or a local light source.

Let us review the expression for surface colour developed in the last section:

surface colour = light colour × ((Kd × diffuse colour × cos()) + (Ks × specular colour × D))

We will adopt a more compact notation of representing the surface colour (surface intensity) as $I(\lambda)$, the diffuse material colour as $Md(\lambda)$, the specular material colour as $Ms(\lambda)$, and the colour (intensity) of light n as $I_r(\lambda)$. The λ signifies that these quantities are colours (functions of the wavelength of light, λ). We will also expand the expression to sum the colour contribution of all lights, and replace $cos()$ with the vector dot product of the light vector and the surface normal, $L \cdot N$, which computes this cosine. Our expression for the colour of a surface is now:

$$I(\lambda) = \sum_{n=1}^{B} I_r(\lambda) \times ((Kd \times Md(\lambda) \times (L \cdot N)) + (Ks \times Ms(\lambda) \times D))$$

The thing to note is that the local illumination model is really evaluated once per light, and that the local illumination model uses the direction of the light, not the location. The implications are that the speed of the colour computation is directly proportional to the number of lights, and that directional lights are faster to compute than local lights since the light vector, L, needs to be computed for each local light every time the illumination model is evaluated.

3.1.4.2 Spotlights and Light Attenuation

In a general model of lights, we would be able to specify the directional light intensity and colour functions and these would be evaluated as the illumination model was evaluated for a surface.[89] Speed considerations make this impractical for interactive rendering, however, and lights are nearly always specified by a constant colour. The compromise provided by many renderers is a renderer implementation of a spotlight function. The positive aspect of this is that there is more control of lighting effects in the renderer and that the implementation is optimised for speed. The negative aspect is that you are limited to the lights provided by the renderer.

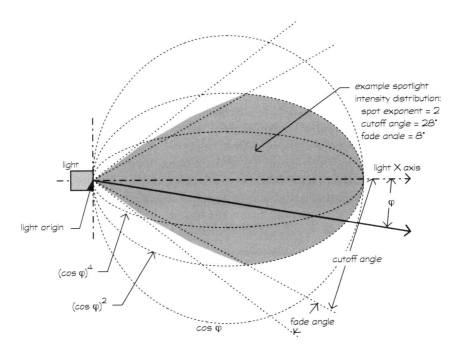

Figure T-90: Spotlight intensity distribution function.

The most common spotlight function raises the cosine of the angle between the axis of the light and the light direction to the surface to a power, Figure T-90. This controls the shape directional distribution function for light intensity. Some renderers also support a cutoff angle and a fade range which limits the cone of illumination provided by the light. Although the `CJoeyLight` object allows

---

[89] The `CJoeyLight` class allows the specification of the light intensity as a function or texture indexed by direction, however, interactive renderers will generally only accept a constant colour specification.

specification of these parameters, the appearance of the rendered image will be a "best approximation" of the specified lighting based upon the capabilities of the renderer. The light type `JOEY_LIGHT_TYPE_SPOT` indicates that the `SpotCutoff`, `SpotFade`, and `SpotExp` (exponent for the cosine function) should be used in specifying the light to the renderer.

Observation of real lights also reveals that as we get further away from the light source, the illumination from the light is reduced (attenuated). The physical behavior of lights is that the illumination decreases in proportion to the inverse square of the distance from the light. In generating imagery, this rate of attenuation often looks bad. It is often more satisfactory to attenuate more gradually or not at all. The `CJoeyLight` class supports a linear attenuation factor, K_{linear}, and a quadratic attenuation factor, $K_{quadratic}$. The actual use of these parameters may vary from renderer to renderer. In the OpenGL implementation of `IRenderDevX`, the light is attenuated for distance by the factor:

$$attenuation\ factor = 1\ /\ \left(1 + (K_{linear} \times distance) + (K_{quadratic} \times distance^2)\right)$$

Light attenuation is only applied to local light sources and spot light sources. Since directional sources are at an infinite distance from the scene, distance attenuation makes no sense for this type of light.

3.1.4.3 Global Ambient Illumination

In addition to light from explicit sources. Illumination also results from light reflected off of other surfaces in a scene. The simplest way to account for this is to use global ambient illumination. This is a constant illumination value independent of direction or location in the scene. The `CJoeyLight` type `JOEY_LIGHT_TYPE_AMBIENT` is used to specify a global ambient light for the scene. Renderers typically allow specification of ambient light colour and an ambient material reflectivity resulting in the expression for surface colour:

$$I(\lambda) = \left(I_{ambient}(\lambda) \times Md(\lambda)\right) + \sum_{n=1}^{b} Ir(\lambda) \times \left((Kd \times Md(\lambda) \times (L \bullet N)) + (Ks \times Ms(\lambda) \times D)\right)$$

The ambient material reflectivity is the same as the diffuse material reflectivity for real materials. To reduce user confusion, the *JOEY* dialogue for the specification of a material does not reveal the ambient material colour, but sets it to be equal to the diffuse colour.

3.1.4.4 Radiosity Illumination

Radiosity is a method for performing a physically based lighting simulation so that a detailed description of the interreflection of light can be generated. This detailed description is generally used in computing a colour per vertex for the model and then the model is rendered with no additional lighting computations. The radiosity lighting simulation and computation of vertex colours is normally run as a batch processing operation.

JOEY has provisions to describe the material and light information required for radiosity lighting simulations in the `CJoeyMaterial` and `CJoeyLight` classes. Interactive renderers can be used for scene planning and for walking through a scene after the lighting simulation has been performed. Using radiosity during interactive manipulation of data in a scene is not currently computationally feasible.

A discussion of model preparation for radiosity rendering and conditioning the output for display is beyond the scope of this text.

3.2 Graphic Representations of Data

Presenting data in a way that promotes user interaction to accomplish the desired data manipulation task is always a difficult challenge. The *viewit3d* example demonstrates that certain representations work best for certain task requirements. Smooth shading works well for examining the final shape. Wireframe is easiest for picking and moving vertices. Bounding volume representations may be required to maintain the interactivity necessary for camera positioning. Tools, such as positioning jacks and grids (that are not even part of the database) help control data manipulations. In most cases, the question will be which abstraction of the data provides the best access for user manipulation. We suggest several options that you might consider as you design data presentation abstractions and manipulation interaction. References that are helpful in designing alternative ways to present data are (McKim 1972), (Tutfe 1983), and (Tufte 1990).

WYSIWYG[90] presentation of 2D data in 2D applications is a great idea because the output media (2D printed output) is closely related to the data on the screen (2D black and white or coloured data). If you can display it, you can probably print it. For 3D, this does not work. There is very little correlation between a 3D object being displayable and it being realisable as a real 3D object made of some real material that looks like what was displayed. WYSIWYG is really only

---

[90] What You See Is (usually) What You Get.

applicable to 3D when the ultimate product is a 2D representation such as print or film. The positive aspect of this observation is that since what you see is only a 2D abstraction of some 3D reality, you have immense freedom in designing 2D abstractions that will convey essential elements of the 3D reality.

MS Visual C++ is an excellent example of an application designed to edit a project (another application) that shares a resistance to WYSIWYG presentation that is similar to 3D data. In this case, a multitude of different presentations of data are used for file editing, presenting program structure, presenting file structure, presenting code structure within a file, presenting class structure and class hierarchy, etc. This is a good reference when you begin to think about other ways to present your 3D data for editing or examination.

3.2.1 Rendering Styles

The rendering styles of solid, wireframe, shaded, and unshaded are the most obvious ways to change the character of displayed 3D data. The rendering styles in *viewit3d* demonstrate how to globally change the rendering style by setting the style that the render device will use as well as locally changing the style by controlling the material and the drawing functions used to display the object.

The most difficult part of using different rendering styles is providing automatic control with user overrides. For example, when the user enters vertex drag mode in *viewit3d*, the mode could automatically be set to wireframe because it is the most appropriate for selecting and dragging vertices. The material dialogue provides one method for user control of rendering style. The addition of a rendering style selection provides another means. Both are adequate for a simple program such as *viewit3d* where there is a limited number of objects and materials, and applying a single rendering style to the entire database is sufficient.

In more complex applications, it is often necessary to have several rendering styles in use simultaneously. In this case, the application must provide tools to help the user associate rendering styles with objects and/or parts of objects in a way that is easily controlled by the user.

3.2.2 Grouping Mechanisms

In order to facilitate faster user interaction, you might consider grouping mechanisms to allow a user to select and change the properties for a group of objects at one time (Hall 1994). Grouping provides an interesting user interface challenge. The basic windows interaction paradigm is a noun-verb or object-action paradigm. The interaction is that of selecting an object, and then selecting the action to be performed upon that object. In grouping, we would like to select the object or object part and then add it to, or remove it from, a group. Determining if selection applies to a group, an object, or a part of an object is a problem. This problem is compounded if overlapping groups are allowed (an object can be part of more than one group).

The drawing facility in MS Word can be examined for some clues as to how grouping can be implemented. Object selection is normally mutually exclusive, that is, if you select an object, the previous object is de-selected. Groups of objects can be selected by either fence picking (surrounding the objects to be selected with a fence) or by holding the <SHIFT> key as objects are selected. This is a dynamic grouping that is ungrouped when the next normal selection is made. It is also possible to permanently group the objects by selecting the group button after a collection of objects has been selected. After grouping, the group of objects can only be manipulated as a group until the group is disbanded. While this interaction is fine for simple drawings, it begins to break down as the data becomes more complex.

One shortcoming of this grouping mechanism is that only a grouping hierarchy can be represented. A group can contain other groups, but an object can only be a member of one group. In creating a large drawing, we might want to create groupings of elements with similar colours, fill styles, etc. If we are using text boxes, the text style associated with the box is a second implicit grouping mechanism that allows simultaneously changing the text attributes of all text boxes belonging to a single style by redefining the style.

One method to manage multiple overlapping groups when objects and groups are named is to use a textual matrix, Figure T-91. This presentation allows unambiguous selection of both individual objects and groups, as well as providing an editing mechanism for group ownership. Colour coding in such a display can also be effectively used to provide other information such as the active object or group, visibility, or rendering style.

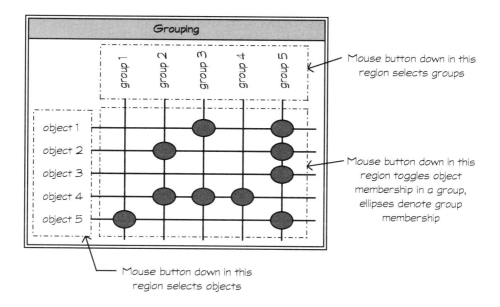

Figure T-91: Matrix representation for editing and picking with multiple overlapping groups.

3.2.3 Shape Abstraction

We demonstrated shape abstraction in *viewit3d* when the geometry was represented either as the complete geometry or as a bounding volume. These are two extremes in the representation of an object. Intermediate level-of-detail abstractions of the shape may also be useful in speeding image rendering time and improving interactivity.

One aspect of shape abstraction that is often overlooked is that it provides a method to simplify the displayed data. *JOEY* provides a framework for communication between the 3D objects and the renderer at render time so that decisions about appropriate level-of-detail can be made in response to the viewing conditions as well as a result of programmatic or user directives.

3.2.4 Visibility and Invisibility

In the 3D world, data is intrinsically more complex because objects cover each other many different ways, depending upon the camera position and the projection into 2D presentations. Objects inside a room are completely hidden if the camera is outside the room and the walls of the room are solid. While 2D constructs are manipulated relatively easily in a 2D presentation, the manipulation of the 3D world becomes more difficult when presented in 2D projections because the inter-object relationships are not easily interpreted from the 2D presentation.

Transparency and invisibility are tools that can be used to simplify the display and make it possible to see otherwise obscured information. When using these tools, the interaction must be carefully kept in sync with what is being displayed. Making an object invisible so that interior detail is revealed may not be useful if the object is not also removed from the list of objects that can be hit tested. If it remains on the hit test list, the user may not be able to pick the interior objects, though they are now clearly visible in the display. Once an object is removed from the hit test list, there must be a mechanism to select the object so that it can be made visible again.

3.2.5 Symbolic Representation

Symbolic representations or symbolic abstractions are often used to represent complex data, or data in which the physical form is not indicative of function. An example of this is electrical or piping schematics. Both of these are usually two dimension representations of something that is realised through construction as three dimensional objects. It is important to provide the option to look at data in any fashion that will reveal additional data. When using additional representations it is important that actions in one representation be synchronised with the graphics of other representations. For example, if the user selects a valve in a schematic representation, that selection should be reflected in the schematic as well as any 3D views of the object.

Another aspect of symbolic representation is presenting abstractions that are easy to manipulate. The light abstraction drawn by *viewit3d* for light positioning, and the positioning jack are examples of this type of representation. The light icon is the graphic representation of a lighting function, while the positioning jack is a graphic representation of a 4x4 transformation matrix. Neither of these is easy to manipulate interactively without such abstractions.

An important consideration which is not accounted for in *viewit3d* is turning these abstractions off when the user wants to examine the data only. You might consider differentiating examination windows from editing windows or having windows moded to be editing or examination windows (in the same way that rendering style was a window attribute in *viewit3d*).

We have presented data representation from the biased point of view of an application working with data that represents a three dimensional physical reality. Another important opportunity for symbolic abstraction is the use of 3D to better represent data does not have a 3D physical reality (or not an observable one). Examples of this are ball and stick molecular models, 3D piping diagrams, graphs of functions of 2 variables, and a multitude of other visualisations of data. 3D represents an opportunity to present more information in a view of data. The opportunities to include 3D tools in applications that do not deal with data that is inherently 3D should not be overlooked.

3.3 Manipulating Data

Most manipulations either create data, delete data, or change relationships between existing data elements. Establishing relationships and maintaining consistency in relationships is often the single most important task of a graphic editor.

Consistency with other Windows programs dictates the use of the noun-verb interaction paradigm in your applications. Very simplistically, meeting this paradigm means that you need to be able to select database elements, and then you need specify some editing action that should be taken. Unfortunately many of the operations a user wants to perform do not map simply onto the 2D projection of a 3D environment. In Section 3.2, we discussed various representations that might be used to reduce visual clutter, increase interaction speed, simplify complex 3D environments, and provide a variety of otherwise hidden information about the data. Here, we discuss using some of these representations to accomplish specific tasks.

3.3.1 Direct, Indirect, Immediate, and Delayed Interaction

In **Practice** and **Implementation** we discussed direct, indirect, immediate, and delayed interaction and how they can be used in an application (as well as the tools available in *JOEY* to facilitate these interactions). We have not yet addressed the advantages and disadvantages of each of these interaction techniques and some of the decisions that must be made in designing the appropriate interactions for your application.

The table below summarises some of the advantages and disadvantages of direct and indirect manipulation. It is often necessary to provide both interaction methods in order to provide tools that allow them to work quickly and efficiently.

	Advantages	*Disadvantages*
Direct Manipulation	- fast approximate positioning - direct correlation between input activity and changes in the display - selection activities are often enhanced by picking from a graphic data representation - relationships of data being manipulated to other data elements is immediately visible	- difficult to get exact positioning unless there are special alignment and constraint tools - if the display update rate falls below about 15 frames/second, input and output seem out of sync - it is more difficult to program
Indirect Manipulation	- exact positioning or attribute input is easy - easy to program	- activities that set attributes and structure are disjointed from the results of the activity

Immediacy in displaying a result (or approximate result) from the manipulation is a requirement for good interaction. However, as models get more complex, the time required to draw the model and to compute constraints and relationships may make it difficult to achieve immediacy. In this case, feedback indicating that the operation is proceeding, feedback indicating the status of the operation, and the option to bail-out are crucial.

3.3.2 *JOEY* Camera Interaction

The most important aspects of the *JOEY* camera interaction are:

♦ A large collection of interaction paradigms are presented to the user. These paradigms include viewing methods that are familiar to anyone who uses mechanical drawings (axis aligned orthographics, isometric, perspective), include the idea of scale (do you move a small object in from of the camera or the camera through a large object?), and provide recovery mechanisms for the user (camera reset).

♦ Constraints in camera positioning aid in controlling camera manipulation. Axis aligned manipulation paradigms and paradigms that are based on an assigned ground plane help prevent the user from getting lost during the manipulation of the camera. If the user does get lost, it is simple to reset to a known viewing position.

♦ A camera dialogue provides precise camera positioning and access to the dialogue for selecting projection and move paradigm types.

♦ Messaging during the interaction gives the application hints for providing performance sensitive drawing so that interactivity can be maintained.

3.3.3 Dialogue Interaction

We refer you to the Microsoft interface guidelines for a discussion of designing dialogue interactions. One consideration in dialogue design is that dialogues with 3D environments are often changing the visual presentation of data. The user should have the option to apply the new data to visually check correctness before closing the dialogue. We also recommend the use of the linear dimension and angular dimension formatting capabilities found in *JOEY* (and using similar methodologies for handling other dimensioned data).

3.3.4 Grab and Drag

The grab and drag interaction cycle implemented in *viewit3d* was somewhat counter to the object-action paradigm that is normally used for windows. Positioning jacks to position the object or light conformed to the paradigm of picking an object and then positioning it. The vertex drag, on the other hand required that the position vertex be set before the, vertex could be picked and the drag be performed. At the end of the drag, the vertex was de-selected. The real question is whether you can avoid moded operation in an application, that is, setting an action type mode before you select the object to be manipulated. Designing for this is brings up the issues of how selection, or hit testing, is implemented. See Section 3.3.6 for more discussion on hit testing.

The most difficult aspect of dragging is controlling the dragging so that the desired goal can be achieved. In a simple editing environment, this often means re-positioning many elements to re-establish relationships after an element has been moved. Inserting a class into a complex figure like the MFC/*JOEY* class hierarchy diagrams at the beginning of **Implementation** required a great deal of fussing to get all the parts and outlines re-connected. This type of problem is exaggerated in 3D by the extra degrees of freedom (both translational and rotational) that the third dimension contributes. The specification of constraints and relationships is an important part of creating a good 3D editing application. In the words of (Sproull 1990), *"What remains hard is modeling. The structure inherent in three-dimensional models is difficult for people to grasp and difficult too for user interfaces to reveal and manipulate. Only the determined model three-dimensional objects, and they rarely invent a shape at the computer, but only record a shape so that manufacturing and analysis can proceed. The grand challenges in three-dimensional graphics are to make modeling easy and to make complex modeling accessible to far more people."* It is all too common that although we can create data, the relationships that were important in selecting the type of data to be created and positioning that data relative to other data are not and can not be save as a part of the data.

When complex 3D data is created and manipulated, it is common that manipulations late in the data creation process will violate decisions and relationships made early in the data creation process, and that these go undetected. Procedures and processes such as alignment, clearance, mating, infill, connection, etc., must be represented as an intent which can be re-evaluated in response to the addition of new data or the shifting of existing data. Maintaining or saving only the result of a process or procedure at a particular point in time does not preserve and/or document the intent of the decisions that lead to using that process or procedure, nor does it assure that the relationships established by that process or procedure will be maintained during any future revisions of the data.

JOEY can provide help in creating and maintaining some relationships, however, most relationships that are important in modeling data are specific to the data. We provide some pointers to references that specifically discuss relationships and constraints to help you in investigating alternatives that may be helpful in your application. A taxonomy of constraint methods is presented in (Hall 1991). The relationship and constraint methods you might consider are:

♦   **Direct Manipulation:**

Direct manipulation places features and figures in relationship to each other; however, no record of the relationships exist other than the resulting geometry. *JOEY* provides a number of constraint techniques modeled after (Robertz 1980), (Haber 1980), and (Fiebush 1981) that lock onto construction grids and pre-defined angles which mimic drafting procedures of working to grids and with typically encountered angles. More recent work that addresses temporary constraints between objects and positioning in three dimensions are (Rogers 1980), (Nielson 1987), (Bier 1986), (Bier 1987), (Bier 1988), and (Bier 1990). The common theme of this work is that locational constraints are temporarily created as a function of the context of the manipulation and there is no record of the constraint once the manipulation is finished.

The advantages of using direct manipulation are that interaction is fast for simple geometries, it works well when the user knows what the geometry should be, editing is simple and intuitive, and programming the interaction is relatively easy. The disadvantages are that there is no record of key geometric features, and there is no way to describe dependencies between features.

♦ **Variational Geometry:**

Variational geometry is a constraint based approach for describing and maintaining geometric relationships within a part (Fitzgerald 1981), (Lin 1981), (Light 1982) or for assemblies of parts (Lee 1985a), (Lee 1985b). This technique is rooted in conventional dimensioned drawing descriptions of parts. Variational geometry relies on describing relationships between features (*characteristic points*) of the geometry, and constraints (area, volume, coincidence, dimensions, etc.) as a set of error functions whose values converge to zero when the constraints are satisfied. The positions of the features are programatically manipulated until the system converges to a solution that satisfies the constraints.

The advantages of variational geometry are that important features are explicitly identified, dependencies are described in the dimensioning, editing topology and constraints is conceptually simple for users familiar with standard drafting and dimensioning practices for machined parts, and the constraints are met simultaneously. The disadvantages are that programming the interaction is not simple, editing by changing dimensions or other goals is non-intuitive and may require large computation times to find new converged solutions, specifying a valid dimensioning scheme becomes increasingly difficult as the model gets more complex, and dimensions can be selected for which the solution does not converge. Variational geometry is probably limited in usefulness to CAD applications that are closely related to disciplines commonly using dimensioned drawings in describing topologically well-defined designs.

♦ **Constructive Specification:**

Constructive specification is similar to the direct manipulation technique except that a record of how the object is constructed is maintained as a part of the data. This is similar to creating a script for constructing an object. By editing the script the object can be changed while the relationships that defined the construction are maintained (Nelson 1985). While the script of an editing session may be easily created, providing an interface for simple, intuitive editing interaction is not very easy. It should also be noted that the construction sequence may not necessarily reflect the important relationships and features in a meaningful way. Specifically, it may not reflect intended permanent relationships but may be merely an expedient way to create some data in the desired location.

The advantages in constructive specification are that the steps in positioning are often analogous to physical assembly and are thus 'natural' to the user, initial specification is simple, and recording the construction process is simple. The disadvantages are that the construction must be sequential (no simultaneous constraints), and that it is not easy to provide an intuitive interface for editing the construction script.

◆ **Parametric Specification:**

Parametric or procedural specification forces all relationships and constraints to be reduced to explicitly computable functions of some input parameters. The variable resolution sphere generator in the OpenGL Programming Guide (Neider 1993) is a good example of this. The generation of a variable resolution sphere based on a platonic icosahedron is specified simply by providing the diameter and the level of face subdivision. While this is the most direct method of maintaining simultaneous constraints in a model, it requires the user to program the relationships between parameters and geometry. Writing and editing the procedures to create complex geometric systems is not an easy task.

The advantages of parametric specification is that it is relatively easy to write a system that can accept parametric object descriptions and display parameters for editing, the parametric description can solve simultaneous constraints and provide limits for parameters to assure valid geometry, and the model can be quickly regenerated after parameters have been changed. The disadvantages are that the user if forced to program objects which may not be a very natural interaction for the users, complex geometry specification is difficult, and although constraints and relationships are embodied in the procedure that generates the object this does not make them easy to identify or change when the procedure is edited.

◆ **Energy Constraints:**

Energy constraints approach the problem of specifying relationships similarly to variational geometry. Error "energy" expressions that converge to zero when a constraint or goal is met are written for each constraint or goal (Witkin 1987). Energy constraints are best used with procedural data generators. The parameters that control the data generation are adjusted to achieve the "best fit" of the constraints (the lowest error energy).

The advantages of this method are similar to variational geometry with the added benefit that any type of goal (geometric, cost, energy, etc.) may be used as long as a value for the error from reaching this goal can be expressed as a function of the geometry and attributes of the object. Additionally, goals can be importance weighted, and the problem can be either under or over constrained by the goals. The disadvantages are similar to variational geometry. Providing an intuitive interface to a system using energy constraints is not easy.

We have obviously only touched lightly on methods that may be used to control and constrain manipulation so that the manipulation results in data changes that satisfy what the user had in mind. Most of the research in this area is relatively recent and application specific. This means that there is little previous work that has created conventions that will limit your creative exploration of techniques to control interaction with 3D environments.

3.3.5 Enhanced Feedback

The Microsoft interface design guide should be used in exploring feedback alternatives that are consistent with other Windows programs. Many graphic operations take unreasonably long to perform and it is important for the user to know what is happening.

3.3.6 Hit Testing

Hit testing is one of the more interesting aspects of 3D applications. *JOEY* solves part of the problem by providing facilities to map the mouse position into a 3D mouse vector and hit frustum, and to then test geometric entities for intersection with the mapped mouse. The question the application must answer is which of the possible choices for the hit item is the user actually interested in.

Let us consider the operation of *viewit3d* for object positioning and vertex positioning. You have probably noticed that the use of a "move vertex" mode often leaves you trying to pick one of the positioning jacks, but being unable to because vertex move mode is turned on, or conversely, trying to move a vertex, but not being in move vertex mode. Or, worse yet, you are still in left camera mode and instead of picking and dragging something, the view moves. All of these are potentially frustrating experiences. They occur because there is not a consistent paradigm with other windows applications.

Let us consider alternate approaches for *viewit3d*. For data positioning, we use the positioning jack and the vertex as the object of the positioning action. Looking at the drawing functionality in MS Word, we note that when a collection of elements are on the screen, the cursor changes as we pass over elements indicating what will happen if we hit the left mouse button. The first mouse click picks the object, changes the display to indicate the object was selected and detailed selection points within the object, and generally results in an object translation if the mouse is moved while the button is depressed, Figure T-92. A double-click brings up an editing dialogue for access to object attributes, position, etc. What we observe about picking in this example is that it is hierarchical. We first pick the object, then we pick a detail of the object.

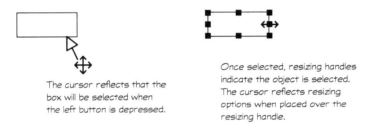

The cursor reflects that the box will be selected when the left button is depressed.

Once selected, resizing handles indicate the object is selected. The cursor reflects resizing options when placed over the resizing handle.

Figure T-92: Hierarchical hit testing for drawing objects in MS Word.

How might we use a similar paradigm in *viewit3d*? Let us first think about other functionality that would exist if *viewit3d* was a real application. In addition to vertex operations, we would probably also have object, edge, and face operations. The positioning jack implements an object operation. Edge and face positioning might be similar to vertex positioning. The object, faces, edges, and vertices all have attributes that we may want to manipulate, and it may be desirable to be able to group these elements for different operations. You might think we are leading up to a grand revelation about manipulating 3D data. Well, unfortunately, we only have some suggestions about how you might fit this problem into the noun-verb manipulation paradigm.

Working with only the functionality that has been implemented in *viewit3d*, you could easily revise the structure so both the positioning jack and the vertices were selectable. The order of hit testing would establish a priority in the event the jack and a vertex were overlapping. Since the jack is often embedded inside a collection of vertices, it would make sense to give the jack first priority so that in can be selected in such a case. Hit testing can be moved into the mouse move so that the cursor reflects an indication of the thing that will be selected. This is fine in the simple case of vertices and a positioning jack, but breaks down completely when face and edge operations are included. A hierarchical picking strategy could be used, i.e. identifying object, then face, then vertex or edge on the face, but this would make it impossible to pick a collection of vertices or edges without some very interesting logic in picking while the <SHIFT> key is depressed.

An alternate possibility is to provide toolbar buttons or a selectability dialogue that lets the user indicate the type of feature that is to be manipulate before specifically selecting the feature. The vertex position toolbar button is similar in nature to this idea. This again creates a moded operation.

With a few additions, *viewit3d* provides a simple application for experimenting with controlling hit testing. The additions are implementing face positioning, edge positioning, and selection of a group of elements by holding the <SHIFT> key. The addition of edge and face positioning can be implemented nearly identically to vertex positioning by using a toolbar button to turn the mode on and off. Using cursor feedback before selection is simply a matter of copying existing hit testing code into the OnMouseMove message handling function and defining some feedback cursors. Group selection requires managing a group of elements, rather than just a single element. Once these changes are made, then the interface can be adjusted to try different presentations of the data manipulations.

3.4 Performance Sensitive Interaction

Performance sensitive interaction is based loosely on the work of (Bergman 1986). If a user is interactively positioning data by dragging, the data must follow the cursor so that the user will know where it will be when the mouse button is released. If the data lags behind the cursor, positioning operations become tedious, time consuming, frustrating, and a barrier rather than an aid to solving a problem. A typical problem with lagging data is that it does not end up where it is expected and the operation needs to be repeated several times to achieve the desired result.

In our experience, a redraw rate of 5 to 15 frames per second is sufficient for interactive operations. For critical positioning operations, higher rates are required than for approximate positioning. This is because the user expects the object to remain where it is when the mouse is released. If there is too much lag, there is a high probability that the object position and the mouse position were out of sync when the button was released. What is acceptable is highly subjective, depending upon both the task and the user, and we recommend that users have the option of selecting a target interaction speed that they feel comfortable with.

A few guidelines are required for reasonable operation of performance sensitive camera operation. As you review the implementation of performance sensitivity in *viewit3d*, you may discover some of these rules of for controlling drawing complexity:

1. The draw routine is set to the original draw routine at the end of the camera move. The user expects to be looking at the object in the same fashion as before the camera move.

2. Once the level of detail is decreased, it cannot increase during the move. A bizarre toggling between two draw routines can occur if this rule is not in place. This happens when the lower level of detail is faster than the upper update rate limit and the higher level of detail is slower than the lower update rate limit. We have found this behavior to be very annoying and confusing, and believe it should be avoided.

3. The initial draw routine in a camera move should be the next most complex draw routine as the last draw routine used in the previous camera move. In most cases, the model does not significantly change between camera moves and thus, the same drawing routine as used in the last camera move will probably be the correct routine for the move. Instead of cycling through all the levels of detail between the default rendering and that required for interactive speed, it is nice to start at the right place. However, using the last displayed level of detail can result in the bizarre behavior that the first frame of the move is drawn in a simplified form, the next in a more complex form, and the next back in the simplified form (as described in the previous note). Starting a camera move at the next most complex level of detail eliminates this problem and provides a reasonable starting point.

This is not the only set of rules you might use to control the level of detail changes, they are offered only as a set of guidelines that we have found to work reasonably well.

An unexplored possibility is monitoring user inactivity and generating increasingly higher quality images while the user is inactive. This would use cycles that are otherwise wasted while a user is on the phone, conversing with colleagues, stepping out for coffee, or even hanging out at home with family; to replace images within designated application windows with increasingly higher quality imagery.

4. Extending *JOEY*

Extensibility is essential in *JOEY* if the applications built today using *JOEY* as a base are to remain viable into future. A common theme of much of the material in this text is that *JOEY* can only provide for a common subset of the functionality required in 3D applications, and the remainder must be supplied by application specific implementations. This chapter provides a brief description of where and how to extend *JOEY*.

4.1 Dimensioning

The model used by *JOEY* for providing linear dimension formatting through application supplied functions can be used for other formatted information. If you are adding common functionality using dialogues and feedback messages for other types of dimensioned information, you might consider similar strategies for increasing the flexibility of those dialogues and messages.

4.2 Adding Render Devices

Adding render devices is not for the weak at heart. The basic template is provided so that you can play with the idea of adding render devices if you are so inclined. There is a large body of render device boilerplate in the OpenGL render device that should be pulled into a support *.dll* for rendering devices. The rationale behind a component object rendering interface has been explored in detail in previous sections and will not be discussed further, instead we will draw attention to some of the details you need to be aware of.

You need your own CLSID for the render device you add. Your render device must be registered, and the *JOEY* registration should reflect the use of your rendering device. You can register your rendering device to be the default *JOEY* renderer or use `CJoeyConfig` and `CJoeyView` facilities to set the current renderer to your rendering device whenever necessary.

The code segment for `CJoeyView::OnDraw` (**Implementation** 3.1.2) should be reviewed to understand the use of the render device when repeatedly drawing to a window. The render device is attached to the window during the *JOEY* view processing of the `WM_CREATE` message. The placement is reset whenever a

WM_SIZE message is processed, and the render device is released during
WM_DESTROY message processing. The device is then use for repeated drawing
cycles, each cycle bounded by calls to UpdateStart and UpdateEnd. In order to
assure that update rate timing functions correctly, the rendering must be
completed and flushed to the screen window before the UpdateEnd function
returns.

JOEY is very careful about the state of the rendering device. Some functions
such as StateLock and StateRestore do not need to be implemented during
testing if the applications used for testing are well behaved and these functions
are not called. *JOEY* uses all of the material functions in the base
implementation of a *JOEY* application, so these must be implemented. *JOEY*
does not use any of the light functions in the base implementation of a *JOEY*
application.

You should never even begin to think about replacing the *JOEY* CArchive
render device. This would result in producing 3D metafiles with a *.j3d* extension
that are completely unreadable by the *JOEY* Viewer. If you want to create your
own 3D metafiles and viewer, perform the file setup and initialisation of your
3D metafile renderer then give it to *JOEY* using CJoeyView::RenderDev and
call the CJoeyView::OnDraw function. Remember to restore the CJoeyView
render device after the cmpletion of the draw to your metafile render device.
This sequence is used by *JOEY* for rendering to Bitmap, CDC, and CArchive
render devices. These are all ephemeral rendering devices, created only for a
single draw, after which they are released.

An important, and perhaps non-obvious, thing to remember is that an instance
of an IRenderDev object is created each time a new rendering device is
required. Although the same rendering device may service different physical
devices (the OpenGL render device services CWnd, CDC, and Bitmap) it is never
switched between devices within *JOEY*.

4.3 Creating a *JOEY* extension *.dll*

If you are creating a *JOEY* extension *.dll*, you are probably adding common
functionality between *JOEY* application classes and the application classes,
Figure T-93, or you are extending the *JOEY* material, grid, camera, light, or
rendering geometry classes, Figure T-94. Adding classes in the application
framework presents little problem. The structure of MFC was used to add the
JOEY classes in a very similar fashion, and your classes are simply another level
of extended functionality.

Adding extension classes to lights, materials, cameras, and other *JOEY* constructs is not so simple, however. Extending these classes for use in an application by deriving application specific classes is straightforward. The problem centers on the *JOEY's* use of these objects in the 3D metafile. *JOEY* asks cameras, grids, materials, and other entities to serialize themselves into the 3D metafile, assuming they can be read at a later time. Since the *JOEY* Viewer is not linked with the libraries that contain these objects, they cannot be serialized into the viewer. The obvious solution is to make use of component object technology to implement a solution similar to that used by OLE compound document containers. This implementation would keep the original object and a default representation (the *JOEY* class from which the object is derived) in the 3D metafile. If the original object existed and could be created, it would be used to represent it's data in the Viewer. Otherwise, the data would be skipped and the default *JOEY* implementation data would be used in the 3D Viewer.

A complete implementation of this extensibility was beyond the scope of the *JOEY* toolkit. While you can create application specific classes derived from the *JOEY* classes, you should be aware of the limitations that exist in writing these extended formats into the *JOEY* 3D metafile.

4.4 3D OLE Extensions

It is clearly desirable to be able to treat 3D objects as servers to 3D container applications. This opens an opportunity to integrate 3D applications that create and manipulate 3D objects in different ways. The problems of describing and maintaining relationships between objects in this context are very real and must be addressed in a very robust way if objects from different 3D server applications are to be truly integrate into a 3D environment inside a 3D container application. 3D OLE extensions are beyond the scope of *JOEY* Toolkit and address a very different area of application integration, though we believe that *JOEY* could be a component in 3D OLE extensions.

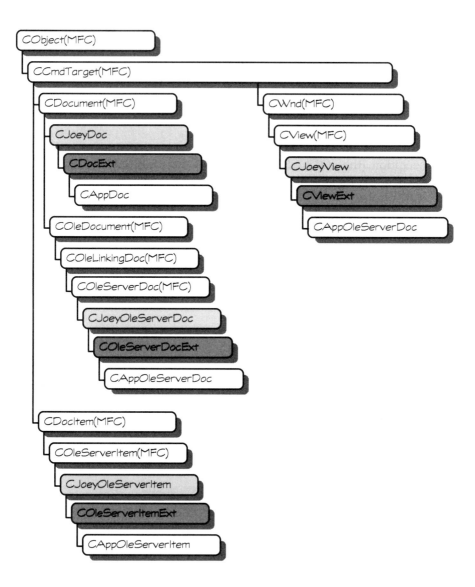

Figure T-93: Application framework extension classes inserted between the *JOEY* class and the application class.

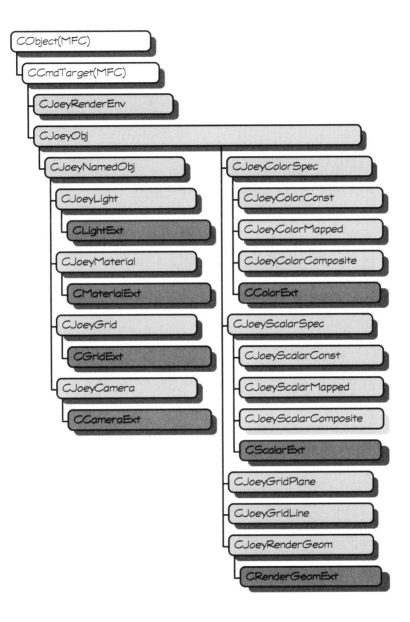

Figure T-94: Extension classes for materials, lights, cameras, etc. in the *JOEY* class hierarchy.

Bibliography

Appel, A. (1967), "The Notion of Quantitative Invisibility and the Machine Rendering of Solids," Proc. ACM National Conference, pp. 387-393.

Arvo, James, ed. (1991), *Graphics Gems II*, Academic Press, London.

Baumgart, B. G. (1975), "A Polyhedron Representation for Computer Vision," Proceedings of the National Computer Conference.

Bergman, L. H. Fuchs, E. Grant, and S. Spach (1986), "Image Rendering by Adaptive Refinement," ACM Computer Graphics, vol. 20, no. 4, pp. 29-37.

Bier, E. A. and M. C. Stone (1986), "Snap Dragging," ACM Computer Graphics (SIGGRAPH 86), vol. 20, no. 4, pp. 233-240.

Bier, E. A. (1987), "Skitters and Jacks: Interactive 3D Positioning Tools," in *Proceedings of the 1986 Workshop on Interactive 3D Graphics* (Chapel Hill, NC October 23-24, 1986), ACM, New York, pp. 183-196.

Bier, E. A. (1988), "Snap-dragging: Interactive Geometric Design in Two and Three Dimensions," Ph.D dissertation, Univ. California at Berkeley, Technical Report UCB/CSD 88/416.

Bier, E. A. (1990), "Snap-dragging in three dimensions," ACM Computer Graphics (SIGGRAPH 90), vol. 24, no. 4, pp. 193-204.

Blinn, James F. and M. E. Newell (1976), "Texture and Reflection in Computer Generated Images," Communications of the ACM, vol. 19, no. 10, pp. 542-547.

Blinn, James F. (1977), "Models of Light Reflection for Computer Synthesized Pictures," ACM Computer Graphics (SIGGRAPH 77), vol. 11, no. 2, pp. 192-198.

Bloomenthal, Jules and Jon Rokne (1994), "Homogeneous Coordinates," The Visual Computer, vol. 11, no. 1, pp. 15-26.

Borges, Carlos F. (1991), "Trichromatic Approximation for Computer Graphics Illumination Models," ACM Computer Graphics (SIGGRAPH 91), vol. 25, no. 4, pp. 101-104.

Carpenter, Loren (1984), "The A-buffer, an Antialiased Hidden Surface Method," Computer Graphics (SIGGRAPH 1984), vol. 18, no. 3, pp. 103-108.

Catmull, E. (1974), *A Subdivision Algorithm for Computer Display of Curved Surfaces*, Ph.D. Thesis, Report UTEC-CSc-74-133, Computer Science Department, University of Utah, Salt Lake City, UT, December, 1974.

Catmull, E. E. (1975), "Computer Display of Curved Surfaces," Proceedings of the IEEE Conference on Computer Graphics, Patteren Recognition, and Data Structures, May 1975, pp. 11-17.

Cornsweet, T.N. (1970), *Visual Perception*, Academic Press, New York.

Crow, Franklin (1984), "Summed-Area Tables for Texture Mapping," ACM Computer Graphics (SIGGRAPH 84), vol. 18, no. 3, pp. 207-212.

Duff, Tom (1979), "Smooth Shaded Renderings of Polygonal Objects on Raster Displays," ACM Computer Graphics (SIGGRAPH 79), vol. 12, no. 2, pp. 270-275.

Feibush, E. (1981), "An Interactive Computer Graphics Geometric Input and Editing System for Architectural Design," Masters Thesis, Cornell Univ.

Fitzgerald, W. J. (1981), "Using axial dimensions to determine the proportions of line drawings in computer graphics," Computer-Aided Design, vol. 13, no. 6, pp. 377-381.

Foley, James D., Andries van Dam, Steven F. Feiner, and John F. Hughes (1990), *Computer Graphics Principles and Practice*, second edition, Addison-Wesley Publishing Co. Reading, Massachusetts.

Glassner, A.S., ed. (1989), *An Introduction to Ray Tracing*, Academic Press, London.

Glassner, A.S., ed. (1990), *Graphics Gems*, Academic Press, London.

Goldberg, A and A. Kay (1976), *SMALLTALK-72 Instruction Manual*, Learning Research Group, Xerox Palo Alto Research Centre, Palo Alto, CA.

Goral, Cindy M, K.E. Torrance, D.P. Greenberg, and B.Battaile (1984), "Modeling the Interaction of Light Between Diffuse Surfaces," ACM Computer Graphics (SIGGRAPH 1984), vol. 18, no. 3, pp. 213-222.

Gouraud, Henri (1971), "Continuous Shading of Curved Surfaces," IEEE Transactions on Computers, June 1971, pp. 623-629.

Haber, R. (1980), "Computer-Aided Design of Cable Reinforced Membrane Structures," Masters Thesis, Cornell Univ.

Haeberli, Paul and Kurt Akeley (1990), "The Accumulation Buffer: Hardware Support for High Quality Rendering," Computer Graphics (SIGGRAPH 1990), vol. 24, no. 4, pp. 309-318.

Hall, R. A. (1990), *Illumination and Color in Computer Generated Imagery*, Springer-Verlag, New York.

Hall, Roy A. (1990), "Manipulating Color," Advanced Ray Tracing Tutorial notes, SIGGRAPH 90.

Hall, R. A. (1991), "Supporting Complexity and Conceptual Design in Modeling Tools," in State of the Art in Computer Graphics, ed. D. F. Rogers and R. A. Earnshaw, Springer -Verlag, New York, pp. 153-183.

Hall, R. A. and M. Bussan (1994), "Abstraction, Context, and Constraint," in State of the Art in Computer Graphics, ed. D. A. Rogers and R. A. Earnshaw, Springer-Verlag, New York.

Hartson, R, and D. Hix (1989), "Human-Computer Interface Development: Concepts and Systems," ACM Computing Surveys, vol. 21, no. 1, pp 5-92.

Hecht, Eugene and Alfred Zajac (1987), Optics, 2nd. edition, Addison-Wesley Publishing Co. Reading, Massachusetts.

Heckbert, Paul S., ed. (1994), *Graphics Gems IV*, Academic Press, London.

Hunt, R. W. G. (1975), *The Reproduction of Color*, Third Edition, John Wiley and Sons, New York.

Joblove, G. H. and D. P. Greenberg (1978), "Color Spaces for Computer Graphics," ACM Computer Graphics (SIGGRAPH 78), vol. 12, no. 3, pp. 20-25.

Judd, D. B. and G Wyszecki (1975), *Color in Business, Science, and Industry*, John Wiley and Sons, New York.

Kaufman, J. E. ed. (1984), *IES Lighting Handbook, 1984 Reference Volume*, Illuminating Engineering Society of North America, New York.

Kirk, David, ed. (1992), *Graphics Gems III*, Academic Press, London.

Lee, K. and D. C. Gossard (1985a), ``A hierarchical datastructure for representing assemblies: part 1," Computer-Aided Design, vol. 17, no. 1, pp. 15-19.

Lee, K. and G. Andrews (1985b), ``Inference of the positions of components in an assembly: part 2," Computer-Aided Design, vol. 17, no. 1, pp. 20-24.

Light, R. and D. Gossard (1982), ``Modification of geometric models through variational geometry," Computer-Aided Design, vol. 14, no. 4, pp. 209-214.

Lin, V. C., D. C. Gossard and R. A. Light (1981), ``Variational Geometry in Computer-Aided Design," ACM Computer Graphics (SIGGRAPH 81), vol. 15, no. 3, pp. 171-177.

Mantyla, M., and R. Sulonen (1982), "GWB: A Solid Modeler with the Euler Operators," IEEE Computer Graphics and Applications, vol. 2, no. 7, pp. 17-31.

McKim, Robert H. (1972), *experiences in visual thinking*, PWS Publishers, Boston.

Meyer, Gary W. (1983), "Colorimetry and Computer Graphics," Program of Computer Graphics, Report no. 83-1, Cornell University, Ithaca, NY.

Meyer, Gary W. (1986), "Tutorial on Color Science," The Visual Computer, vol. 2, no. 5, pp. 278-290.

Meyer, Gary W. (1988), "Wavelength Selection for Synthetic Image Generation," Computer Vision, Graphics, and Image Processing, vol. 41, pp. 57-79.

Myers, Rob (1986), "Pictorial Conversation: Design Considerations for Interactive Graphical Media," USENIX Computer Graphics Workshop, Monterey, California, Nov. 1986.

Neider, J., T. Davis, M. Woo (1993), *OpenGL Programming Guide*, Addison-Wesley Publishing Co. Reading, Massachusetts.

Newell, M.E., R.G. Newell and T.L. Sancha (1972), "A Solution to the Hidden Surface Problem," Proceedings of the ACM National Conference 1972, pp. 443-450.

Nielson, G. M. and D. R. Olsen Jr. (1987), "Direct Manipulation Techniques for 3D Objects Using 2D Locator Devices," in *Proceedings of the 1986 Workshop on Interactive 3D Graphics* (Chapel Hill, NC October 23-24, 1986), ACM, New York, pp. 175-182.

OpenGL Architecture Review Board (1992), *OpenGL Referennce Manual*, Addison-Wesley Publishing Co. Reading, Massachusetts.

Perlin, K (1985), "An Image Synthesizer," ACM Computer Graphics (SIGGRAPH 85), vol. 19, no. 3, pp. 287-296.

Phong, Bui Toung (1975), "Illumination for Computer Generated Pictures," Communnications fo the ACM, vol. 18, no. 8, pp. 311-317.

Plücker J (1830), "Über ein neus Coordinaten system" (in German), Journal für die Reine und Angewandte Mathematick, vol. 5, pp. 1-36.

Robertz, W. (1980), "A Graphical Input System for Computer-Aided Architectural Design," Masters Thesis, Cornell Univ.

Rogers, D. F. and Satterfield, S. G. (1980), "B-spline Surface for Ship Hull Design," ACM Computer Graphics (SIGGRAPH 80), vol. 14, no. 3, pp. 211-217.

Rogers, David F. and J. Alan Adams (1990), *Mathematical Elements for Computer Graphics*, second edition, McGraw-Hill Publishing Company, NewYork, New York.

Rupel, A. (1983), "Graphic Based Applications - Tools to Fill the Software Gap," Digital Design, vol. 3, no. 7, pp. 17-30.

Smith, A. R. (1978), "Color Gamut Transformation Pairs," ACM Computer Graphics (SIGGRAPH 78), vol. 12, no. 3, pp. 12-19. Sproull, R. F. (1990), "Parts of the Frontier are Hard to Move," ACM Computer Graphics, vol. 24, no. 2, pg. 9.

Sproull, R. F. (1990), "Parts of the Frontier are Hard to Move," ACM Computer Graphics, vol. 24, no. 2, pg. 9.

Sutherland, I.E., R.F. Sproull and R.A. Schumacker (1974), "A Characterization of Ten Hidden-Surface Algorithms," Computer Surveys, vol. 6, no. 1, pp. 1-55.

Tufte, E. R. (1983), *The Visual Display of Quantitative Information*, Graphics Press, Chesire, Conneticut.

Tufte, E. R. (1990), *Envisioning Information*, Graphics Press, Chesire, Conneticut.

Upstill, Steve (1990), *The RenderMan Companion*, Addison-Wesley Publishing Company, Reading, Massacchusetts.

Wanger, Leonard R., James A. Ferwerda, and Donald P. Greenberg (1992), "Perceiving Spatial Relationhips in Computer-Generated Images," IEEE Computer Graphics and Applications, vol. 12, no. 3, pp. 44-55.

Watkins, G.S., *A Real Time Visible Surface Algorithm*, Ph.D Thesis, Technical Report UTEC-CSc-70-101, NTIS AD-762 004, Computer Science Department, University of Utah, Salt Lake City, Utah.

Weiler, K. and P. Atherton, "Hidden Surface Removal Using Polygon Area Sorting," SIGGRAPH 1977, pp. 214-222.

Weiler, K. J. (1986), "Topological Structures for Geometric Modeling," Ph.D. dissertation, Rensselaer Polytechnic Institute, Troy, NY.

Whitted, Turner (1980), "Processing Requirements for Hidden Surface Elimination and Realistic Shading," Digest of Papers, COMPCON, spring 1982.

Witkin, A., K. Fleisher, and A. Barr (1987), "Energy Constraints On Parameterized Models," ACM Computer Graphics (SIGGRAPH 87), vol. 21, no. 4, pp. 225-232.

Williams, Lance (1983), "Pyramidal Parametrics," ACM Computer Graphics (SIGGRAPH 83), vol. 17, no. 3, pp. 1-11.

Index